The Polar Pivot

THE POLAR PIVOT

Great Power Competition in the Arctic and Antarctica

Ryan Patrick Burke

LYNNE
RIENNER
PUBLISHERS

BOULDER
LONDON

This material is based on research and fieldwork funded by the Air Force Office of Scientific Research. Any opinions, findings, conclusions, or recommendations expressed herein are mine alone and do not necessarily reflect the views of the US Air Force Academy, the US Air Force, the Department of Defense, or any other organizational affiliation.

Published in the United States of America in 2022 by
Lynne Rienner Publishers, Inc.
1800 30th Street, Suite 314, Boulder, Colorado 80301
www.rienner.com

and in the United Kingdom by
Lynne Rienner Publishers, Inc.
Gray's Inn House, 127 Clerkenwell Road, London EC1 5DB
www.eurospanbookstore.com/rienner

© 2022 by Lynne Rienner Publishers, Inc. All rights reserved

Library of Congress Cataloging-in-Publication Data
Names: Burke, Ryan, author.
Title: The polar pivot : great power competition in the Arctic and
  Antarctica / Ryan Patrick Burke.
Description: Boulder, Colorado : Lynne Rienner Publishers, Inc., 2022. |
  Includes bibliographical references and index. | Summary: "Explores the
  rising tensions among China, Russia, and the US in the Arctic and
  Antarctica and argues that the new geopolitical environment demands a
  shift in US defense policy"— Provided by publisher.
Identifiers: LCCN 2021036838 (print) | LCCN 2021036839 (ebook) | ISBN
  9781626379947 (hardback) | ISBN 9781955055161 (ebook)
Subjects: LCSH: Polar regions—Strategic aspects. | Security,
  International—Polar regions. | Great powers. | United States—Military
  policy.
Classification: LCC G593 .B87 2022 (print) | LCC G593 (ebook) | DDC
  320.1/20911—dc23
LC record available at https://lccn.loc.gov/2021036838
LC ebook record available at https://lccn.loc.gov/2021036839

British Cataloguing in Publication Data
A Cataloguing in Publication record for this book
is available from the British Library.

Printed and bound in the United States of America

∞ The paper used in this publication meets the requirements
of the American National Standard for Permanence of
Paper for Printed Library Materials Z39.48-1992.

5 4 3 2 1

Contents

List of Tables and Figures   vii

1 On Thin Ice: The Polar Melting Pot   1
2 Security, Sovereignty, and Influence in the Polar Regions   23
3 The Four Cs: Commons, Claims, Covenants, and Cosmos   45
4 Polar Peer Powers: China and Russia   75
5 US Polar Policy and Strategy   111
6 The Polar Trap: Conditions for Conflict   141
7 Toward a US Grand Strategy   171
8 Balancing on the Pivot: The Future of Polar Security   201

Bibliography   233
Index   247
About the Book   261

Tables and Figures

TABLES

4.1	Polar Powers	86
4.2	Polar Players	86
4.3	Polar Perceivers	87
4.4	Polar Peripherals	88
4.5	Russian Arctic Policies, 2020 vs. 2035	94

FIGURES

1.1	The Arctic Region	6
1.2	The Antarctic Region	8
3.1	Lomonosov and Mendeleev Ridges	53
4.1	Polar Typology	79
4.2	Northern Sea Route vs. Suez Canal	99
8.1	Combatant Command Boundaries in the Arctic	210
8.2	Combatant Command Boundaries in Antarctica	211
8.3	Arctic Shipping Routes	218

1

On Thin Ice: The Polar Melting Pot

SINCE 1945, THE INTERNATIONAL SECURITY COMMUNITY HAS dedicated itself to describing, explaining, and predicting nuclear warfare and deterrence. For all the analyzing and assessing, however, the phenomenon has occurred only twice in recorded history, and within a span of three days. When, where, and how nuclear warfare might occur again has been the subject of much debate. As of this writing, there are five nuclear weapons states (United States, United Kingdom, France, Russia, China) recognized by the 1970 Nuclear Nonproliferation Treaty (NPT).[1] Four other states (India, Israel, Pakistan, North Korea) possess nuclear weapons but are not part of the NPT.[2] Of the eight nuclear weapons–possessing states in addition to the United States, two are formal US allies (United Kingdom and France); two are strategic partners (Israel and India); and one is a nonaggressor (Pakistan). The remaining nuclear states (Russia, China, North Korea) are formidable adversaries, at least in terms of military power that could threaten Western interests. Russia and China, specifically, are considered "great power competitors"* and among the most pressing twenty-first-century security challenges for the

---

*In October 2021, the US Department of Defense directed that the phrase "great power competition" be replaced with "strategic competition" in official correspondence. I use both phrases interchangeably throughout the book, while recognizing this is not the Defense Department's intent.

United States. So it should follow, then, that the international security community would and should pay attention to these great power competitors and those areas most likely to be the locations for resulting great power competition, confrontation, and potential conflict. The challenge is predicting where this might occur and why.

The polar regions of the Arctic and Antarctica are among the few areas with simultaneous Russian and Chinese presence in pursuit of national interests. The polar regions should occupy significant space in the current international security dialogue; but they do not, at least compared to the continued infatuation with analyzing every detail of nuclear warfare despite having a sample size of only two. And ignoring this observation of today will lead to the international security problems of tomorrow. In the twenty-first-century great power competition with Russia and China, the polar regions of the Arctic and Antarctica will be areas of both competition and military conflict if we do not attend to them today.

In the chapters that follow, I examine the evolving issue of polar militarization, defense, and security affairs in the context of twenty-first-century great power competition. I approach the discussion from a US perspective and with an eye toward Russia and China as great power rivals. As a central theme to the narrative, I argue that the United States has a strategic blind spot in the polar regions that others seek to exploit. I will present evidence throughout the book that the polar regions are on course to become contested regions that—absent reorientation of US priorities, posture, and presence—will eventually give way to military conflict. With this in mind, I contend that it is the polar regions, not Iraq, Afghanistan, Syria, or even the South China Sea, that should be the principal focus of future US military power projection efforts in the twenty-first century.

As the book progresses, I ask and attempt to answer the following questions: What is the historical significance of the polar regions in military affairs? Given this significance, who are the actors influencing the polar region security dynamic in the twenty-first century? What are their positions relative to each other—in other words, which states can most influence the future of the Arctic and Antarctica? For those with the greatest influence potential in polar region affairs, what are their polar region agendas? Given these competing agendas in an era of renewed great power competition, how will the polar regions influence and serve as backdrops for great power competition in the twenty-first century? After arguing that the polar regions are relevant to future great power competition, I then ask, and attempt to answer: What does the United

States need to do in order to shape and influence the polar regions in the context of future great power competition and US interests? In other words, how should the United States posture itself for a future fight?

Answering these questions requires a layered analysis of the polar regions' geography and geology; historical trends and punctuations in international security contexts; issues of sovereignty and influence; great power rival interests and orientation to the regions; US polar policies and postures; and military and diplomatic strategies. After examining the myriad factors shaping and influencing potential polar warfare and great power competition, I analyze comparable and historical context informing related critical theories for application to the polar regions in the evolving great power competition. Using existing theory as a basis for further analysis, I develop my own theoretical framework for a US approach to polar defense and security orientation and influence. From this new concept, I discuss what this strategy might look like in practice before concluding with a series of policy and strategy recommendations for future US polar orientation in twenty-first-century great power competition.

As we begin this assessment of the polar regions in the context of great power competition, we must remind ourselves that polar militarization and warfare—inclusive of both the Arctic and Antarctica—are seldom-discussed topics in academic and practitioner communities for reasons we will address. Even with a rapidly evolving polar security dialogue emerging among scholars and practitioners, this subject still lacks comparable theoretical, conceptual, and analytical depth of the myriad topics in military affairs in the post–World War II era. From strategic deterrence in the Cold War to counterinsurgency operations in the global war on terror, hundreds of topics and subtopics permeate the ether within security studies, strategic studies, and international relations literature. Polar defense and security enjoys relative ambiguity in comparison to the more *en vogue* topics of the late twentieth and early twenty-first centuries. There is one paper on polar security for every fifty papers on counterinsurgency (or so it seems). Therefore, there is ample room for contribution and substantive analysis on a topic of comparative obscurity, and until the resurgence of renewed great power competition, of questionable relevance since the 1950s.

As the primary source documents for US national security and defense postures, the current (as of this writing) versions of the National Security Strategy, National Defense Strategy, and National Military Strategy each emphasize a pivot to great power competition or rivalry with China and Russia. "Great power competition"—or, more recently, "strategic competition"—is the flagship phrase of modern defense policies and strategic guidance. Despite this, none of these primary source documents discuss the polar regions in any detail. Yet the polar regions are the only geographic locations at present in which the United States can potentially find itself in a competitive or even contested domain simultaneously with both Russia and China—and few are actually talking about it.

The conversation is changing, however. In today's geopolitical environment, the polar regions matter. China and Russia seek, at the least, influence in the poles, as evidenced by evolving interest and orientation. Despite this, scholars and practitioners struggle to communicate, in a compelling enough manner to drive action, why the poles are important to future great power competition and US standing in international security.

This book aims to further the conversation and advance our understanding of the complexity and importance of the polar regions. It aims to make scholars and policymakers more aware of the polar regions' significance for future great power competition and to advocate for more resources and attention to these increasingly critical regions in the international security discourse. Through these efforts to raise awareness and advocate for more attention, the book aims to compel US action to meet this evolving security concern. With that we should ask: What are the polar regions and how and why will these regions influence the future great power competition?

What Are the Polar Regions?

The polar regions are some of the least-studied and least-known areas on Earth. Known as the "frigid zones," the regions surrounding the geographical North and South Poles are—relative to most of the Earth's populated areas and other climatic regions—remote and desolate. These frigid zones within the northern and southern polar circles are dominated by cold as well as seasonal darkness or constant sunshine. In the northern polar region, the Arctic, floating sea ice covers most of the Arctic Ocean throughout the year. In the southern polar region, the Antarctic ice sheet blanket 98 percent of the continent of Antarctica with ice over a mile thick in some places.[3] In general, the term *polar regions* refers to the regions within the polar circles of the Arctic Circle in the Northern Hemisphere and the Antarctic Circle in the Southern Hemisphere. Throughout the discussion, I will refer generally to the polar regions inclusive of the Arctic and Antarctica, but suffice to say they are not mirror images of each other and are instead, quite literally, polar opposites. Each enjoys its own unique characteristics warranting distinction and consideration as we consider their futures relative to renewed great power competition.

THE ARCTIC

The conventional—and current due to dynamic drift—international definition of the Arctic stipulates the region as all area north of the Arctic Circle, or 66°33' north latitude, leading many to colloquially refer to the Arctic as the "High North." Whereas 66°33' north specifies the Arctic Circle proper, the climatic zone above 60° north latitude includes most of Alaska, all of Greenland, Iceland, most of Scandinavia, and the northern half of Russia. This region is only slightly warmer than the area north of the Arctic Circle and is the lowest northern latitude to experience the midnight sun during the summer months, a natural phenomenon associated exclusively with the polar regions. As such, some consider the Arctic anywhere you can see the midnight sun, or north of 60° north. As if the Arctic Circle or the climatic zone north of 60° north latitude are not specific enough, others apply a more precise climate indicator to their definition of the Arctic. This third definition holds the Arctic to include any area north of the 10 degree Celsius (50 degree Fahrenheit) July isotherm, or a geographic contour line indicating constant temperature patterns (the solid line in Figure 1.1).

The 50 degree Fahrenheit isotherm includes the northernmost regions of Alaska and Russia, the Alaskan Aleutian Islands, and the Bering Sea. It notably excludes most of Scandinavia, and includes all of Greenland and a large section of northern Canada. The 50 degree Fahrenheit isotherm indicates that not all Arctics are equal, an important distinction we will come back to later. However, the 50 degree Fahrenheit isotherm, in that it excludes Scandinavia and most of northern Russia, is too limiting for our discussion. From a legal standpoint, US code stipulates the Arctic as territory north of the Arctic Circle, but further includes "United States territory north and west of the boundary formed by the Porcupine, Yukon, and Kuskokwim Rivers; all contiguous seas, including the Arctic Ocean and the Beaufort, Bering, and Chukchi Seas; and the Aleutian chain."[4] For our purposes as we consider current and future defense, security, and great power competition in the Arctic, we will adopt the US legal definition of the Arctic, inclusive of the Aleutian Island chain.

At approximately 6 million square miles, the Arctic Ocean is the smallest of the world's oceans.[5] It is the least-known due to its mostly

Figure 1.1 The Arctic Region

Source: Central Intelligence Agency, *World Factbook*, https://www.cia.gov/the-world-factbook.

year-round sea ice above 75° north, seasonal darkness, and generally harsh conditions. It is also the least-accessed of the world's oceans. With an average depth of 3,000 feet, the Arctic Ocean is not a deep ocean compared to the Pacific and Atlantic, but does have some locations reaching depths of 18,000 feet or more. The many islands, archipelagoes, and peninsular extensions within the Arctic Ocean necessitate the designation of several marginal seas on its periphery, including the Norwegian, Greenland, Beaufort, Chukchi, East Siberian, Laptev,

Kara, Barents, and Bering Seas.[6] Sea ice forms seasonally in the marginal seas, where most enjoy ice-free waters during the warmer months between 60° and 75° north. North of 75° latitude, the sea ice extent is, today, constant year-round save for the many leads (navigable fractures within ice expanses) and resulting pockets of open water stemming from them.

The continued melting of sea ice and opening of the Arctic Ocean creates economic opportunity for nations with both the interest and the capability to reach the Arctic's vast energy resources and vital commerce lanes. Per some estimates, there is upward of $35 trillion worth of untapped oil and natural gas in the Arctic, as well as untold sums of precious minerals and biological resources in this transforming region.[7] A US government estimate notes the Arctic region could have about 90 billion barrels of oil, 1,700 trillion cubic feet of natural gas, and 44 billion barrels of liquid natural gas.[8] The massive economic proposition coupled with the annual decrease in sea ice in the Arctic Ocean enables greater maritime access and makes for a renewed sense of urgency for those with interests in shaping the Arctic's future and benefiting from its potential resource bounty. Arctic sea ice continues to decline by about 13 percent per decade and has done so since 1980.[9] Such a steady decrease in sea ice and expanding navigable waters underscore the significance of the opportunity for ambitious states to stake their claim and influence the Arctic's future. And this is precisely where the situation in the Arctic becomes complicated.

With a host of sovereign borders extending into the Arctic Circle and bordering the Arctic's marginal seas, this is a region teeming with interest due to both geography and the dynamic environmental changes leading to enhanced economic opportunity. Arctic governance, then, as an inherent multinational proposition, is challenging and ripe for competing interests and resulting tension.

In short, the Arctic is an area of evolving international interest furthered by its changing geography. What was once an inhospitable, impassable, and largely ignored region (relative to others) is now, in the twenty-first century, becoming more hospitable, passable, and emphasized in the international conversation. Absent a legitimate governing body—as we will discuss later—and with expanding international interests, the Arctic may become the Wild West of the Northern Hemisphere. And while the northern polar region commands the preponderance of the day's attention from scholars and practitioners interested or involved in international affairs and security, the southern polar region, too, has an evolving interest profile.

ANTARCTICA

The Antarctic is the southern polar region south of the Antarctic Circle containing the geographic South Pole and the continent of Antarctica. The conventional definition of the Antarctic encompasses the area of the Southern Ocean—all water and landmass below 60° south latitude, or the continent of Antarctica and the immediate surrounding water bodies (see Figure 1.2). As the southernmost and fifth largest continent on Earth, Antarctica has a landmass of 5.5 million square miles, over 98 percent of which is covered by ice that is over a mile thick in some places.[10] A polar desert, it is the coldest, driest, and windiest place on

Figure 1.2 The Antarctic Region

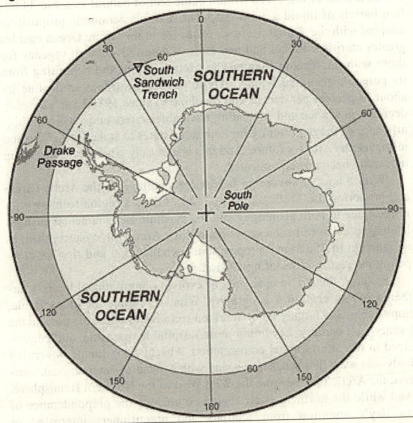

Source: Central Intelligence Agency, *World Factbook*, https://www.cia.gov/the-world-factbook.

the planet, with fewer than 5,000 transient residents at any given time housed throughout the dozens of research stations spread across the continent. Depending on the season, the Antarctic ice sheets expand and contract, covering nearly 7 million square miles of ocean in the winter and about 1 million square miles in the summer.[11]

Temperatures vary widely on Antarctica based on location, season, and elevation, with the average coastal temperatures (the warmest part of the continent) around 15 degrees Fahrenheit.[12] Antarctica registered Earth's coldest temperature on record, at −128 degrees Fahrenheit on July 21, 1983. The warmest temperature ever recorded in Antarctica, at the time of this writing, was 69 degrees Fahrenheit on February 9, 2020. The extraordinary difference in temperature variance between the higher and lower elevations of Antarctica drives most research station locations to the coasts, where the temperatures are more tolerable for sustained human activity. In the summer months on the Antarctic coasts, temperatures are comparable to late summer or early fall in Fairbanks, Alaska, with average temperatures reaching near 50 degrees Fahrenheit. Unlike Antarctica's coastal regions, which see a range of weather patterns and precipitation, the interior of the continent is a polar desert mostly isolated from influential weather patterns. As few weather fronts make their way to Antarctica's interior, this area remains cold and dry.

Despite the conditions, there is an abundance of wildlife as well as scores of natural and biological resources and scientific uniqueness on the continent, driving dozens of countries to maintain research stations throughout Antarctica. That dozens of countries operate some form of permanent infrastructure on the continent, used exclusively as a research domain, and all without a single government or indigenous population, is something of a global anomaly that begs discussion for context.[13]

Outside of year-round occupied research stations or bases, there is no permanent human habitation on Antarctica and no native population.[14] Since the Russians claimed Antarctica's discovery in 1820, the southern continent has seen a steady increase in activity in the 200 years since.[15] From Shackleton's famed Antarctic expeditions in the early 1900s to cruise ships today, Antarctica is a place of novelty and intrigue for many. Still, the bucket-list travelers and adventurers account for a small fraction of the annual visitors to Antarctica. Rather, most who make the southerly trek do so in the name of science. With this multinational interest on an identity-less continent, it is no wonder there is a standing Antarctic Treaty stipulating the prohibited and permitted activities on Antarctica. In this way, the Antarctic Treaty System drives the conversation and likewise serves as the starting point for discussion about Antarctica's place in the international security dialogue, to include the overlapping and competing territorial claims that we will examine later.

Until recently, discussing Antarctica and international security in the same context raised eyebrows. As we progress into renewed twenty-first-century great power competition, the two are no longer mutually exclusive. Antarctica is creeping back into relevance in the international security landscape, and with good reason. To this end, we turn our attention to great power competition, what it is, why it is occurring, where it will likely go in the future, and the significance of the polar regions in this context.

Outside of scholarly discourse on the matter, there has been much interest in the polar regions, both military and otherwise, throughout the past eight decades, such that expecting great power competition to arrive in the poles at some point in the twenty-first century should be assumed. With that, we must consider the changing geopolitical landscapes in an increasingly globalized world in the early twenty-first century. Increasing globalization also brings increased knowledge and experience. As the world learns more of the changes in the polar regions, we also learn more about their potential yet unrealized economic value. Melting ice and improved technology enable greater polar region access. As access broadens, resources present themselves. And as resources present themselves, especially in the global commons, competition ensues as countries seek to exploit some of the last untouched regions on Earth. In the era of sustained US and allied focus on the global war on terror throughout the Middle East, Asia, and North Africa, great power competition has returned to other regions of the world. As the war on terror dwindles into the history books, US defense postures and policies have continued their shift toward renewed great power competition.

GREAT POWER COMPETITION RENEWED

What is great power competition? The buzz phrase of Washington during the Trump administration, "great power competition," describes the international security environment with rising state powers threatening the US-led world order. The Biden administration's Interim National Security Strategic Guidance, published in March 2021, refers to this phenomenon as "rivalry" rather than competition.[16] Regardless of word choice, the United States is increasingly wary of authoritarian state power positions in the twenty-first century. Since the end of World War II, the United States has enjoyed status as the global superpower—the lone hegemon standing atop the world stage absent a suitable foe, be it military, economic, or otherwise. In simple terms, great power competition is—in a way—analogous to the childhood game King of the Hill, the objective of which is to be on top of the hill. Others charge the hill in the quest for summit dominance and status among peers. Typically, the strongest kid remained at the top in constant defense of the summit from the charges of weaker kids. In this way, since World War II the United States has been king of the hill—perched upon the international security summit looking down at weaker states, most of which are too afraid to attempt a challenge. As king of the hill, the United States has defined the world order according to its terms since 1945, despite challenges during the Cold War.

Scholars and policymakers long considered the Soviet Union a competing power on the global stage during the Cold War. Though their strength, and thus their true threat, was widely debated, the Soviets possessed enough military strength and a strong nationalist identity to gain US attention and influence activities across the diplomatic, informational, military, and economic spectra. Whether the Soviet Union was ever a legitimate threat to the United States during the Cold War is the subject of continued academic debate. Regardless of position, the consensus is that the United States and the Soviets were in a competition for global influence. This was as much a competition about conflicting ideology as it was a competition about whose missile was bigger. To some, the Soviet Union was, along with the United States, a great power such that the Cold War was very much a twentieth-century great power competition. Even still, the consensus among academics and policymakers holds that the United States was never at risk of losing its status as the global hegemon to the Soviet Union. The same cannot be said for the renewed twenty-first-century great power competition of today.

Following the Soviet Union's collapse in the early 1990s, the United States, fresh off a decisive military victory in the Gulf War, distanced itself from the rest of the international pack. Save for smaller military skirmishes in Africa and the Balkans, the United States enjoyed relative peace and autonomy in the 1990s. After the terrorist attacks of September 11, 2001, the United States thrust itself into a global war on terror, first in Afghanistan and then in Iraq. The war on terror is the longest sustained military conflict in US history, costing trillions of dollars and thousands of American lives. Beyond the financial toll and loss of life, the war continues to serve as a distraction while rising powers advance their position on the metaphorical hill. As the United States continued meddling in the Middle East, Asia, and Africa in the war on terror during the 2000s, Russia and China rose to more prominent positions on the world stage. Growing economies fueled the expanding militaries that enabled greater power projection and influence. Budding economies and emerging militaries also encouraged brazen action and rhetoric. Today there is an ideological struggle between Western democracies and autocracies.[17] Central to this struggle are the United States, as the global superpower and champion of Western ideology, and emerging autocratic, anti-Western, revisionist competitors China and Russia.

As the war on terror fades, the US defense and national security establishment has shifted its focus away from countering terrorism and toward great power competition with Russia and China. Foundational national security documents codify this shift in focus as a rebalancing effort, redirecting diplomatic, military, and economic resources to the Asia Pacific region. In the context of this rebalance, the Trump administration's 2017 National Security Strategy adopted the term "great power competition" as a "dismissed . . . phenomenon of an earlier century."[18] Though the 2017 strategy did not define great power competition, it squarely seated China and Russia at the center of the discussion, labeling both as "revisionist powers" and unambiguously stating their intent to "change the international order in their favor."[19] The strategy claimed that Russia and China sought regional and global influence through expanding "military capabilities designed to deny America access in times of crisis and to contest our ability to operate freely in critical commercial zones during peacetime."[20] Along this thread, the 2018 National Defense Strategy identified "reemergence of long-term, strategic competition" with these revisionist powers as the "central challenge to U.S. prosperity and security." The defense strategy doubled down on the security strategy's assertion of Chinese and Russian ambition, claiming that both sought "to shape a world consistent with their authoritarian model" and influence the economic, security, and diplomatic decisions of other nations.[21] Finally, the unclassified 2018 description of the National Military Strategy sowed the thread by listing the "reemergence of great power competition" with Russia and China as the top in the list of relevant security trends in the National Defense Strategy.[22] Today, the Biden administration is actively developing its national security and defense policies. Until then, the national security and defense establishment left over from the Trump administration, via its foundational documents, has established great power competition with Russia and China as the principal national and international security threat in the twenty-first century. But competition implies spoils. What are they?

WHAT ARE WE COMPETING FOR?

The continued rise of Russia and China in the twenty-first century now threatens the era of unipolarity, or hegemony, the United States enjoyed since World War II. If we are to accept the notion that these revisionist great powers pose a legitimate threat to the US-led world order, then we must consider the reality of a multipolar world with more than one influential power. As we usher in a new era of strategic competition and potential conflict, the question we must ask is: What are we competing for? And why? Answering this question should, in theory, inform future US posturing and security approaches. Should the United States seek to maintain a unipolar world in which it remains atop the hill as the global hegemon? If so, does this necessitate the continued liberal hegemonic ambition of preponderance and interventionism? If not, what are the changes the United States can and perhaps should make to reflect the evolution of renewed—and perhaps unwinnable—great power competition?

The superficial board game answer to the "What are we competing for?" question is world domination. But a game of Risk is not reality. The more complex and less hyperbolic answer trends toward the desire for global influence and the ability to set and enforce the rules in one's favor. Russia and China see the world order as one reflecting US and Western values and antithetical to their regimes and philosophies. As the global hegemon, the United States has reigned supreme over the world order due to its unmatched military and economic clout. As such, the United States has—for seventy-five years—been the biggest influencer on the world stage, able to mold and shape international relations and security to suit its own agenda while promoting global prosperity and security greater than that of a world in which the United States did not set the global agenda.

In metaphorical terms, the renewed twenty-first-century great power competition is a game of chess—a global environment of strategic posturing and advancing toward one's objective of checkmate or, in the case of today's security environment, hegemony. As opposed to chess's two-player format, this twenty-first-century game of strategic chess is a three-way competition with two players—Russia and China—decidedly against and seeking to supplant the third—the United States.

In the stakes of twenty-first-century chess, the spoils are hegemonic power status and the ability to influence economic, security, and diplomatic matters to suit the winner's agenda. To be a global hegemon in the twenty-first century requires a combination of policy, posture, presence, and power in every corner of the world stage, including the polar regions. The poles today host a range of diplomatic, military, and economic interests and propositions compelling competition among great powers and even subordinate states seeking to move up a step or two on the global power ladder.

In the Arctic and Antarctica, trillions of dollars' worth of undiscovered natural and biological resources can reshape global trade and the economic positions of those with access and control. But these resources exist within the global commons—shared and ungoverned spaces of the world for all to access. There is a competition to access and benefit from the resources within the commons, and there are few institutions strong enough to effectively deter malign actor intent. Absent recognized territorial claims, competition within the resource-rich international polar commons is left checked only by international covenants—institutional agreements maintaining the superficial luster of legitimacy but in truth and reality lacking any actual binding deterrent for self-motivated states deviating from such agreements and intent on securing rights to untapped commodities. Beyond polar commodities, the international community is in competition over influence for access to the cosmos, or outer space. As the last truly ungoverned but also strategically relevant locations, especially for projecting power in space, the polar regions are equally rooted in competition over claims and territoriality. Influence requires presence and capabilities. The states with the most presence and capabilities will generate the most influence and thus the most control—presumably—over the strategic value, be it realized or anticipated, of the polar commons. Greater influence translates to more power—and the most powerful state in the game of international chess enjoys status as global hegemon and the one who most molds the world order in its own favor.

In the context of expanding influence via the commons and territory, we can look into the depths of the history books for examples of how each has compelled conflict sufficient to extend the same logic to the current situation in the polar regions. That said, while we can look to historical antecedents, we need only look back to Vladimir Putin's rise to power in Russia or Xi Jinping's rise in China for modern examples of the same as informative frames by which to consider the future of the polar regions given today's international dynamics.

RUSSIA AND CHINA AS GREAT POWER COMPETITORS
In 2007 under President Vladimir Putin's direction to restore Russian great power status, Russia began resurrecting Soviet-era Arctic bases. That same year, the country planted a Russian Federation flag on the North Pole seabed in an international declaration of Arctic ownership and propaganda.[23] In 2008, Russia invaded Georgia and conducted a combined air, naval, and land military campaign that resulted in Russia's continued occupation of two Georgian territories to this day.[24] Russia continued its expansionist aggression with the 2014 invasion of Ukraine and subsequent annexation of the Crimean Peninsula, now administered as a Russian federal subject, or controlled political territory.[25] Later that year, Russia established its Northern Fleet Joint Strategic Command, whose priority focus is the Arctic. Since then, Russia has continued its Arctic military infrastructure and capabilities development to include regular aerial reconnaissance missions throughout the Arctic and near Alaskan airspace. Russia requires foreign vessels traversing the Northern Sea Route to allow a Russian captain to board and navigate the route, against international maritime law but on the basis of disputed Russian claims about territorial waters relative to the continental shelf.[26] Russia has also deployed nuclear-capable hypersonic weapons systems to the Arctic and continue aggressive rhetoric toward the United States and its allies.[27] There is no evidence of passivity or isolationism, and with the reelection of Putin through 2036, Russian political and military trajectories are likely to continue along this path well into the future. Finally, in a 2019 speech, Putin addressed growing speculation of expanding Russian-Chinese relations, referring to such as "an allied relationship in the full sense of a multifaceted strategic partnership."[28]

As if to complement Russian aggression and great power restoration efforts, China has also asserted its status as a global power player in the twenty-first century. With a rapidly growing economy, the Chinese have invested billions of dollars into military modernization efforts. Moreover, China's long-standing practice of debt-trap diplomacy continues advancing the Chinese Communist Party's global presence through expanded infrastructure projects and economic relationships with the preponderance of the world's countries. The hallmark of this effort, China's 2013 Belt and Road Initiative, seeks to develop Chinese presence in more than 70 countries and has established partnerships with 142 and counting.[29] Under President Xi Jinping since 2013, the People's Republic of China has become a global force of economic and military influence. Its most controversial effort to date, though, is its extension of territorial claims into the South China Sea international waterway since 2012.

The international community casts China's continued creation of artificial islands for military and economic purpose as a breach of international law and disruption to the regional and global economy by extension. This ongoing and expanding territorial assertion adds greater tension to the international discourse and continues to bring China and the United States closer to each other in their respective naval exercises in the region. Finally, China's polar region interests are similarly evolving with their development of nuclear icebreakers—its self-proclaimed status as a "near-Arctic state" and its increasing presence in Antarctica, sometimes for questionable or unknown reasons.[30] The evidence of Chinese and Russian aggression is undeniable, and their intent equally so. We will discuss these and other matters in subsequent chapters. For now, the prevailing position in the international security discourse holds China and Russia as twenty-first-century great power competitors to the United States. The degree of threat and competition continues to be debated, but that China and Russia seek greater global influence in the twenty-first century is a largely agreed-upon fact. What the community cannot and does not agree on, it seems, is whether the polar regions of the Arctic and Antarctica should be part of the conversation.

COMPETITION IN THE POLAR REGIONS

Those contending that the polar regions are irrelevant to renewed great power competition are not paying attention. Instead, they cling to the notion that the polar regions are of little value to the world order and the great powers vying to shape it. More to the point, this camp contends that even if the polar regions did present some known value to the future international security landscape, thus compelling military presence in some form, the regions themselves are distant, austere environments sufficient to deter sustained military activities. Between seasonal darkness, navigation challenges, unforgiving temperatures, and unpredictable icepack, the polar regions, according to some, are too harsh for even the most committed militaries. In some ways this has proven true. The polar regions are among the least-populated regions on Earth and, with the exception of the period immediately following World War II, have seen equally little military attention through the years. As the polar regions become more accessible, their obscurity and irrelevance is shifting toward fame and relevance.

The February 9, 2020, temperature reading of 64.9 degrees Fahrenheit at Esperanza Base weather station in Hope Bay was an Antarctic milestone.[31] One day of high temperatures alone is insignificant. What is significant is the frequency of higher-than-average temperatures recorded on Antarctica over time. As ocean temperatures rise, so do Antarctic surface temperatures. And as Antarctic surface temperatures increase, so does the rate of perceived melt or, at the very least, perceived accessibility. The Arctic is trending toward a similar future. According to the National Oceanic and Atmospheric Administration, 2019-2020 was the warmest summer on record and nearly 3 degrees Fahrenheit hotter than average.[32] The largest remaining Arctic ice shelf is breaking apart, and the continuing observation of sea ice decline at 12-13 percent since the 1980s had led the scientific community to generally agree that—assuming continuation of this trend—the Arctic will see ice-free summers for the first time in recorded history by 2050.[33]

Regardless of reason, be it human-driven warming or natural climatic variations that have occurred throughout Earth's history, scientists agree: the climate is changing; the oceans are getting warmer and rising; and the ice—in both polar regions—is melting. Climate change skeptics' predictions based on trend analysis and extrapolation are flawed. Scientists predicted in the 1970s that the world would soon run out of oil, yet in 2020 we continue to discover new oil reservoirs and resource-rich environments. Maybe the ice will not continue to melt, but maybe it will. Either way, the United States cannot afford to dismiss the observable realities of today and the predictions of the changing polar environments of tomorrow, while simultaneously enabling great power rivals China and Russia to assert themselves at the poles in the absence of substantial US presence and interest.

Great power competitors are paying attention to what the United States does or does not do in its global engagements. These actions or inactions have shaped and will shape future Russian and Chinese perceptions of US strength and resolve. When the Obama administration failed to enforce the 2012 "red line" in Syria with promised military action if the Assad regime used chemical weapons, the world noticed.[34] In the years following, the Chinese rebuked international law and US finger-wagging and built artificial islands in the South China Sea; Russia invaded and annexed another country's sovereign territory. As both great powers move on the polar regions, the United States continues to watch. Training with North Atlantic Treaty Organization allies in Norway, sending fighter squadrons to Alaska, and sending navy surface action groups into the Barents Sea have all been part of the "steady northward creep" of the United States to Arctic security posturing.[35] For the United States to retain its hegemony, this is not enough. But should the United States seek hegemonic maintenance in the twenty-first-century world order? We will address these and other questions throughout the rest of the book. Either way, the polar regions matter in the future geopolitical and geostrategic equation.

The polar regions will be—and already are to an extent—a competitive domain in the twenty-first-century great power competition. Competition will continue to drive confrontation. Increasing confrontation may lead to contestation. To prevent the polar regions from becoming contested environments, and eventually succumbing to conflict that will affect the US homeland and the global economy, the United States must follow a more aggressive course of both policy and strategy to safeguard its interests and promote favorable power balances in and around the polar regions. The recommended policies and strategic concepts for polar region employment must be informed by relevant context and the lessons of history influential to strategic theory that inform the application of the national instruments of power.

STRUCTURE OF THE BOOK

Over the course the remaining chapters I will discuss polar region dynamics in the international security context of current and future great power competition with an eye toward military, defense, and security policies, postures, and practices.

Chapter 2 opens with a discussion of the polar regions through the lens of international security relevance and punctuations since World War II. I discuss significant shaping events in polar region dynamics through the years, emphasizing only what I consider the most influential matters contributing to the evolving polar region security discussion today. This overview hints at and outlines the nature of the conversation and how the polar regions have arrived at the point they are today: at the nexus of international peace and security.

In Chapter 3, I transition to discussing the four categories I argue to be most influential to the current and future polar region security sphere, or what I call the polar Cs: commons, claims, covenants, cosmos. I discuss each of the four polar Cs in context of their influence on today's and tomorrow's polar region landscape. I address such topics as historical claims to both regions, competing claims and the basis for each, international polar institutions like the Arctic Council and Antarctic Treaty, as well as current and future space operations and interests enabled via the polar regions and their critically important geography. I detail why each of the polar Cs, as broad categorical descriptors, have and will continue to encourage and incentivize great power competition between Russia, China, and the United States.

In Chapter 4, I offer a frame for analyzing polar actors and their relative capabilities and intent for future polar region influence. I turn my attention to those with actual influence in the regions as measured by policy, posture, presence, and power. I argue that, if left on the same trajectory absent change, the polar regions will devolve into contested militarized domains in the twenty-first century, spurred by particular polar region actors with the necessary combination of capability and intent to influence polar affairs, or their relative threat.

To differentiate among the polar actors relative to their perceived threat, I present a polar typology: a four-by-four frame for both Arctic and Antarctic actors categorizing and plotting each according to my assessment of their polar capabilities and intent. I further describe these four polar actors within the typology as polar peripherals, polar perceivers, polar players, and polar powers. The discussion extends from the polar powers designation and emphasizes Russian and Chinese polar policies informing the national narrative and their respective polar orientations. These policies inform much of what the revisionist great powers are actively pursuing in the polar regions, including the arguably malign actions each is undertaking in their quest for polar region influence. This chapter provides a comparison for the proceeding chapter's discussion on current US polar policies and informed postures relative to what China and Russia have developed.

In Chapter 5, I provide a policy analysis of the current polar posture of the United States, or lack thereof, since Richard Nixon. I then examine trends in the National Security Strategy, National Defense Strategy, and National Military Strategy and their collective emphasis on great power competition. I discuss the military significance of the polar regions to US hegemony and how they are unique in that they span multiple geographic combatant command areas of responsibility, and yet, save for US Northern Command, none of these commands' current posture statements address security challenges or concerns in the polar regions.

From there, I summarize the latest Department of Defense Arctic Strategy as well as the other services' Arctic strategies relative to the objectives stated in the National Security, Defense, and Military Strategies. I further compare the Arctic strategies to existing treaties and international governance and discuss what can and cannot be done considering the established limits. I present missed opportunities in each for polar policy inclusion and discuss briefly that continued omission of polar policies or the adoption of toothless policies lacking budgeted intent will lead to a United States that is strategically outpaced and disadvantaged in the polar regions by the rise of great power competitors such as China and Russia.

Finally, I present three potential scenarios and outcomes for the future of the poles based on the analysis of current US policy. In that context, I argue that the polar regions are quickly becoming the priority power-grab regions for rising great power competitors. Whereas the United States stands as the current global hegemon, the rise of China and Russia in the polar regions—coupled with the lack of orientation of the United States—is creating conditions ripe for realization of the Thucydides Trap, or what I refer to as the polar trap.

In Chapter 6, I outline the leading scholarly narratives informing the polar strategic blind spot and the conditions necessary to realize the polar trap. I detail the predictive implications of these circumstances should they actually occur and the problem scenarios created as a result. I spend the remaining discussion of the chapter focused on the future implications of the polar trap for the United States and what the risks are to succumbing to this historically predictable fate.

In Chapter 7, I extend the logic of the polar trap as the basis for presenting an alternative strategy for influence, or what I refer to as transactional balancing globally and polar balancing within the polar regions. I review seminal concepts in current US grand strategy and focus attention on the debate between liberal hegemony (strategy of engagement and global military presence) and offshore balancing (generally a strategy of restraint save for specifically identified areas of geopolitical and strategic significance). Using this decades-old debate (i.e., Should we engage or should we restrain?), I build the case for an alternative strategy of polar influence that satisfies both restraint and the platforms of engagement advocates given the significance of the polar regions to future great power competition. Building from this argument, I present the framework and conditions for polar balancing as a proposed alternative approach for polar influence in the twenty-first-century great power competition. The proposed strategy describes, explains, and predicts what the future great power competition will look like should the United States adopt this polar orientation. In doing so, the chapter addresses the issues identified in Chapter 2 relative to enhanced polar infrastructure and capabilities; attends to the realities of the polar spheres of influence noted in Chapter 3; addresses the rising polar posture and influence from competing great powers discussed in Chapter 4; fills in some of the policy gaps noted in Chapter 5; and perhaps most important might put the United States on course to avoid becoming victim to the polar trap identified in Chapter 6.

Chapter 8 concludes the book by first detailing a series of recommendations for executing polar balancing in twenty-first-century great power competition. Here I label the proposed approach the polar pivot. Essentially, if the United States adopts the recommended polar balancing approach in Chapter 7, Chapter 8 is the blueprint to execution. As part of the pivot, I outline a strategic framework inclusive of polar region goals and recommended lines of effort toward these goals. I recommend changes to the US military combatant command structure; recommend US military service-specific orientations to the polar regions; and encourage numerous revisions to polar military operational capabilities and readiness. Finally, I revisit the pressing security and presence situation in the poles; the polar Cs shaping the polar security scape; the polar typology describing the power balance and imbalance in the regions; the lack of US policy orientation toward these regions compared to the substance of competitors' policies to the same; the real risks of the polar trap resulting from the lack of US orientation; and the adoption of polar balancing via a twenty-first-century US polar pivot. I detail the lasting implications of an unrealized polar conflict situation should the United States refuse to reorient to the poles and further attempt to bring attention to this seldom-discussed issue critical to US national security and global interests. While this may not be an issue of today, it certainly will be one of tomorrow.

Notes

1. "The Nuclear Nonproliferation Treaty (NPT) at a Glance," March 2020, https://www.armscontrol.org/factsheets/nptfact.
2. "Nuclear Weapons: Who Has What at a Glance," August 2020, https://www.armscontrol.org/factsheets/Nuclearweaponswhohaswhat. North Korea withdrew from the NPT in 2003.
3. "Ice Sheets," n.d., https://www.nsf.gov/geo/opp/antarct/science/icesheet.jsp#:~:text=It%20averages%202%2C160%20meters%20thick,all%20the%20world's%20fresh%20water.
4. 15 US Code § 4111. "Arctic" defined.
5. Whelan, "The Oceans of the World by Size."
6. Ostenso, "Arctic Ocean." Some oceanographers include the Bering Sea as an Arctic marginal sea, given it is within the 50 degree Isotherm of Arctic climate conditions. For the purposes of this book and to remain consistent with the US legal definition, I consider the Bering Sea among the Arctic's marginal seas.
7. Dillow, "Russia and China Vie to Beat the U.S."
8. Gautier et al., "Circum-Arctic Resource Appraisal"; Desjardins, "This Infographic Shows."
9. Meier et al., *Sea Ice Outlook Interim Post-Season Report*.
10. "Ice Sheets."
11. National Snow and Ice Data Center, "All About Sea Ice: Arctic vs. Antarctic," April 3, 2020, https://nsidc.org/cryosphere/seaice/characteristics/difference.html.

12. The highest elevations in Antarctica average temperatures below −70 degrees Fahrenheit.
13. Teller, "Why Do So Many Nations Want a Piece of Antarctica?"
14. The closest thing to actual human settlement on Antarctica is Argentina's Esperanza Base on the Antarctic Peninsula. Argentinian military personnel and their families can be stationed here for extended periods. There is a small school building and other limited infrastructure to support nonresearch activities. It is said that residents moving to Esperanza Base must have their appendix removed prior to arrival, as an example of the remote nature of this duty assignment for personnel and their families.
15. Moran, "200 years of exploring Antarctica."
16. Biden, *Interim National Security Strategic Guidance.*
17. Friedman, "The New Concept Everyone in Washington Is Talking About."
18. Donald J. Trump, *National Security Strategy of the United States of America* (Washington, DC: Executive Office of the President, 2017), p. 27.
19. Ibid.
20. Ibid.
21. Mattis, *Summary of the 2018 National Defense Strategy,* p. 2.
22. Joint Staff, *Description of the National Military Strategy 2018,* p. 2.
23. Parfitt, "Russia Plants Flag on North Pole Seabed."
24. Pruitt, "How a Five-Day War with Georgia."
25. Council on Foreign Relations, "Conflict in Ukraine."
26. Staalesen, "Russia Sets Out Stringent New Rules."
27. "Russia Tests Hypersonic Missile in Arctic, TASS Cites Sources," *Reuters,* November 30, 2019, https://www.reuters.com/article/us-russia-arctic-missiles/russia-tests-hypersonic-missile-in-arctic-tass-cites-sources-idUSKBN1Y40BB.
28. *Russia Analytical Report,* October 21–28, 2019, https://www.russiamatters.org/news/russia-analytical-report/russia-analytical-report-oct-21-28-2019.
29. "Countries of the Belt and Road Initiative," March 2020, https://green-bri.org/countries-of-the-belt-and-road-initiative-bri?cookie-state-change=1607466378905.
30. Durkee, "China.'"
31. "Antarctica Melts Under Its Hottest Days on Record," February 13, 2020, retrieved July 5, 2020, https://earthobservatory.nasa.gov/images/146322/antarctica-melts-under-its-hottest-days-on-record#:~:text=On%20February%206%2C%202020%2C%20weather,widespread%20melting%20on%20nearby%20glaciers.
32. National Oceanic and Atmospheric Administration, "Northern Hemisphere Just Had Its Hottest Summer on Record," September 14, 2020, https://www.noaa.gov/news/northern-hemisphere-just-had-its-hottest-summer-on-record#:~:text=August%202020,-According%20to%20scientists&text=The%20Northern%20Hemisphere%20had%20its%20hottest%20August%20on%20record%20with,five%20warmest%20occurring%20since%202015.
33. Twila et al., "The Expanding Footprint of Rapid Arctic Change." There are some regions of the Arctic Circle that are regularly ice-free during the summers. However, to date, the area above of 80° north latitude is typically covered in year-round icepack. This year-round ice cap is predicted to be ice-free by the summer of 2050.
34. Rhodes, "Inside the White House."
35. "America and Britain Play Cold-War Games with Russia in the Arctic," *The Economist,* May 10, 2020, https://www.economist.com/europe/2020/05/10/america-and-britain-play-cold-war-games-with-russia-in-the-arctic.

2

Security, Sovereignty, and Influence in the Polar Regions

THE POLAR REGIONS HAVE NOT ALWAYS BEEN ON THE PERIPHery of the international security conversation. In fact, there was a time in the period immediately following World War II when both the Arctic and Antarctica were among the chief international security concerns of the United States. To better comprehend why the polar regions are creeping back into the security conversation, it is important to know and understand the significance of the polar regions to international security through the years—an exercise in understanding the relevant context shaping the regions for how we see them today. While acknowledging there are dozens of operations, expeditions, agreements, and like matters for discussion, I choose here to focus on only what I consider to be particularly influential matters to the evolving polar region dialogue as it relates to future great power competition. In this way, I discuss myriad national interests and military operations focused on each of the poles, but recognize that it is not an exhaustive list.

THE POLAR REGIONS AND INTERNATIONAL SECURITY
To group both poles as one in the context of international security is a broad—and misguided—generalization. Both the Arctic and Antarctica have their own unique histories such that this is, to use the common phrase, an apples and oranges comparison. That said, both polar regions

are fruit, so to speak. Thus, the deeper we get into polar region analysis and comparison, the more similarities we see, such that we can discuss each region via a common thread of significance to the global security environment, albeit acknowledging the particular nuance of each as separate and distinct regions in their own right. As well, to examine the entirety of polar security issues takes us beyond the scope of this book. I focus on contemporary and future polar security and defense issues, so I will maintain a forward-looking agenda throughout. But to best understand the current and future environment, we must also have a working knowledge of past events that have shaped and influenced the landscape of the polar regions today in terms of international affairs.

Surveying relevant polar punctuations through the years is a useful exercise in developing the context by which we will later examine current and future polar operations and state interests. By surveying the past history of the polar regions relative to military operations and the like, we can develop a sense of the importance of these regions to an ongoing global security dialogue, as well as better understand the lessons of history and experiences in these unforgiving regions and how such informs the conversation today. Given the niche significance of the polar regions to international security history, the question is: Where to begin?

While acknowledging the great historical significance of cold weather on the Grand Armée's retreat from Russia in 1812, Napoleon and his forces operated well south of the Arctic Circle in their March to Moscow.[1] Even "America's Forgotten Invasion" of northern Russia in 1918–1919, known as the Polar Bear Expedition, remained just south of the Arctic Circle. Here, US troops braved –50 degree Fahrenheit temperatures in then unexperienced conditions for US forces.[2] The lessons learned from these campaigns are valuable and remain compelling depictions of the enormous challenges embedded within sustained cold weather operations. In the years following World War I, the polar regions, and particularly Alaska for the United States, generated more military intrigue and strategic relevance.

The Poles Before, During, and After World War II: Strategic Indicators

The prelude to World War II in the mid-1930s saw evolving Japanese aggression in the Pacific coupled with Italian and German advances in Europe. As the worldwide situation grew more precarious, military leaders took note of the evolving threats and necessity of geographic advantage. In a February 1935 speech to what was then the US House

Military Affairs Committee (the equivalent of today's House Armed Services Committee), famed Army Air Corps (later US Air Force) general Billy Mitchell quipped that "Alaska is the most strategic place in the world" and that "he who controls Alaska controls the Arctic."[3] Mitchell's reference to the Arctic in 1935 stems from his insistence that Alaska was the most likely avenue of approach for the Soviet Union in the event of military conflict. Considering the Alaska Purchase from Russia in 1867, this may well be one of the best real estate investments for the United States in history. Sought mostly for its anticipated economic value, the $7.2 million Alaska Purchase also brought the added benefit of deterring further Russian settlement in the massive northern territory.[4] While the United States and the Soviets were not at war in 1935 nor during any point World War II, the Soviets' proximity to Alaska and their great power status in the 1930s was reason enough for Mitchell to advocate the strategic necessity of Alaska in the midst of evolving global tensions. As the Arctic garnered more interest from ambitious and expansionist-minded states in the latter half of the 1930s, Mitchell's assertion would come to fruition seven years later in an air war over Alaska's Aleutian Island chain.

The Aleutian Islands Campaign

During the war from 1941–1945, Finland, Germany, Norway, and the Soviet Union fought various campaigns in the European Arctic. In the Pacific theater, Japan's expansionism targeted Alaska's Aleutian Island chain. In June 1942, the Japanese invaded the United States and secured two small islands in the Aleutian chain. These small Japanese garrisons were the only US territory held by adversaries during the war. Though the motivation for Japan's Aleutian claim was most likely as a distraction for the eventual Battle of Midway in the Pacific, the strategic implications of adversarial occupation on US soil were—at the time—significant and led to expanded conversation regarding the strategic value of Alaska and the Arctic as a future potential battlespace and avenue of approach. Through the combined air and ground campaign to reclaim the lost territory from Japan, US troops succumbed more to the harsh weather and environmental conditions than from actual combat, much as they did during the many cold weather campaigns of World War I.[5] The extreme conditions of operating militarily in an Arctic climate during the Aleutians campaign raised questions about the ability for sustained operations in such climates in the future. As the Arctic saw actual polar warfare during World War II, Antarctica, too, had garnered some interest before and after the war.

SEND IN THE MARINES . . . TO ANTARCTICA?

Antarctica has "always been a mirror for the changing global balance of power and geopolitical rivalry."[6] In the years before and after World War II, Antarctica was an occasional topic of intrigue. Before it became shrouded in conspiracy theories and fears of malign actor exploitation in the immediate postwar era, Antarctica was a focus of Adolf Hitler's prewar supply preparations. In a search for whale oils used in the production of margarine—which the Germans apparently consumed in great quantities—Hitler dispatched a naval expedition to Antarctica in December 1938.[7] Though the expedition sought new resources, the Germans also intended to survey and claim portions of the southern continent as part of the voyage. Publicly unknown until 1958, the German Antarctic expedition in 1938–1939 added circumstantial context to a bizarre conspiracy about Hitler's fate at the end of the war that further embedded Antarctica within the international security discourse.[8]

Some conspiracy theorists believe—despite a mountain of supporting evidence—that rather than shooting himself in the head in his Berlin bunker, Adolf Hitler, sensing impending defeat in 1945, fled to Antarctica, where the Germans had constructed an elaborate fortress in secrecy.[9] As multiple German U-boats were captured off the coast of Argentina in the summer of 1945 and dozens more were reported missing in action that same year, prominent figures of the time such as Joseph Stalin gave weight to this disappearing-act narrative, though Stalin insisted that Hitler sought refuge in Argentina rather than Antarctica.[10] Such speculation and curiosity surrounding known and unaccounted-for German U-boat activity in July and August 1945 furthered fantastic claims of a secret Nazi base in South America or even Antarctica. As the United States investigated these stories, President Truman in 1946 commissioned a US naval expedition to Antarctica known as Operation High Jump. Perhaps coincidental, perhaps not, the US branded High Jump as an Antarctic photo-mapping and reconnaissance expedition; it was one of several US expeditions to Antarctica from 1929 to 1956.[11]

Taking advantage of the coming Antarctic summer, Operation High Jump embarked on August 26, 1946, and reached Antarctica in December that year. The brainchild of seasoned Antarctic explorer navy rear admiral Richard Byrd, High Jump was commanded by Byrd's Task Force 68 colleague, fellow veteran Antarctic explorer, and future polar warfare scholar, navy rear admiral Richard Cruzen. Under the tutelage of the navy's most experienced Antarctic leaders, both of whom held prominent roles in past US Antarctic expeditions, High Jump was the first US photo-mapping effort of its kind in Antarctica. Unsurprisingly, searching for secret Nazi bases and Adolf Hitler were not among the publicly stated priorities. Instead, High Jump's primary mission was to establish the Antarctic base Little America IV. Subordinate to this mission, the operation had six objectives:[12]

1. Training personnel and testing equipment in frigid conditions.
2. Consolidating and extending US sovereignty over the largest practicable area of the Antarctic continent (this was publicly denied as a goal even before the expedition ended).
3. Determining the feasibility of establishing, maintaining, and utilizing bases in the Antarctic and investigating possible base sites.
4. Developing techniques for establishing, maintaining, and utilizing air bases on ice, with particular attention to later applicability of such techniques to operations in interior Greenland, where conditions are comparable to those in the Antarctic.
5. Amplifying existing stores of knowledge of hydrographic, geographic, geological, meteorological, and electromagnetic propagation conditions in the area.
6. Supplementary objectives of the Nanook expedition (the Nanook operation was a smaller equivalent conducted off eastern Greenland).

Being a naval expedition, High Jump's objectives were decidedly military in nature. Establishing sovereignty, surveying basing locations and feasibility, and developing techniques and procedures for sustained cold military weather operations, as a summation of the operational objectives, indicates a United States intent on continuing its presence on and influence of Antarctica. In all, some 4,000 soldiers, sailors, and marines deployed to Antarctica embarked aboard thirteen ships and thirty-three aircraft from August 1946 to February 1947.[13]

The leading admirals of the operation, Byrd and Cruzen, were already synonymous with Antarctic exploration. Byrd's involvement in High Jump was his fourth Antarctic expedition at the time, and both he and Cruzen served prominent roles in the 1939–1941 US Antarctic Service Expedition.[14] Their leadership in High Jump only furthered both admirals' credibility of voice in their subsequent writings on the significance of the poles for future international security.

Admiral Byrd, having led the first US base-establishing expedition to Antarctica in 1929, spent decades exploring the polar regions and "preaching the importance of Antarctica."[15] In the days following his departure from Antarctica at the conclusion of Operation High Jump,

Admiral Byrd interviewed with Chilean newspaper *El Mercurio* and warned of future polar region threats and considerations. Reporter Lee Van Atta, who interviewed Byrd following High Jump, wrote:

> Admiral Richard E. Byrd warned today that the United States should adopt measures of protection against the possibility of an invasion of the country by hostile planes coming from the Polar Regions. The Admiral explained that he was not trying to scare anyone, but the cruel reality is that in case of a new war, the United States could be attacked by planes flying over one or both poles. This statement was made as part of a recapitulation of his own polar experience, in an exclusive interview with International News Service. Talking about the recently completed expedition, Byrd said that the most important result of his observations and discoveries is the potential effect that they have in relation to the security of the United States. The fantastic speed with which the world is shrinking—recalled the Admiral—is one of the most important lessons learned during his recent Antarctic exploration. "I have to warn my compatriots that the time has ended when we were able to take refuge in our isolation and rely on the certainty that the distances, the oceans, and the poles were a guarantee of safety."[16]

Echoing these sentiments in a 1948 lecture at the Naval War College, Byrd's polar region compatriot Cruzen, too, warned of the dangers of overlooking the polar regions in future international security and military considerations: "Before the war little or no consideration was given to the strategic potentialities of the Polar Regions, either north or south. As a result, our pre-war strategic thinking and our military and naval training was largely confined to the tropic and temperate zones."[17]

Both admirals, having been profoundly influenced by their own experiences in polar operations, continued their advocacy of the polar security discourse through the years. Though particularly oriented south to Antarctica, both Byrd and Cruzen experienced Arctic operations as aviators earlier in their careers. Just as the admirals embarked for Antarctica in August 1946, a complementary US Arctic operation was under way with similar military reconnaissance and installation-establishing objectives in Greenland.

HIGH NORTH INTERESTS IN THE 1940s–1950s

In 1945–1946, the US Navy undertook efforts to test maritime equipment above latitude 65° north, referred as Operation Frostbite. Following Frostbite, the navy deployed an expedition to Greenland in the summer of 1946 with the intent to further train personnel in polar operations and assess future weather station locations.[18] Focused on the Thule area along Greenland's northwest coast, the expedition rooted further US interests in the region and enabled the construction of Thule Air Base in subsequent years. This effort also coincided with the 1946 attempt of the United States to purchase Greenland from Denmark in an effort to secure access for military basing, among other things. On the significance of the United States purchasing Greenland—an autonomous island under the control of Denmark—then-secretary of war Robert Patterson wrote to the undersecretary of state, Dean Acheson, that "it might be a good idea to take prompt action toward securing (Greenland) from Denmark (even to the extent of purchasing the entire island, if necessary), the military rights which have been outlined by the Joint Chiefs of Staff."[19]

The US interest in purchasing Greenland for its strategic implications is well documented. After Denmark and the United States signed the Defense of Greenland Agreement, the United States deployed troops to Greenland in 1941.[20] With Operation Nanook, the United States continued its military footprint in Greenland in the summer of 1946 and subsequently offered Denmark $100 million for the purchase on December 14 of that year.[21] Denmark declined the offer but the United States had already begun the construction of military infrastructure on what *Time Magazine* called "the world's largest island and stationary aircraft carrier."[22] *Time* even compared Greenland's significance in US national defense and security to Alaska saying that it "would be as valuable as Alaska" for enhanced bomber power projection and "invaluable, in either conventional or push-button war, as an advance radar outpost [and] a forward position for future rocket-launching sites."[23]

Looking back at the evolving Cold War rhetoric in the postwar 1940s, historians recounted the fear the United States had relative to the transpolar routes and the lack of US Arctic orientation. Reviewing comparable operations of the time like Floodlight, Polaris, and Eardrum, Farquhar noted that the seldom-traveled transpolar routes "suggested the possibility of a surprise attack, an atomic pearl harbor with no-notice or means of defense."[24]

Owing to these and other concerns of a future high Arctic Soviet military threat, the United States continued its dialogue with Denmark over its interest in and presence on Greenland. In a diary entry recalling Denmark's admission into the North Atlantic Treaty Organization (NATO) in 1949, Denmark's trade minister wrote that the decision was, in part, motivated by "the USA's *de facto* partial occupation of Greenland (which we do not possess the power to prevent)" and the perception of Western favor this would bestow Denmark in rising tensions with the Soviet Union.[25] In April 1951, Denmark and the United States revised the 1941 Defense of Greenland Agreement to reflect Denmark's new NATO status and evolving defense priorities. Articles 2 and 3 of the revised 1951 Defense of Greenland Agreement gave the United States rights to "improve and generally to fit the area for military use."[26] The agreement further stipulated expanded military arrangements from the original 1941 version, including not only the ability for US military base construction but also access to such facilities on Greenland by NATO armed forces. The intent of these and other provisions in the revised agreement is to, per Article 1, "promote stability and well-being in the North Atlantic Treaty area by uniting their efforts for collective defense and for the preservation of peace and security and for the development of their collective capacity to resist armed attack." In accordance with this language and following the breakout of the Korean War in 1950, the United States began construction on its northernmost military installation, Thule Air Base in northwest Greenland, a short time later.

With the ongoing threats to the spread of communism in the post–World War II era, the United States found itself once again in conflict resembling polar warfare in Korea.[27] The United States, fearing an uncontained communist threat, adopted its modern-day military philosophy of preponderance, or liberal hegemony. Under the concept of liberal hegemony, the United States sought global military and diplomatic presence sufficient to influence matters and promote democratic values far from its shores. With this in mind, the polar regions again came into focus in the 1950s as regions necessitating both presence and influence in the evolving world order.

Leveraging earlier military deployments and infrastructure investments, the United States began construction on Thule Air Base in 1951. Originally purposed for the US Air Force's Strategic Air Command (the equivalent of today's Air Force Global Strike Command), Thule served as a hub for US reconnaissance sorties and bomber training flights, cold weather training, and polar flying operations. Thule also housed the northernmost elements of the now-retired Defense Early Warning Line's radar array, stretching from Alaska to eastern Greenland.[28] Today, Thule is housed under Air Force Space Command and figures prominently in ballistic missile early warning detection for North America. As concerns about Soviet expansion consumed the national security narrative in the early 1950s and oriented US attention north toward the Arctic, the South Pole, too, was generating interest in the international discourse relative to Soviet ambition.

ANTARCTIC DETERRENCE

Prior to World War II and to capitalize on the successes of Byrd's and others' Antarctic expeditions, the United States sought "permanent occupation and scientific exploration" of Antarctica through the programs such as the US Antarctic Service Expedition.[29] During the war, the Axis powers of Germany, Japan, and Italy "used Antarctica in their war operations."[30] This compelled both the United Kingdom and Argentina—among the original claimants of Antarctic territory—to increase naval activity around Antarctica, specifically in an attempt to maintain freedom of navigation through the Drake Passage.[31] After the war and having established four previous Antarctic bases under the Little America program from 1929 to 1947, the United States was a leading nation in Antarctic exploration at the time. But the United States was not the only nation interested in continued Antarctic influence.

The United Kingdom was the first state to lay claim to Antarctic real estate in 1908. Claims from Argentina, Chile, Australia, New Zealand, Norway, and France followed years later. In 1948 and after a series of territorial claims disputes, Chile, Argentina, and the United Kingdom signed a tripartite agreement that prohibited naval activity below 60° south latitude. As an onlooker to this early attempt at Antarctic demilitarization but a prominent military actor in Antarctica, the United States—absent an active claim to the continent—sensed international tensions mounting. In 1948, the United States proposed an international agreement among the claimant nations while also asserting itself as the eighth nation claiming sovereign Antarctic territory. The proposal lobbied for Antarctic governance administered via the United Nations, but more important the proposal clearly excluded the Soviet Union from the Antarctic conversation and contributed to broadening tensions in the region.[32] Though Chile and Argentina rejected the proposal, the implications of Soviet exclusion reverberated throughout a world gripped by rising Cold War pressures.

Tensions over disputed, unrecognized, and competing claims in Antarctica continued into the 1950s, though not with the Soviet Union. In 1952, four years after a British Antarctic base on Hope Bay burned to the ground, Argentina established Esperanza Base only a few hundred meters from the abandoned British installation. Shortly thereafter, the United Kingdom dispatched a team to the site of the old base for a reconstruction effort. Upon landing at the site and near Argentinian forces on Esperanza Base, Argentinian military personnel fired machine gun warning shots over the heads of the British survey team as they landed. This incident prompted the British personnel to retreat to the

British-held Falkland Islands. Upon learning of the incident, the Falklands governor embarked with the Royal Marines aboard a British naval vessel en route to Hope Bay, in violation of the previously signed tripartite agreement. The arrival of the Royal Marines compelled an Argentinian retreat and allowed subsequent reconstruction of the British base, as originally intended.[33]

The Hope Bay incident of 1952 was, and is as of this writing, the only documented hostile military action to occur on Antarctica. Under known Antarctic hostilities and expanding international interests, the United States again dispatched a military operation to the southern continent in 1955–1956 to prepare for the upcoming year of worldwide scientific study and collaboration known as the International Geophysical Year. Operation Deep Freeze, as it is still called today, was the first in the now long-running annual operation of US military assets supporting scientific research in Antarctica. Among the early accomplishments of the operation, US personnel set foot on the geographic South Pole and also landed the first plane at the pole. The United States would establish its first permanent base at the South Pole on January 1, 1957, under the support of its operational assets.[34] In all, twelve countries conducted research in Antarctica during the International Geophysical Year: the United States, the United Kingdom, the Soviet Union, South Africa, Norway, New Zealand, Japan, France, Chile, Belgium, Australia, and Argentina.

Despite active hostilities only five years prior, the 1957–1958 International Geophysical Year demonstrated the capabilities and willingness of the international community to set aside their differences and collaborate on scientific research in Antarctica. The successes are lauded and widely held as the impetus behind the subsequent development of the 1959 Antarctic Treaty.

THE ANTARCTIC TREATY

Article 6 of the Antarctic Treaty defines Antarctica as all land and ice shelves south of 60° south latitude.[35] The treaty is the guiding framework for Antarctic activity, outlining the boundaries for Antarctic research and exploration. Led by the United States, twelve original signatories negotiated the Antarctic Treaty in 1959—the same twelve countries that had demonstrated Antarctic interests during the International Geophysical Year. The treaty was later enacted in 1961 and came into force on June 23, 1961. The Antarctic Treaty and its complementary components form the entirety of the Antarctic Treaty System.[36] It outlines fourteen articles, of which few receive most of the attention as directive stipulations ensuring some activities and restricting others. The first line of the first article of the Antarctic Treaty holds that "Antarctica shall be used for peaceful purposes only."[37] It also outlines the specifics of scientific, environmental, and tourist activities on the continent subject to the provisions of the treaty.

Today, there are fifty-four parties to the treaty including the original twelve signatories. Forty-two countries (in addition to the original twelve) have endorsed the treaty since its establishment in 1959. Of these fifty-four countries party to the treaty, twenty-nine have consultative (decisionmaking) status in Antarctic Treaty consultative meetings. To reach consultative status, countries must demonstrate sufficient interest in Antarctica by "conducting substantial research activity there, such as the establishment of a scientific station or the despatch [sic] of a scientific expedition."[38] As of this writing, there are approximately seventy permanent research stations in Antarctica representing the twenty-nine countries with consultative status.[39] The twelve original signatories of the treaty are granted permanent decisionmaking status, while the remaining seventeen countries with consultative status must demonstrate continued interest by way of research activity to maintain their status. In this way, the twelve original signatories are seen as most influential in consultative discussions.

The treaty broadly supports scientific research while also providing the regulatory framework for ensuring the protection of Antarctica's diverse bionetwork, of which some species of fauna are found only here. Of the many stipulations of the Antarctic Treaty and the associated agreements since forming the entirety of the Antarctic Treaty System, the guidepost and most consequential of them is the treaty's prohibition of "any measures of a military nature, the carrying out of military maneuvers, as well as the testing of any type of weapons."[40] Though the treaty does allow militaries to support scientific research and other activities of a "peaceful purpose," which in most cases tends toward logistics support and heavy airlift of cargo and personnel, the treaty's broad characterization and prohibition of military activities effectively served as the first arms control agreement of the Cold War. For all of the treaty's lauded successes as a collaborative agreement to avoid escalatory tensions, its ability to fully deter prohibited military activities has been challenged.

As the treaty went into force in 1961, it took only four years before its provisions were tested, by ten Argentinian soldiers who set off to Antarctica on what was referred to by Argentine media as a "Sovereignty Patrol." In Operation Ninety, and unbeknownst to the Americans and Soviets, the Argentineans pursued an expedition to Antarctica that "opened a groove of land in the White Desert to allow to operate large aircraft with conventional landing gear."[41] Consistent with the Argentine military's firing of their weapons in 1952 as the only documented hostile act on Antarctica, Operation Ninety is the only documented military maneuver on Antarctica since the adoption of the Antarctic Treaty in 1961. From that point, international relations and security issues in Antarctica leveled out.

Countries continued their research activities and developed more, bigger, and permanent bases and stations on the continent. Past US presidents paid attention to the polar regions, but tended to consider them on the periphery to the litany of more proximal issues on the international security spectrum, and thus relegated the poles to an afterthought in defense and security conversations following the signing of the Antarctic Treaty. It was not until President Richard Nixon directed his National Security Council to develop an Arctic policy that the United States saw its first true instance of a polar security policy platform since World War II.[42] In 1970, Nixon also established the basis for US Antarctic policy by reinforcing the US commitment to the Antarctic Treaty as the foundation for its own policy.[43] While the Antarctic region enjoyed the relative peace of international collaboration and cooperation, the situation in the Arctic—as a geographically adjacent region to the ongoing Cold War—was heating up.

THE ARCTIC IN THE LATE TWENTIETH CENTURY

During the Cold War period from the 1950s to the 1980s, the Arctic saw both rising sea levels and rising international tensions.[44] Noted as an area of increased threat from Soviet aggression, the Arctic evolved into a region of NATO concern. Continuing in the Stalinist tradition of "Red Arctic" propaganda, the Soviets constructed some fifty Arctic military bases during the Cold War period.[45] As Canada–United States relations galvanized with the commonly perceived Soviet threat, the two nations collaborated on the Defense Early Warning Line project in the 1950s as an advanced early warning radar array designed to detect incoming Soviet bombers and other threats over the Arctic. Across the Atlantic, the United States continued its basing expansion efforts in Europe.

In 1955, for example, the United States and Norway agreed to a bilateral pre-positioning basing program for the US Marine Corps. It enables the marines to store wartime materiel across a multicave system spread throughout Norway.[46] As a forward strategic stockpile, this pre-positioned equipment enhances operational responsiveness and compresses the future battlespace by ensuring necessary combat equipment is closer to the potential fight. The Cold War–era innovation of the pre-positioning model also serves as the premier cold weather equipment stockpile and enables the marines to rapidly supply and sustain a combat force in the European theater and elsewhere. Similar to the evolving interest in the European land domain during the Cold War, the strategic importance of the maritime and air domains also became clear.

The Greenland–Iceland–United Kingdom Gap became apparent to NATO during the 1970s. With the growing significance, NATO allies focused naval detection and monitoring operations across the gap to track and deter Soviet submarines from traversing it.[47] Meanwhile in North America, the Defense Early Warning Line was replaced with the North Warning System in the late 1980s before officially being deactivated in 1993. A northern-tier radar array in Alaska and Canada designed to identify incoming ballistic missile threats, the North Warning System still serves today to complement US and Canadian threat detection in the northern regions. The upgrade to the North Warning System in the 1980s complemented increased US Air Force reconnaissance operations in Alaska and the Arctic Circle during this time as well.[48] Though tensions remained high, military posturing persisted, and aggressive rhetoric dominated into the late 1980s until an albatross of US-Soviet relations spurred one of the most significant developments in Arctic relations history.

In a 1987 speech outlining his foreign policy prescriptions and owing to the rising tensions in the High North, Russian premiere Mikhail Gorbachev insisted that the Arctic should no longer be a battlefield. Known as the Murmansk Initiative, Gorbachev's agenda sought to reshape the global perspective on the Arctic from a military domain and instead to a zone of international collaboration and discourse, not unlike Antarctica. Some saw this as a disarmament proposal between the Soviet Union and the United States and a contributing catalyst for the eventual discussions to establish the Arctic Council.[49] Despite tension during this time, the Arctic remained conflict-free in the traditional sense. A short time later and leveraging the dissolution of the Soviet Union and Cold War tensions against the period of comparative peace in the early 1990s, the United States organized an effort to establish a similar collaborative structure for the Arctic as it had done for the Antarctic in the 1950s.

The Arctic Council

Following the Murmansk Initiative, and like the development of the Antarctic Treaty System, the United States took the lead in the development of the Arctic Council in the mid-1990s. Established in September

1996 by the Ottawa Declaration, the Arctic Council is the "leading intergovernmental forum promoting cooperation, coordination and interaction among the Arctic States, Arctic indigenous communities and other Arctic inhabitants on common Arctic issues, in particular on issues of sustainable development and environmental protection in the Arctic."[50]

Currently, the Arctic Council stands as the Arctic's institutional body representing the collective voice of the eight Arctic states: Canada, Denmark, Finland, Iceland, Norway, Russia, Sweden, and the United States. The council serves principally as a forum for discussing Arctic matters among Arctic States and other Arctic-interested communities. The council has eight Arctic states with territory in the Arctic Circle (five of which border the Arctic Ocean); six permanent participants representing Arctic Indigenous communities; six working groups responsible for conducting research on behalf of the council; and numerous Arctic observers representing non-Arctic states, intergovernmental and interparliamentary organizations, as well as nongovernmental organizations that the Arctic Council sees as valuable contributors to furthering the council's interests. These are distinctions to examine later.

Since its inception, the Arctic Council has stood as the foundation and facilitator of peace and collaboration for Arctic affairs. It has been hailed as a resounding success in international cooperation and serves still today as an example framework for bringing a diverse network of voices and interests to the table for common discussion and discourse. The Arctic Council serves in this way a similar function to the Antarctic Treaty System and ensures that the representative voices of its relative polar actors are both heard and considered in how the collective body attempts to guide and govern activities in the Arctic commons. For all of its perceived relevance and utility in informing and influencing Arctic actor relations and advancing Arctic interests common to the international community, the Arctic Council lacks a security and defense charter, thus raising its fragility among the international community as a legitimate deterrent for malign activity, or likewise as a sufficient incentive for international compliance. Only four years after its 1996 adoption, the Arctic Council unknowingly faced its biggest threat in the 2000 election of Russian president Vladimir Putin.

THE PUTIN EFFECT

The year 1996 was the apex of the twentieth-century unipolar movement of the United States. The US economy was surging, its diplomatic influence was rising, and its military power was unmatched. At the height of global hegemony, the United States enjoyed the insularity and security of favorable geography but still projected power where and when necessary in support of its global agenda. Following the decisive Gulf War victory and save for small military engagements in Somalia and the Balkans—neither of which threatened the US homeland or Western ideology—the 1990s was a time of US economic, diplomatic, and military superiority. The geopolitical plates were entrenched in their positions, unmoved with the United States as the global hegemon since 1945. The first shift of the geopolitical balance occurred with the 2000 election of Russian president Vladimir Putin.

A former Soviet intelligence officer and aggressive military-minded politician, Vladimir Putin's long and storied position as president of the Russian Federation began in 1999 when he assumed the role as acting president before his formal election in March 2000.[51] During his first two terms, from 2000 to 2008, Putin presided over eight years of Russian economic expansion and a return to international significance following the dissolution of the Soviet Union—what Putin once called the "greatest geopolitical catastrophe of the Twentieth Century."[52] An aggressive leader, Putin watched intently as the United States committed itself further into the global war on terror throughout the 2000s. As the United States became distracted and overextended in Iraq and Afghanistan, Putin saw opportunity in the Arctic—a region that had gone largely unattended militarily in the post–Cold War era. A tired, distracted, and complacent United States focused on combating radical jihadist ideology was uninterested in the Arctic or Antarctic. Russia and Putin saw the Arctic, in particular, for both economic and military opportunity and largely devoid of international attention to serve as a potential obstacle.

From the start of his presidency, Putin's desire to restore Russian global influence and superpower status was obvious. In 2001, Russia lobbied the United Nations to recognize nearly half a million square miles of Russian claims on the Arctic Shelf.[53] The United Nations (UN) in 2007 rejected the Russian shelf claims, prompting Russia to buck the UN rejection by symbolically planting the Russian Federation flag on the North Pole seabed in August that year.[54] Putin's Arctic ambition was then and remains today undeniable.

The 2007 flag-planting on the North Pole was just as symbolic as it was strategic. This event served both as the representative gesture of intent and as the metaphorical punch in the face to the United Nations and Arctic Council that Russia deemed itself king of the Arctic. The planting of the flag, in myriad ways, not only visually asserted Russian

Arctic ambition under Vladimir Putin but also demonstrated to the world that Russia viewed itself as the lone Arctic power that would seek to set the rules in the High North.

The 2007 flag-planting also signaled Russian Arctic re-prioritization. Russia's Arctic expansion effort since has been aggressive and tenacious. Even as Putin relinquished the presidency in 2008 and reprised his role as Russian prime minister until 2012, his Arctic ambition persisted. Reassuming the presidency in 2012, Putin continued to push the limits of permissibility in the Arctic, but did so quietly. In the years since the 2007 flag-planting and under Putin's influence, Russia restored Soviet-era Arctic bases and constructed new ones, but did so with little fanfare and propaganda. By 2014, Russia, under Putin's ambition to restore great power status to a rebuilt country, had refurbished dozens of Arctic military facilities and constructed dozens more while simultaneously modernizing Russia's naval fleet and expanding polar capabilities. The Russian Ice Curtain, as some have come to refer to it, is now a formidable military asset profile of Arctic offensive and defensive capabilities, both static and mobile, and all constructed, expanded, and fielded during a time of comparatively absent US interest and orientation to the same.[55]

Now as the US national security establishment begins to acknowledge the expanding Russian Arctic portfolio and debate Moscow's intent, Washington finds itself wondering: How did this happen? The Arctic is a twenty-first-century security dilemma in the making. As Putin pushed Russian Arctic advancement, the United States turned a blind eye in favor of continued focus on Iraq and Afghanistan. And as America's longest war fades to the history books, the Arctic emerges as a potential twenty-first-century battlespace right in America's backyard. With more and greater military capabilities in the Arctic, coupled with emerging access to untapped natural and biological resources, the Arctic compels Russian attention. Russia has nearly 15,000 miles of total Arctic coastline and by some estimates relies on Arctic resources for over 20 percent of its economic output. Russian aggression to mineral mining claims will "open a new sphere for maritime competition" in the Arctic.[56] This, coupled with the growing interest in the Arctic as an international maritime domain, provides all the motivation Russia, under Putin, needs to ensure continued access to and influence of the Arctic region in the twenty-first century. Russia's rapid Arctic militarization is generating more interest among the other Arctic states, such that a budding security dilemma now threatens to upend the long-standing post–Cold War paradigm of Arctic exceptionalism and thrust the High North into the fray of renewed great power competition.

As Russia expands its military capabilities and presence in the Arctic, punctuated by the establishment of its Arctic-focused Northern Fleet Joint Strategic Command in December 2014, NATO has expanded its own military presence in and orientation to the Arctic with annual military exercises in Norway and other locales. Naval exercises in the Arctic Ocean and its marginal seas once again occur regularly. In 2019, for the first time in almost thirty years, a US Navy carrier strike group sailed into the Arctic Ocean. The Harry S. Truman Carrier Strike Group's deployment to Arctic waters was the first such US naval operation north of the Arctic Circle since 1991.[57] Since the Truman Strike Group's North Atlantic deployment, the United States continues to pursue freedom of navigation operations, patrolling the maritime commons and engaging in more regular cold weather training.

Also in 2019, the Theodore Roosevelt Carrier Strike Group participated in Exercise Northern Edge in Alaska while the USS *Gravely* conducted operations north of the Arctic Circle off the Greenland coast as part of the navy's reorientation and commitment to preparing for Arctic operations.[58] Cold weather naval presence has continued since these renewed Arctic forays. In May 2020, a navy surface action group sailed into the Barents Sea—the epicenter of the Russian navy—to "assert freedom of navigation" in international waters.[59] This prompted the Russian Northern Fleet—based in Severomorsk on the Kola Peninsula—to announce it would conduct live-fire naval exercises in the region. With the knowledge that Russia can now sink US naval ships from land-based cruise missiles in the Arctic, coupled with the known Russian bastion defense concept within the Arctic's marginal seas as part of its Ice Curtain, the United States takes such rhetoric seriously but also refuses to cower.

Other annual joint and multinational cold weather training exercises in Alaska and Norway have become annual events, like Icex, Arctic Edge, and Cold Response. Onetime events such as Trident Juncture—the largest naval exercise since the Cold War—provided NATO coalition forces the opportunity to simulate cold weather warfare and to expand NATO's Arctic awareness and capabilities into the twenty-first century.[60] Similarly, US Marine Corps rotational force deployments to Norway ensure the marines stay true to their hymn by training in "every clime and place," even if it means in the "snow of far-off northern lands."[61] But exercises and occasional naval presence above the Arctic Circle is intermittent at best and lacks the commitment of static Arctic presence. To this end, the United States took a step toward a bigger Arctic commitment in 2020.

In spring 2020, the US Air Force reactivated fighter squadrons at Eielson Air Force Base, Alaska—the northernmost US military base in

North America and just south of the Arctic Circle. Now with two fighter squadrons, the Eielson F-35 contingent is the largest concentration of fifth-generation fighters anywhere in the world and reflects a welcomed and necessary—even if thirteen years late—reorientation of US national security priorities toward the Arctic. The deployment of F-35s to Alaska's northernmost base coincides with upward of $1.4 billion of Alaskan military infrastructure development since 2016, indicates a renewing US commitment to Arctic defense and security, and is also a visible and necessary response to continued Russian pokes at US northern defenses through the years.[62]

Along with increased basing infrastructure in the Arctic, Russian air activity in the Arctic has kept pace. Continued Russian sorties in the Alaskan Air Defense Identification Zone through the years have compelled dozens of US intercepts.[63] Given their frequency and bravado of daytime Russian flights into the known Air Defense Identification Zone, it is foolish to believe the Russians are accidentally flying within 200 miles of the Alaskan coastline. Russia is testing US response, capabilities, timing, response direction, assets deployed, and actions on contact. It is difficult to imagine a scenario in which Russia is *not* using each encounter as a data point informing a database of predictable US military activities. Whereas most of the Russian sorties to date have been reconnaissance planes, Russia maintains fighters in the Arctic that, per Moscow's claims, are even mounted with nuclear-capable hypersonic missiles. The North Warning System cannot reliably track and warn against emerging over-the-horizon weapon systems like Russian hypersonic missiles, and Putin knows it.[64]

There can be no doubt of Putin's intent to reestablish Russia as a global superpower. And there can be no doubt of Putin's view of the Arctic as a primary domain for geostrategic influence to this end. As Russia expands its military presence in the Arctic and further extends the boundaries of both its claims and acceptable actions, others have noticed. Increased Russian military attention toward the Arctic has created the blueprint for a new security dilemma whereby the increase of military presence and capabilities by one nation compels an increase in the same among other stakeholders, thus serving to make the domain that much more dangerous rather than secure. The Arctic after the Cold War—and prior to Putin's rise to Russian power—was a comparably ignored domain, devoid of regular military surface presence and international competition. Its unforgiving conditions and isolated environment kept it both figuratively and literally above the geostrategic fray.

Today, and almost entirely due to Vladimir Putin's twenty-first-century Arctic prioritization, the High North no longer enjoys its relative irrelevance in the geostrategic equation. The international security contours have extended north; the trend lines point toward rising tensions and potential conflict in the Arctic as a result. Thanks to Putin, great power competition has arrived in the Arctic. The "Putin effect," then, has been to introduce a security dilemma into the Arctic that promises to expand. Putin is thus responsible for the evolving nature of the Arctic as a future battlespace and the conflict that may one day occur. Moreover, Putin's insistence on Russian Arctic presence and influence has not only compelled US and NATO northward orientation, but also raised equal questions among scholars and practitioners regarding Russian-Chinese polar collaborations in the Arctic as well as Antarctica.

A Sino-Russian Polar Alliance?

Whether Russia and China are actually friends is anyone's guess. Neither Moscow nor Beijing acknowledges the existence of a formal alliance and instead elect to classify the relationship in terms of "coordination."[65] China's Foreign Minister Wang Yi categorizes Russian-Sino relations as "bilateral strategic coordination," whereas Russia insists it is a "strategic partnership of coordination."[66] Semantics to some, significant to others. Regardless of adjective, the evidence of Sino-Russian partnership is both obvious and indicative of aligned interests, at least for now. Though tension exists, Russian and Chinese interests do align elsewhere. So whereas a formal military and diplomatic Sino-Russian alliance is unlikely anytime soon, a partnership of strategic coordination is not only likely, but happening; we only have to look to the polar regions for proof.

China and Russia both seek a new world order that supplants the United States as the global hegemon. Their collective efforts toward polar region presence and influence indicate their recognition of both the significance of the polar regions to the global order as well as the lack of US orientation to the same such that the polar regions present areas of opportunity and exploitation for power-hungry states. China's self-proclamation as a "near-Arctic state" punctuates its 2018 Polar Silk Road white paper policy and demonstrates its interest in both being present in and influencing Arctic dynamics in the twenty-first century.[67] To the south, China sends icebreakers and polar aircraft to Antarctica, using Russian airfields no less.[68] Likewise, Russia's military buildup in the Arctic is something of a precursor to its now-evolving Antarctic interests and activities. There are enough individual points of polar partnerships between the two that when considered in the aggregate it is difficult to dismiss as coincidental or superficial. China and Russia may not be militarily allied, but they are most certainly aligned in polar interests and their coordinated efforts—it seems—to extend their influence to both regions while simultaneously edging out the United States in the process.

I will examine Russian and Chinese polar policies and activities in greater detail in subsequent chapters. To this end though, our discussion has arrived—after a brief survey of polar punctuations since the late 1930s—at the present day's polar dynamic. In 2021 and at the time of this writing, the polar regions have reemerged as significant regions for the current and future international security discourse. Whereas a committed faction of scholars and policymakers continue their insistence that the polar regions remain peaceful, isolated, and shared spaces of common good and access, there is a competing and emerging position—one I fervently argue—holding that the polar regions have already become regions of competition that will soon lead to military confrontation and eventual conflict. In this way, we must consider the polar regions for what they are today and what they offer to compel great power competition. In the context of great power competition, the polar regions present a series of considerations unlike other regions that, when considered as a collective, make them arguably more strategically important to great power competition and international security than any other region of the world. When we consider the polar regions in terms of these categories, their apparent significance is undeniable.

Notes

1. Van Creveld, *Supplying War*, pp. 65–74.
2. Nelson, *The Polar Bear Expedition*.
3. Lisa Murkowski, "Floor Speech: Unveiling Arctic Legislation to Reinvigorate America's Arctic Role," US Senate, Washington, DC, December 11, 2018, https://www.murkowski.senate.gov/press/speech/floor-speech-unveiling-arctic-legislation-to-reinvigorate-americas-arctic-role.
4. "Purchase of Alaska, 1867," https://history.state.gov/milestones/1866-1898/alaska-purchase.
5. "Battle of the Aleutian Islands," June 30, 2020, https://www.history.com/topics/world-war-ii/battle-of-the-aleutian-islands.
6. Brady, *China as a Polar Great Power*, p. 11.
7. Lüdecke and Summerhayes, *The Third Reich in Antarctica*.
8. Niiler, "Hitler Sent a Secret Expedition to Antarctica."
9. "Antarctica," http://antarctica.greyfalcon.us/highjump1.html.
10. Beschloss, "Dividing the Spoils"; Summerhayes and Beeching, "Hitler's Antarctic Base."

11. The first US Antarctic base in the Little America series was established by Admiral Richard Byrd in 1929 (Little America I). The United States subsequently established Little America II in 1934, Little America III in 1940, Little America IV in 1946, and Little America V in 1956. The bases, each established in locations near their predecessors, served only temporary purposes, as each was either buried in snow or drifted out to sea via glacial movement.

12. US Navy, *Report of Operation HIGHJUMP: U.S. Navy Antarctic Development Project 1947* (Washington, DC: Office of the Chief of Naval Operations, 1947).

13. Kearns, *Where Hell Freezes Over.*

14. Dewing and Kelsay, "Records of the United States Antarctic Service," p. 1.

15. Byrd, "All-Out Assault on Antarctica," p. 141.

16. Summerhayes and Beeching, "Hitler's Antarctic Base," p. 17; Atta, "A Bordo del Monte Olimpo en Alta Mar," p. 23.

17. "Polar Operations" lecture delivered by Rear Admiral R. H. Cruzen (US Navy) at the Naval War College, Newport, R.I., October 6, 1948.

18. Salsig, "Operation Frostbite"; "Operation Nanook: Baby It's Cold Outside!" Ship's log, USS *Atule*, July 4, 1946, https://web.archive.org/web/20110717175906/http://uss-atule.com/operation-nanook.

19. Nelson, "Wanna Buy Greenland?"

20. Berry, "Cryolite."

21. Ibid.

22. "Deepfreeze Defense," *Time*, January 27, 1947, https://web.archive.org/web/20110516124103/http://www.time.com/time/magazine/article/0,9171,778870,00.html.

23. Ibid.

24. Farquhar, "Arctic Linchpin," p. 40.

25. Beukel, "The Greenland Issue," p. 54.

26. *Defense of Greenland: Agreement Between the United States and the Kingdom of Denmark*, April 27, 1951.

27. Though the Korean War was fought well below the Arctic Circle, temperatures and conditions often resembled that of the polar regions during the conflict. The Battle of Chosin Reservoir, for instance, saw temperatures as low as −36° Fahrenheit by some estimates.

28. Takahashi et al., "Autonomy and Military Bases," p. 7.

29. Hatherton, "Antarctica Prior to the Antarctic Treaty," p. 29.

30. Maquieira, "Antarctica Prior to the Antarctic Treaty," p. 51.

31. Ibid.

32. Ibid., pp. 52–53.

33. Beck, *The International Politics of Antarctica*, p. 35.

34. Wallwork and Wilcoxson, *Operation Deep Freeze.*

35. *The Antarctic Treaty*, Conference on Antarctica, Washington, DC, October 15, 1959, art. 6.

36. The Antarctic Treaty System encompasses the provisions of the Antarctic Treaty and other such documents governing activities in and around Antarctica. Others include the Protocol on Antarctic Environmental Protection to the Antarctic Treaty (1991); the Convention for the Conservation of Antarctic Seals (1972); and the Convention on the Conservation of Antarctic Marine Living Resources (1980).

37. The Antarctic Treaty was signed in 1959 but was not enforceable until 1961. "The Antarctic Treaty," http://www.ats.aq/e/antarctictreaty.html; National Research Council, *Antarctic Treaty System.*

38. *The Antarctic Treaty*, art. 9(2).

39. Bishop, "A Look into the International Research Stations of Antarctica."

40. *The Antarctic Treaty,* art. 1.
41. "A Historical Fact to Remember: Marambio Antarctic Base," October 29, 1969, https://translate.google.com/translate?sl=es&tl=en&js=y&prev=_t&hl=es-419&ie=UTF-8&u=http%3A//www.marambio.aq/index1.htm&edit-text=&act=url.
42. Weingartner and Orttung, "U.S. Arctic Policymaking Under Trump and Obama."
43. "U.S. Antarctic Policy: Historical Perspective," accessed July 18, 2020, https://www.nsf.gov/geo/opp/antarct/usaphist.jsp#:~:text=In%20October%201970%20President%20Richard,or%20object%20of%20international%20discord.
44. "Investigation of Arctic Sea Level Rise: Preliminary Conclusions," accessed July 18, 2020, https://www.whoi.edu/science/PO/arcticsealevel/conclusions.html.
45. McCannon, *Red Arctic;* Melino and Conley, "The Ice Curtain."
46. "Marine Corps Prepositioning Program—Norway (MCPP-N)," May 2017, https://www.candp.marines.mil/Organization/MAGTF/Marine-Corps-Pre-Positioning-Program-Norway-MCPP-N.
47. Rhode, "The GIUK Gap's Strategic Significance."
48. "North Warning System," December 17, 2012, http://www.forces.gc.ca/en/news/article.page?doc=north-warning-system/hgq87x9w.
49. Åtland, "Mikhail Gorbachev," p. 290.
50. Arctic Council, *Declaration on the Establishment of the Arctic Council;* Arctic Council, "About," https://arctic-council.org/en/about.
51. McFaul, "Russia's 2000 Presidential Elections."
52. Hopko, "What Putin Must Hear in Munich."
53. Commission on the Limits of the Continental Shelf (CLCS), "Outer Limits of the Continental Shelf Beyond 200 Nautical Miles from the Baselines: Submissions to the Commission: Submission by the Russian Federation," December 20, 2001, https://www.un.org/Depts/los/clcs_new/submissions_files/submission_rus.htm.
54. Parfitt, "Russia Plants Flag on North Pole Seabed."
55. Conley and Rohloff, *The New Ice Curtain.*
56. Cohen, *The Big Stick,* p. 184.
57. Eckstein, "Truman Carrier Strike Group."
58. Eckstein, "Theodore Roosevelt Strike Group."
59. Eckstein, "U.S., U.K. Surface Warships."
60. "Trident Juncture 2018," October 29, 2018, https://www.nato.int/cps/en/natohq/157833.htm.
61. "The Marines Hymn," https://www.marineband.marines.mil/about/library-and-archives/the-marines-hymn.
62. Slaughter, "F-35 Fleet Doubles at Eielson."
63. Burke, "Great-Power Competition."
64. Humpert, "Russia Elevates Importance of Northern Fleet."
65. Dresen, "The Prospects for a Sino-Russian Strategic Partnership."
66. "Chinese, Russian FMs Hold Phone Conversation over Bilateral Coordination," December 20, 2019, http://en.people.cn/n3/2019/1220/c90000-9642227.html; "China, Russia Agree to Upgrade Relations for New Era," June 6, 2019, http://www.china.org.cn/world/2019-06/06/content_74859445.htm.
67. "China's Arctic Policy," January 2018, http://www.scio.gov.cn/zfbps/32832/Document/1618243/1618243.htm.
68. Tiezzi, "China to Establish Antarctic Air Squadron."

3

The Four Cs: Commons, Claims, Covenants, and Cosmos

CHANGING GEOPOLITICAL LANDSCAPES IN AN INCREASINGLY globalized world brings renewed focus on evolving geostrategic competition. Increasing globalization also brings increased knowledge and connectivity to the far reaches of the world. Today there are several categorical factors anchoring the analysis and significance of the polar regions for the future international security environment.

Mike Sfraga, director of the Woodrow Wilson Center's Polar Institute, provides one of the most useful (and clever) lenses to view the current situation in the Arctic. In Sfraga's *Navigating the Arctic's Seven C's,* he considers climate, communities, commodities, commerce, connectivity, cooperation, and competition as informative frames for today's Arctic analysis.[1] Sfraga's seven Cs are inclusive of considerations beyond defense and security, though arguably the former informs the latter. Useful as it may be, the Arctic seven Cs excludes Antarctica. We need a frame that looks at the polar regions, inclusive of both poles, focused on the evolving great power competition with an eye toward defense and security affairs. In both accepting the admittedly derivative nature and building on Sfraga's seven Cs, I offer the polar Cs of commons, claims, covenants, cosmos.

With the polar Cs, I begin where Sfraga concludes at competition and extend to current and future defense and security considerations in both poles. Each C links the state of current polar competition to its progression along a continuum, and I discuss here the likely reasons that polar affairs will progress from strategic competition to confrontation to conflict. By examining the polar Cs as competition leading to potential conflict, we begin to see the conditions manifesting for militarized disputes in the polar regions. In this case, they are not emerging but rather have already arrived.

I acknowledge the issues and discussions related to climate, communities, commodities, commerce, connectivity, and cooperation as contributing elements to progressing toward competition in not just the Arctic but the Antarctic as well. The competition sphere serves as the logical point of departure. Building from competition, the next question is: Beyond scrapping for resources and commodities, what is the basis of the current competition in the polar regions preceding confrontation that will give way to conflict? Or, what would compel states to get into a hot fight in the cold?

There are myriad considerations within the great power competition spectrum such that a generalized argument pitting broad categories as the foci will, to some readers, be a gross omission of the many factors deemed relevant and influential to the conversation. Accepting this broad characterization of great power competition aims while excusing the omission of numerous other elements allows us to focus on the trends and implications for future competition as it pertains to the focus of this book: the polar regions. With the polar Cs, I provide a framework to view the conversation and analysis of great power competition in the polar regions, but in a way that helps grasp state motivations for competition to evolve, and for potential conflict.

COMMONS

The global commons are the world's unowned, unclaimed, or unpossessed regions and resources: the shared domains typically in the world's seas and oceans, airspace, and—with improving technology—even outer space.[2] The global commons are shared resources for the use and benefit of all. Whereas territorial claims and possessions are held by a people, government, or both, the global commons remain unencumbered and are thus free to navigate and use. As a result, the commons are unique in that they are regions of shared access and activity, often with dozens of states present at any given time. The commons, being that they are not legally controlled by any one state, are typically governed by international laws, norms, conventions, and codes of conduct. But the mere existence of so-called global governance mechanisms is insufficient to deter some from attempting to influence, or even command, the commons to their own benefit. The historical conversation regarding the global commons centers on international maritime domains, or the world's shared seas and oceans. With advancing technology and increasing accessibility, the global commons have extended into outer space. But save for those states with active space programs sufficient to project power into the cosmos, the global commons generally refers to the shared spaces of the maritime and air domains.

As shared regions beyond the authority of a government's sovereign territory (and with some consideration given to exclusive economic zones to be discussed later), the polar commons are unlike any other space on Earth. Outside the territorial boundaries of its border states, the Arctic is a common domain of floating sea ice and ever-expanding international maritime channels. The Antarctic is a common domain that is part international maritime waters in the Southern Ocean and part ungoverned land and ice on the continent of Antarctica. The political, economic, environmental, and even diplomatic dynamics of each region are different, and we must resist the urge to assume that the Arctic's challenges in the defense and security sphere are identical to Antarctica's. But commonality exists in each region's strategic relevance to international security in that multiple states seek to expand their regional and ultimately global influence via presence and influence in the poles. That states seek presence and competing influence in the polar commons is a fundamental rejection of the very idea of the commons as shared, communal spaces for all to access, navigate, and—depending on international law—even benefit from. The race to be present and influence the polar commons, left unchecked, is in itself a competition that will erode notions of the polar regions as global commons. Rather, the polar regions are becoming contested commons and challenging the very notion of freedom of the commons in the twenty-first century.

The United States considers freedom, access, and command of the commons a cornerstone of its foreign policy.[3] In this way, the United States has for decades sought ways to shape and command the global commons for both its own benefit and that of the global community.[4] In the era of renewed great power competition with revisionist adversaries intent on challenging freedom of the commons in the polar regions and elsewhere, the United States has doubled down on its commitment to assert itself as a defender of the seas and the commander of the commons, an enduring goal that necessitates orientation to the polar regions as the newest regions where freedom of the commons will be threatened.[5]

In a canonical 1962 essay on the goals of foreign policy, Arnold Wolfers defines "milieu goals" as goals pertaining to a nation's attempt to shape the environment in which it operates.[6] As the United States and others operate in the global commons, US military and political leaders have held freedom of the commons as a "milieu goal" since World War II. The changing global environment is changing the commons. The Arctic is becoming more accessible, passable, and in some areas hospitable such that it has become a regular topic in the commons conversation. The same can be said for Antarctica. As temperatures rise and ice melts—in both polar regions—international interest grows. As technology improves and access increases, the Arctic and Antarctic are established parts of the global commons network and increasingly relevant in the conversation. Polar interests are evolving and with them come attempts to influence, and even seize and control. As a self-proclaimed defender of the commons, the United States must not overlook the polar commons just because they are on the map's periphery. Moreover, as a defender of the commons, the United States feels compelled to use military power to deny attempts to exploit the commons from hostile actors.[7]

To those who decry such a suggestion as dismissive of international legal framework supposedly governing international maritime waters, remember that international law is a consensus mechanism requiring voluntary compliance among the actors operating within international boundaries. Russia and China have, to date, demonstrated voluntary deviation from international maritime law in the Arctic and South China Sea, respectively.[8] Compliance with international maritime law, then, becomes dependent on naval power projection from the United States and others committed to deterring malign actions, compelling compliance, and thus ensuring freedom of navigation in the maritime commons. To this point, Eliot Cohen reminds us that the United States needs a "strategic concept that informs its approach to those areas of the world that no state commands, which it does not aspire to control, but in which chaos would threaten US interests."[9]

As Cohen and others argue, among the most consequential challenge facing the United States today is strategic competition with Russia and China and the status of the commons and similar ungoverned spaces.[10] The polar regions now host strategic competition with so-called great power rivals within common domains. It is the polar regions that should necessitate orientation, interest, and commitment from the United States to maintain global leadership or a favorable balance of power. Either way, command of the commons is the foundation of influence.[11] An "out of sight, out of mind" dismissal of the polar regions from this equation risks the United States losing its uncontested global influence.

The difficulty, in addition to being ungoverned spaces reliant on international consensus, is that the polar regions are generating simultaneous interest from strategic rivals China and Russia. Moreover, Russia and China have demonstrated a broader commitment than the United States in both policy and practice to prioritizing the polar regions in the twenty-first century. In the post–Cold War era, the victory over the Soviet Union led the United States to polar domain apathy, and resulting polar strategy atrophy. The United States failed to maintain and modernize the North Warning System or expand its polar military infrastructure, at least in the Arctic, where such activity remains permissible. With the Soviet Union no longer a viable threat in the 1990s, the United States reoriented itself toward combating instability and terrorism in the Middle East, Asia, and Africa. The global war on terror distracted Washington and presented opportunities for Moscow and Beijing to expand their influence. There is active competition occurring in the polar regions that will give way to conflict if nothing is done to redirect the current course.

The real issue is that there is a conceptual bias both defining and situating the commons in the global narrative. In reality, the commons do not exist today as they once did. Once shared space and governed via collective agreement and cooperation, the twenty-first-century commons are now drivers of geopolitical and strategic competition as precursors to conflict. Russia and China, through their actions toward the polar regions in particular, are challenging the very notion of US unipolarity and command of the global commons since World War II. Refusing to acknowledge that the United States no longer adequately defends the commons, or has insufficiently deterred international violations, ignores reality. With evidence of a growing multipolar movement and Russia and China extending aggressive behavior into the maritime commons in flagrant rebuke of international norms and agreements, the next logical question asks: At what point will these actions extend into territorial claims in previously agreed-upon commons?

Claims

Sovereignty and territoriality are not the same. The treaties that led to the Peace of Westphalia established and codified the notion of sovereignty via recognized territorial boundaries in 1648 and marked the end of the Thirty Years' War.[12] Chief among the contentious issues that led to conflict in the Thirty Years' War was the extension and imposition of conflicting religious convictions from one state to another and the belief in subject homogeneity. Attempts to pacify and unify under a common religion and rule were met with aggressive resistance, sparking widespread conflict and loss of life for decades.[13]

Arguably the most consequential outcome of the Peace of Westphalia was the creation of borders among the many states involved in the conflict and the recognition that a state may act in accordance with its own wishes within the defined and agreed boundaries, rather than be subjects of or subjected to the whims of those beyond its borders. The concept of sovereignty—and disputes over the same—would influence myriad European conflicts from the Napoleonic Wars to the German Unification in the proceeding centuries. Though internal strife, political disagreements, religious feuds, and even personal animosities fueled some of the subsequent European conflicts, the central tenet and consistent with each was the question of sovereignty and territorial bounds. Under persistent conflict, Europe's borders remained fluid and disputed until the conclusion of World War II.

The objective truth is that geography does not change; politics do. Several additional conflicts were fought over sovereignty in the latter half of the twentieth century and into the early twenty-first. The 2014 Russian military annexation of Crimea is among the most brazen violations of sovereignty thus far in the twenty-first century.[14] The Russian annexation has implications for other competitive and possibly contested regions. By annexing Crimea, Russia effectively redrew the map for the first time in decades, proving that even in the modern era, borders and territorial claims are subject to challenge by those with sufficient motivations and means. In this way, we can assert that the logic of (territorial) contestation holds even in the twenty-first century.

We have become globally complacent in assuming border security just because there are lines on a map. Absent a physical or natural barrier, country and territorial borders are merely recognized lines delineating one state's boundary from another. Violating institutional norms compelling recognition of such boundaries was once unconscionable. Growing global tensions, increasing audacity, dwindling resources, and competition for power, influence, and resources are compelling a new paradigm of aggressive expansionism. As ungoverned spaces sitting on potentially trillions of dollars in potential resource bounties, the polar regions are ripe new targets for great power politics, strategic competition, and territorial expansion.[15] With all of this at stake and international tensions on the rise, what is keeping the polar regions from succumbing to forceful Russian or Chinese claims?

While the history of territorial claims in Antarctica runs deep, more recent are the disputed territorial claims in the Arctic. Regardless, both regions are subject to ongoing, competing, and internationally disputed claims. To assume the existence alone of quasi-self-governing international organizations is sufficient to deter deviation and ensure compliance dismisses the lessons of history. Maintaining the status quo depends on self-regulation, the latter of which China and Russia continue proving their unwillingness to do. Almost as a complement to the 2014 Russian annexation of Crimea, China has, since 2012, bucked international maritime law and the 1982 United Nations Convention on the Law of the Sea (UNCLOS) in its artificial island construction efforts in the South China Sea. Stemming from disputed territorial claims, China's island-building campaign draws persistent international condemnation and raises questions regarding the legitimacy of UNCLOS in steering conduct in international commons, most notably to this discussion in the Arctic.

ARCTIC CLAIMS

UNCLOS governs maritime conduct in international waters. The United States has not ratified UNCLOS and therefore does not consider itself subject to UNCLOS's parameters. Though the United States generally operates in accordance with UNCLOS as a matter of principle, it reserves the right to deviate from UNCLOS stipulations. And while Russia has ratified the convention, Moscow has lobbied the United Nations (UN) three times—in 2001, 2015, and again in 2021—to grant extended territorial waters in the Arctic.[16] To date, Russia remains unsuccessful in its petitioning to the UN Commission on the Limits of the Continental Shelf (CLCS), but this indicates Russian commitments to Arctic influence via expanded and enforceable territory in the High North. Controlling Arctic territory yields economic benefits via the anticipated Arctic resource pool, with estimates holding that 20 percent of Russia's gross domestic product relies on Arctic resources.[17] This points to the symbolism of Russia's 2007 flag-planting expedition on the North Pole seabed. And Russia is not the only nation with Arctic claims. The Arctic is host to myriad claims and country interests, some of which are duly recognized as legitimate by the international community; others are not.

Lacking a common landmass (or permanent ice sheet) like Antarctica, the Arctic Circle is the stage for disputes over continental shelf boundaries and how those boundaries define international domains from territorial waters and airspace, and exclusive economic zones, as well where countries define the air defense identification zones that are part of international airspace but are considered buffer zones compelling military response if crossed. The international standard for territorial waters, according to UNCLOS, is 12 nautical miles from the coastal baseline, or low-water point along a coast. There are differences for archipelagic baselines, but in general, the 12-nautical-mile standard is widely recognized as territorial water.[18] Beyond this, UNCLOS further stipulates the criteria for exclusive economic zones as the jurisdictional area "over the exploration and exploitation of marine resources in its adjacent section of the continental shelf, taken to be a band extending 200 miles from the shore."[19] In other words, these zones are international waters in which a country has exclusive economic rights—but that others may traverse—and extend 200 miles from the coastline or seaward boundary.[20] In adopting the coastline standard, the designation of exclusive economic zone is objective and undisputed. The point of contention within this definition, and one that drives competing and contested Arctic Circle claims disputes to this day, is the phrase "adjacent section of the continental shelf."

Per Article 76 of UNCLOS, coastal states can claim rights over "seabed resources" beyond their 200-mile exclusive economic zones, provided the state can demonstrate an extension of the continental shelf using scientific measuring procedures and confirmed data.[21] Extending from the Russian coast across the Arctic Circle, adjacent the North Pole, and ending at the intersection of the Canadian and Danish (via Greenland) exclusive economic zones, the Lomonosov Ridge is center to the resource claims debate in the Arctic. Additionally, the Mendeleev Ridge (or Rise) extends along another disputed area of the Arctic Circle between Russian- and Canadian-claimed waters (see Figure 3.1).

Russia in 2001 petitioned the CLCS to grant the Lomonosov and Mendeleev Ridges as extensions of its continental shelf, thereby increasing Russian claims to the Arctic Ocean and its seabed resources. The CLCS did not render a ruling to Russia's petition, instead directing more research and investigation into the matter. In 2015, Russia submitted a revised petition to the CLCS again requesting extension of the continental shelf to include the Lomonosov and Mendeleev Ridges.[22] The UN requested further information from Moscow and withheld a ruling pending additional clarification of the request. Most recent, in April 2021, Russia revised its previous submission by extending its continental shelf claims further, this time including elements of the Canadian and Eurasian Basins, among others, and prompting Western Arctic watchers to claim that Moscow is "claiming the entire Arctic Ocean as

Figure 3.1 Lomonosov and Mendeleev Ridges

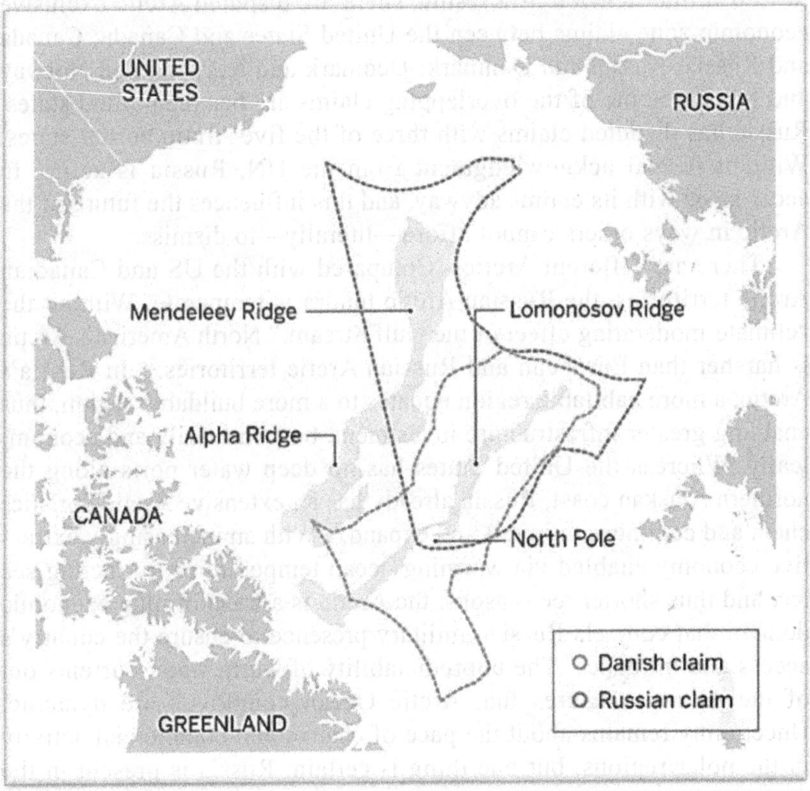

Source: Geological Survey of Denmark and Greenland.

their continental shelf."[23] This is the latest in an ongoing series of disputed Arctic claims between Russia and Denmark in particular.

In 2007, for example, Denmark claimed that the Lomonosov Ridge was an extension of its continental shelf via Greenland.[24] Russia's claims contradict Denmark's and are left to the UN to determine. As of this writing, the CLCS has not ruled on Russia's latest claim, but this has not stopped Russia from assuming the economic rights to Arctic waters and seabed resources beyond its recognized exclusive economic zone. These competing continental shelf claims are some among several disputed claims in the Arctic.

The intricacies and nuance of each disputed claim are covered in greater detail in numerous other venues.[25] The point here is that the

Arctic is an area of dispute—a contested commons that is advancing toward further tension as a result. There are disputed Arctic exclusive economic zone claims between the United States and Canada; Canada and Russia; Russia and Denmark; Denmark and Norway; and Norway and Russia. Some of the overlapping claims are between allied states. Russia has disputed claims with three of the five Arctic border states. Without formal acknowledgment from the UN, Russia is acting in accordance with its claims anyway, and this influences the future of the Arctic in ways others cannot afford—literally—to dismiss.

There are different Arctics. Compared with the US and Canadian Arctic territories, the Russian Arctic tundra is temperate. Without the "climate-moderating effect of the Gulf Stream," North America's Arctic is harsher than European and Russian Arctic territories.[26] In Russia's Arctic, a more habitable region equates to a more buildable region, thus enabling greater infrastructure investment, both militarily and economically. Whereas the United States has no deep water ports along the northern Alaskan coast, Russia already has an extensive Arctic logistics chain and continues to invest and expand.[27] With an increasingly extractive economy enabled via warming ocean temperatures, retracting sea ice, and thus shorter ice seasons, the Arctic is a transforming economic domain that compels Russian military presence to ensure the country's access and influence. The unpredictability of warm water currents out of the Atlantic ensures that Arctic Ocean conditions are dynamic. Uncertainty remains about the pace of change and commercial activity in the polar regions, but one thing is certain: Russia is present in the Arctic and continues to leverage its position toward its goal of securing uncovered resources, to include some 25 percent of the undiscovered hydrocarbons in the Arctic, 80 percent of which are in areas of competing territorial claims.[28] As more countries extend commercial activities into the Arctic, this inevitably raises the specter of increased competition, likely confrontation, and resulting conflict. The Arctic's progression toward being a site of conflict is more advanced than Antarctica's, but there are similar international dynamics at play in the Southern Hemisphere that make it an equally compelling environment relative to the competition-confrontation-conflict perspective.

Antarctic Claims

There are twelve country flags at the geographic South Pole, representing the original signatories of the Antarctic Treaty, but they are purely ceremonial. None represents an internationally recognized territorial claim. No state has planted their flag in either polar region with an expectation of formal recognition. Unlike the Arctic and Russia's North Pole flag-planting, to date Antarctica has been spared provocative publicity stunts. At present, seven countries claim Antarctic territory. While none are recognized via formal boundaries, Norway, France, the United Kingdom, New Zealand, and Australia recognize each other's claims, as none of the respective claims overlap. Chilean, Argentinian, and British claims do overlap along portions of the western Antarctic ice sheet, the Antarctic peninsula, and the Ronne ice shelf.[29] The only unclaimed portion of Antarctica is the Marie Byrd land adjacent the Amundsen Sea. Aside from this area, the remainder of the Antarctic continent is home to historically rooted—and some contested—territorial claims dating to the early twentieth century. These claims and the tensions surrounding them are part of the impetus behind the creation and adoption of the Antarctic Treaty in 1959 and its enforcement in 1961.

The Antarctic Treaty was careful neither to nullify nor to recognize territorial claims on Antarctica. Instead, the crafters elected to leave claims open to international interpretation of those states with significant Antarctic interests. This is an important consideration in the history of Antarctic claims relative to current and future international dynamics on the continent. The nuanced discussion of these claims is, like for the Arctic, beyond the scope and intent here. The consistent point is that, also like the Arctic, there are competing territorial claims in Antarctica representing the interests of at least seven countries. Others like the United States and Russia (then the Soviet Union) without territorial claims at the signing of the treaty reserved the rights to make future claims but have yet to do so.[30]

Absent sovereign states, the polar regions present a unique issue of territoriality, the likes of which countries have been fighting wars over for centuries. We must acknowledge the history of conflict stemming from issues of territoriality coupled with the currently disputed Antarctic claims and evolving resource propositions, and in so doing resist the notion that the mere existence of the Antarctic Treaty is sufficient to deter malign actions and intent. Make no mistake: the mechanisms of collaboration, these polar covenants, are a remarkable achievement of international cooperation, but they are more fragile now than ever. Those who say that Antarctica is now and forever will be a peaceful scientific preserve on the basis of the Antarctic Treaty's existence alone assume universal and indefinite compliance.

Both Russia and China have proven that they are willing to violate international law, invade sovereign territory in Russia's case, and engage in aggressive and incendiary international rhetoric all in the name of advancing their national agendas toward greater global influence. International agreements, the covenants we assume to be binding and compulsory, are a reflection of intent and promise at the time of ratification. As the international security environment changes, so does interest and intent. Competition over claims and territoriality, both in the Arctic and in Antarctica, is a blueprint for conflict just as it has been for centuries. But the international community continues to insist that the existence of international institutions like the Arctic Council and Antarctic Treaty are sufficiently credible to maintain the status quo in these increasingly competitive, contested, and soon-to-be conflicted regions.

COVENANTS

There are several international organizations, institutions, councils, treaties, policies, laws, codes, and norms informing polar region behaviors. In all of their substance, however, these guiding frames have one critical vulnerability: enforceability. Be it the Antarctic Treaty, the Arctic Council, or the myriad other forms of contractual agreements or forums stipulating the bounds for polar activities, each lacks the necessary power to serve as a deterrence or compliance mechanism in the face of malign intent. While departures from international covenants, agreements, codes, and even norms are rare, we have seen—and will continue to see—instances of such occurring in the international environment such that we cannot blindly assume their existence is, alone, sufficient to prevent conflict in competitive and contested regions. With that, the Antarctic Treaty serves as the primary example of a decades-old and successful international covenant, but one that may also be nearing the end of its utility in a rapidly changing geopolitical landscape.

THE ANTARCTIC TREATY

> The Antarctic region was, proportionate to the degree of human activity that took place there, as conflictive as any other area and showing every sign of progressive deterioration.[31]

Looking at Antarctica we tend to assume its isolation gifted it peace. It is one of the only places on Earth where claimed territories exist absent state sovereignty and where conflict has not occurred. Antarctica is an ungoverned space ripe with resources, novelty, and intrigue. But the result of multinational interest coupled with ungoverned space is inevitably conflict. The historical record brings an obvious point to bear when examining the catalysts of conflict: territorial disputes and matters of sovereignty are often the drivers. Whereas conflict over territory has focused on areas of value in terms of economic or cultural significance, population alone is not a necessary precondition for armed conflict.[32] With no permanent human settlements (yet) outside of research stations, Antarctica is the least-populated place on Earth. But it too is not immune from human conflict. In this way, the Antarctic Treaty was, and remains, a conflict resolution mechanism.[33]

The Antarctic Treaty lies at the nexus of territoriality and nationality. The tension between those states favoring territoriality and those favoring nationality in Antarctic governance served as the primary driver for the treaty's language in 1959. Considering the territoriality versus nationality debate, the Antarctic Treaty necessitated a common framework that all signatories would adopt to regulate activities. Among the treaty's stipulations and protocols are prohibitions on mineral mining, nuclear explosions, and nuclear waste disposal. Such prohibitions are necessary to prevent extractive exploitation of Antarctica's resource-rich environment, especially in an area of the world with embedded historical tension. Though disputed, some estimates hold that Antarctica has the third largest oil reserves on Earth at some 200 billion barrels.[34] Such a claim may be broadly misinterpreted and circulated, leading to an increased sense of international significance.

According to David MacDonald, "the potential for energy minerals (coal, oil, and gas) in Antarctica is extremely low."[35] MacDonald and others disputing this claim hold that the original data from the 1980s estimates, rather than surveys, the actual size (and assumed existence) of oil reserves in Antarctica.[36] MacDonald further warns of resisting what he refers to as the "Eldorado complex" in Antarctica—or "the idea that unknown lands will be a treasure trove of resources."[37] But such a claim is equally countered in its own context. We know more about some elements of Mars than we do about some aspects of Antarctica. So whereas some dispute the notion that extractive resources exist in any compelling quantity on Antarctica, their disputes are equally biased in the same data-absent conjecture informing estimates to the contrary.

Those disputing broad claims of massive Antarctic oil reserves typically come from conservation or similar organizations seeking to quell global interest and assumed competition in Antarctica sufficient to question their intention and biases. Despite a concerted effort among scientists and environmentalists seeking to isolate and protect

Antarctica from exploitation, several countries are investing and seeking greater influence on the continent. As more countries seek presence and influence—for whatever reasons and informed by whatever sources—in the ungoverned Antarctic, the probability of competition increases. Peaceful use, rather than competition and tension, is precisely what the Antarctic Treaty seeks to promote through its many stipulations. Even with its specificities, there are embedded disputes that the treaty, in its deliberate language, makes no attempt to resolve.

For as precise and unambiguous as some articles of the treaty are, Article 4 is equally nebulous and thus enables continued claims disputes on Antarctica even to this day. Article 4 of the Antarctic Treaty states:[38]

1. Nothing in the present treaty shall be interpreted as
   a. a renunciation by any Contracting Party of previously asserted rights of or claims to territorial sovereignty in Antarctica;
   b. a renunciation or diminution by any Contracting Party of any basis of claim to territorial sovereignty in Antarctica which it may have whether as a result of its activities or those of its nationals in Antarctica, or otherwise;
   c. prejudicing the position of any Contracting Party as regards its recognition or non-recognition of any other States right of or claim or basis of claim to territorial sovereignty in Antarctica.
2. No acts or activities taking place while the present treaty is in force shall constitute a basis for asserting, supporting or denying a claim to territorial sovereignty in Antarctica or create any rights of sovereignty in Antarctica. No new claim, or enlargement of an existing claim, to territorial sovereignty in Antarctica shall be asserted while the present treaty is in force.

In this way, Article 4 recognizes existing territorial claims to Antarctic sovereignty made prior to its adoption, and allows for non-claimant nations like the United States and the Soviet Union—having conducted activity and established infrastructure in Antarctica without claims to sovereignty—to assert their "basis of claim" in the future. In other words, the treaty does not preclude states from protecting future rights to make claims on Antarctica. This wording matters and will shape future deviations from the treaty. In effect, the treaty acknowledges territorial sovereignty on Antarctica on the basis of previous claims, but also acknowledges the position of other states to not recognize such claims, and allows states to reserve the rights to future claims on the basis of activities. In sum, the Antarctic Treaty interpretation is open for debate and creates conditions for future tensions and potential conflict.

The carefully crafted treaty architecture is equally ambiguous and potentially exploitative. China has been active in Antarctic research since the 1980s, after its ratification of the Antarctic Treaty. Because China's Antarctic presence occurred after treaty ratification, and per the wording in Article 4 of the treaty, these activities cannot be the "basis of claim" for Chinese Antarctic sovereignty. However, this restriction remains insofar as China remains party to the Antarctic Treaty. Should China elect to vacate its commitment to the treaty, it can assert sovereignty over its expanding presence on Antarctica, as it would no longer be subject to the restrictions of the Antarctic Treaty System. This would set a new norm of activities on Antarctica, much like in the South China Sea, serving to advance Chinese economic, research, and even military interests before other states could work to prevent it. We can extend similar logic to Russian actions on Antarctica, though it is more likely Russia would wait for China to first depart from Antarctic Treaty commitments and then follow suit. That said, Russia's approach to the Arctic and its Arctic Council involvement is a comparable analog to China's potential actions toward the Antarctic Treaty that should be equally met with a curious if not worrisome eye.

The Arctic Council

Though the Arctic Council presides over Arctic matters, it lacks the capacity and authority to actually govern. As such, Arctic "governance" is a misnomer. As a quasi-governing body, the Arctic Council "does not and cannot implement or enforce its guidelines, assessments or recommendations."[39] Beyond this, the Arctic Council deliberately omitted defense and security issues from its charter at the time of adoption. The Arctic Council has since revisited this omission due to the changing physical and international security environment, but such a focus deviates from the original intent of the Arctic Council as a collaborative institution focused principally on environmental cooperation. This deliberate omission has decided effects on the Arctic today and has laid the foundation for an Arctic security dilemma motivating militarization and geostrategic competition. This is complicated by the fact that the Arctic lacks a legitimate medium for security and defense dialogue representing both state and nonstate actors with Arctic interests.

The 1972 Incidents at Sea Agreement, the 1989 Dangerous Military Activities Agreement, and the 2014 Code for Unplanned Encounters at Sea all attempt at directing and limiting military interactions in the maritime commons.[40] So logic holds that these would also extend into the Arctic as a domain of the commons. Still, the dynamics of the Arctic domain are different such that these covenants fail to provide the necessary forum for Arctic-specific defense and security discussions. Moreover, they are decidedly oriented to the maritime sphere.

With increasing Arctic militarization on the land fringes as well as in the air and maritime domains, these institutions fall short of a comprehensive framework for Arctic defense and security discussions. Other forums like the Arctic Security Forces Roundtable, the Arctic Chiefs of Defence Staff meetings, and the Arctic Coast Guard Forum have sought to host discussions on military affairs in the High North by bringing together key Arctic stakeholders, including Russia. Following the Russian Federation's annexation of Crimea in 2014, most of these forums removed Russia from the dialogue and subsequently fizzled away.

The Arctic Coast Guard Forum remains an active setting with rotating leadership, but—similar to the Arctic Council—does not specifically address military and defense issues as part of its charter to "foster safe, secure and environmentally responsible maritime activity in the Arctic."[41] Similarly, the 2017 Polar Code—established by the International Maritime Organization—covers a "full range of design, construction, equipment, operational, training, search and rescue and environmental protection matters relevant to ships operating in the inhospitable waters surrounding the two poles."[42] But again, conspicuously, there is no mention of military and defense issues.[43]

In a way, the Arctic Council's resistance to adopting a security and defense charter is a microcosm of the broader issue of blind hope among stakeholders insisting the Arctic will forever remain a peaceful domain. Whether wishful thinking rooted in ignorance or blatant apathy, the fact that the Arctic and all its international forums have no dedicated platform for defense and security dialogue injects risk into contemporary Arctic affairs. It is the lack of formalized defense and security dialogue that created the conditions for competition in the High North over strategically valuable land like Greenland and Norwegian islands in the Svalbard archipelago such as Spitsbergen and Jan Mayen.[44]

THE SVALBARD TREATY

Svalbard, and Spitsbergen as its largest island, is a Norwegian archipelago about 600 miles north of Norway and about 1,000 miles south of the geographic North Pole. Spitsbergen is one of the northernmost inhabited areas in the world; it is home to only 2,100 people compared to the estimated 3,000 polar bears.[45] Despite its remote and rugged terrain, Svalbard is one of the most critical strategic nodes for the evolving Arctic security situation, especially for supporting deep-space communication. The Svalbard Treaty, like the Antarctic Treaty, generally restricts military activity in Svalbard, but there is growing interest in this little-known territory as a big player in the Arctic.

The Svalbard Treaty currently has forty-six parties adhering to its stipulations. In addition to Article 1 establishing Svalbard as a geographically separated part of Norway, Article 9 of the treaty prohibits the "establishment of any naval base" and "any fortification in the said territories, which may never be used for warlike purposes."[46] This does not prohibit Norway from using its military to defend Svalbard's sovereignty. That said, Norway has no military infrastructure on the islands, relying on its coast guard to patrol Svalbard's maritime regions. Such efforts are proving problematic, as ongoing tensions between Russia and Norway over commercial fishing rights and territorial versus international waters have raised Svalbard's profile in the lens of the North Atlantic Treaty Organization (NATO) lens.[47] That, coupled with Russia's continued coal mining and Chinese research personnel on the islands, has led to evolving interest in Svalbard's future strategic significance.

While prospects of conflict over Svalbard and the Arctic appear low, unlike other areas that enjoy relative security of proximate NATO military infrastructure, Svalbard is particularly isolated, which also makes it strategically that much more valuable. The archipelago in general, but Spitsbergen in particular as the flagship island, is vulnerable to China and Russia gaining leverage in the Arctic via future posturing. Spitsbergen is a desirable location in the event of an Arctic conflict, as its unique position could serve as a critical node in supporting operations.[48]

Given the lack of military capabilities in Svalbard, its geographic value in the race for Arctic influence, and the absence of formal military and defense dialogue among Arctic stakeholders, Russia could pursue militarization and contested control of the archipelago. In 2019, Norway discovered Russian Spetsnaz units operating in Svalbard, an explicit violation of the Svalbard Treaty. And while China has maintained its Yellow River research station on Svalbard since 2004, analysts now believe the Chinese are covertly using it for military satellites.[49] For these reasons, the US military has taken a growing interest in Jan Mayen, another remote Norwegian island closer to Greenland than the Norwegian coast, and questionably within the Svalbard archipelago, as an indicator of strengthening US-Norwegian relations and Arctic attention.[50]

Jan Mayen is isolated like Spitsbergen, but also situated squarely in the middle of the Greenland–Iceland–United Kingdom Gap. Though it lacks a suitable port for NATO navies, Jan Mayen's airfield has a mile-long runway capable of receiving smaller cargo aircraft like the C-130.[51] Given the absence of a comparable treaty limiting military activities (because it is considered outside the Svalbard limits for the purposes of the treaty), Jan Mayen's strategic location makes it another valuable option in the NATO Arctic posture, most importantly as a suitable alternative to the rest of the Svalbard archipelago and Spitsbergen island. In this way, Jan Mayen can serve as an additional node connecting NATO's Arctic posture, and one that may be even more necessary given the probability of further Arctic tension. This is one of many possible Arctic flashpoints to watch in the coming years.

That's How the Covenant Crumbles

The covenants guiding polar region activities are going to crumble in time. As competition continues, it will generate greater interest and more presence from strong states. As more countries ascend to or descend on the polar regions and compete for resources, territory, and influence, the potential for confrontation and conflict increases steadily. Even with the risk of nuclear proliferation via a polar region conflict continuum, humanity's capacity for and insistence on militarized dispute as a default form of conflict resolution persists throughout history. Subscribing to the notion that "this time it will be different" is a gambler's fallacy in action. Scholars have made similar arguments relative to these fragile polar institutions and their relation to competing territorial claims for decades: "It is not difficult to foresee that if for any reason the Antarctic Treaty arrangement were to collapse, and the strategic interests of the major powers revived, a likely consequence might be that these potential territorial claims would be made effective, thereby introducing additional complications in the already complex Antarctic scenario."[52]

Such a scenario is far from an impossibility. As a seemingly common thread regarding Antarctic tensions, both Argentina and Chile keep a permanent military presence in Antarctica in support of their respective scientific research activities on the continent. Others, like Russia, China, and the United States, regularly send military personnel to Antarctica under the label of research support. The persistent concern with regular or permanent military presence on a demilitarized continent is that those with self-advancing Antarctic agendas are cloaking the true nature of their military activities, or are using paramilitary agencies and civilian contractors to execute military missions.[53] Such activities are becoming an increasingly routine phenomenon in contested areas and active battlespaces, so much so that they will likely occur in the polar regions in time.

Increasing global tensions coupled with ungoverned spaces and commons home to untold commodity riches are a recipe for competition and eventual conflict. Polar stakeholders have evolved from a sense of quasi-cooperation in each region in the post–Cold War era to, as information and capabilities improve, a competitive dynamic. With great powers both present and competing in the polar regions for access to resources, spurred by disputed claims, or lacking rules governing the contested commons, the situation will further escalate. As the modern-day polar security dilemma evolves, polar stakeholders will move from a competitive domain toward further militarization and eventual confrontation (examples of which we have already seen in the Arctic between Russia and the United States). Increasing probability for confrontation has raised the probability that contestation and conflict will result. This is, of course, theoretically prevented via the existence of and mutual adherence to the international agreements, treaties, and codes supposedly governing polar region activities. Between competing territorial claims and contested commons, the thirst for access to commodities driving commerce in a dog-eat-dog world is sufficient to compel aggression from states even far removed from the regional boundaries.

Further indicative of the evolving territorial interests and potential for future claims, China maintains evolving interests in both polar regions that may extend into eventual territorial claims similar to those on the South China Sea. In their January 2018 white paper, the Chinese Communist Party's State Council Information Office outlined its polar interests for the world to read. The Polar Silk Road policy emphasized protection of the environment, pursuit of scientific research, and support of multinational governance in the region.[54] Though China advocates multinational governance in the Arctic, there is no indication of its intent to comply with such a mandate.

Extending interests to Antarctica, China continues to enhance its diplomatic and economic ties to Australia and New Zealand, as gateway countries to the southernmost continent. Beijing has also increased Antarctic operations in both research and tourism and raised some questions about its true intent on the continent in its refusal to grant unrestricted access to multinational inspectors surveying Chinese Antarctic research facilities.[55] They justify this through their interpretation of what Anne-Marie Brady calls Antarctica's "undetermined sovereignty": "In an area of undetermined sovereignty, a state may construct a case to argue for sovereignty rights by means of discovery, by naming geographical sites and mapping, and by continual presence and occupation."[56]

To this point, there are indicators of Chinese and Russian cooperation on facility access on Antarctica. To what end is anyone's guess, but given the continued expansionist rhetoric from both, it is enough to warrant curiosity. We need to recognize the poles and their surrounding areas as contested commons and act accordingly. Such spaces are, historically, the subject of struggle. Territoriality via contested claims is alive and thriving in the polar regions; we need only look at the objective evidence to reach this conclusion.

Antarctica is an island continent with no land borders to any nation. The fifty-four parties to the current Antarctic Treaty and more than seventy countries represented via research stations on the Antarctic continent all agree via their presence to comply with the treaty in its entirety. Not as isolated and lacking an actual land mass, the Arctic region borders five countries, each of which by being an Arctic border state are members of the Arctic Council (the additional three countries lacking Arctic borders but part of the Arctic Council are Finland, Sweden, and Iceland). In addition to other participants and observers, the Arctic Council serves as the forum for collective voice on Arctic matters. Though each of these institutions carries the luster and label of a legitimate governing body, neither the Antarctic Treaty nor the Arctic Council has legal authority and instead relies on consensus and—when lacking consensus—international pressures of compliance from the countries party to the respective agreements.

Some argue that these institutions, being that they comprise states with diplomatic, economic, and military standing in the world, are sufficient to compel compliance. To date, this is (mostly) accurate. But what would compel a country to depart from its promise to comply with a treaty or agreed-upon code of conduct? Is it conceivable that there are states whose interests now, given the evolving security environment, conflict with their promises of decades prior? Of course we hope that this not be that case, and we hope to continue along the path of peaceful polar relations. But hope is not a course of action. We cannot hope that such deviations never occur and hope that the party states remain committed to decades-old agreements, despite an evolving and increasingly competitive globalized world. It is foolish to assume indefinite compliance by all party or council member states, such that we must return to and acknowledge two evolving realities: that the polar covenants are no longer fit for purpose in the twenty-first century, and that the polar regions are contested commons ripe for competition and conflict.

This is not to say that the polar regions are doomed to competition and conflict in the twenty-first century. Absent an acknowledgment of these facts and the evolving security scape around the world, coupled with inaction aimed at preventing regional exploitation, the polar regions will be the next areas of geostrategic competition for resources and sovereignty, just as others have been the focus of such competition and conflict in the past. But the race to plant the flag, claim territory, and thus consume the spoils of the claim is not the only polar region consideration in the context of future great power competition. The polar regions are critical nodes in the evolving global space race, a race that will influence future strategic competition. Those with polar presence enjoy an advantage in space capabilities and operations that, to date, is a little-known benefit of the polar regions.

Cosmos

Great powers will fight future wars over the commons, including the celestial commons: the cosmos. The space domain has never been more relevant. With the 2019 establishment of the US Space Force (USSF), the United States demonstrated its commitment to the space domain as a twenty-first-century defense priority. The USSF will "protect U.S. and allied interests in space and to provide space capabilities to the joint force."[57] As China and Russia foster their own space capabilities and seek new pathways of influence, the United States must follow suit. Satellite communications are an enabling capability for military forces operating in the air, land, maritime, and cyber domains. Currently, the US Department of Defense integrates both military and commercial satellites into its defense-wide communications systems to link its forces across the globe. There are limits to military communications—especially in tactically remote environments lacking additional commercial infrastructure—but in general the system enables globally distributed, reliable military communications. This is not the case in the polar regions.

As a general rule from cell phones to satellites, the further from civilization, the weaker the signal. Above 65° north latitude in the Arctic, communications are limited and sporadic. And while submarines in the Arctic Ocean do provide some form of communication link, above 70° north, space-enabled surface communications are almost nonexistent. Given that the Arctic is mostly a maritime region, there are few options for permanent base construction and satellite ground station terminals for communications relays. The extent of the static, ground-based Arctic communications receipt and relay infrastructure is limited to the installations along the northern edges of the Arctic border states. For the United States, Thule Air Force Base, in Greenland, is the northernmost installation enabling satellite communications.

There are no assigned aircraft at Thule, as its primary mission is to support the "global network of sensors providing missile warning, space surveillance and space control."[58] Between Thule and other northern installations linked to the Space Force's wideband global satellite communications network, the US military maintains adequate coverage in the Arctic between 65 and 70 north. Farther north, communications begin to fracture. Even with the Space Force's Enhanced Polar System satellites used for military communications, the capabilities are still limited such that US Northern Command (NORTHCOM) continues to request budgetary allocations to fund improved Arctic connectivity and communications capacity.

In the fiscal year 2021 budget request, NORTHCOM listed improved Arctic communications infrastructure as its top unfunded priority. Requesting $130 million for enhanced Arctic connectivity is an indication of the current and future strategic significance of the Arctic to homeland defense and great power competition posturing.[59] We can also conclude from this that NORTHCOM anticipates more military presence and increasingly complex distributed Arctic operations in the near future to justify the request. Then–NORTHCOM commander General Terrance O'Shaughnessy's declaration of the Arctic as a "battlespace" in a March 2020 House Armed Services Committee hearing only advances the narrative that the Arctic has moved beyond competition and is now advancing toward conflict.[60] Therefore, the space domain will be vital for future Arctic military operations. This is a competitive, congested, and contested domain in itself, and so securing a position in the Arctic space-enabled communications race is a strategic imperative for the United States. But space competition and its progression toward conflict is not limited to the Arctic alone. Antarctica, too, presents an operational and strategic consideration for the United States relative to evolving exploitative great power space interests.

In terms of radio signals and interference, Antarctica's skies are the clearest in the world. Lacking radio interference found in other areas, Antarctic skies enable uniquely clear and undisturbed space communications, research, and visibility. As a continental ice-covered landmass, Antarctica affords countries the foundation to build static satellite tracking and relay infrastructure, further facilitating space-based communications. But for the same reasons Antarctica is ideal for space research given its isolation and reduced interference, it is an equally attractive location for military activities. From surveillance networks to remote control of offensive weapon systems, the clear Antarctic skies are a military space force's ideal ground-based operating environment (at least for clarity's sake).[61]

There are planned fiber optic projects linking Antarctica to New Zealand, but currently all inbound and outbound Antarctic communications rely on satellite relays. With the Antarctic Treaty System prohibition on Antarctic military activity, satellite communication keeps the dozens of research stations and thousands of personnel on Antarctica connected to the outside world. The United States leverages US military personnel, networks, and capabilities for Antarctic communications. McMurdo Station, the chief US Antarctic research hub, receives Armed Forces Network (AFN) feeds as its source of television entertainment. Antarctic researchers on McMurdo Station enjoy the AFN the same as military personnel deployed overseas around the world, so much so that the AFN is even serviced and maintained by US military personnel on Antarctica.[62] In addition to partnering with the US Antarctic Program to enable researchers to watch the Super Bowl at 77.5° south, the US military's involvement in Antarctic communications has a strategic component.

In June 2016, the National Science Foundation (NSF) partnered with the Strategic Command (STRATCOM) to be able to access Department of Defense satellites and extend Antarctic satellite communications on to the department's Defense Satellite Communications System, a collection of military communication satellites.[63] Whereas the NSF and US Antarctic Program couch this relationship as an access and communications enhancement for Antarctic research operations, given that the US military controls the satellite network, one has to question the limits of military operations *on* Antarctica relative to this NSF–Department of Defense partnership.

The NSF's use of military communications infrastructure supports the US Antarctic Program's research mission in myriad forms and consistent with the 1961 Antarctic Treaty System provisions. In this way, the Defense Satellite Communications System's support is analogous to the US Air Force's continued logistical support of the US Antarctic Program via Operation Deep Freeze. The military provides the platform—be it communications or transport—to facilitate Antarctic research missions. However, with Russia and China continuing their push to expand their presence on Antarctica, what is the US tolerance threshold for continuing to provide defense platforms for nondefense matters in Antarctica?

According to Anne-Marie Brady, China seeks to expand its offensive and defensive military posture on Antarctica, as evidenced by years of expanding interest, policy orientation, and now presence on the continent. With the completion of its BeiDou global navigation satellite system in June 2020, China now has a fully operational, state-controlled analog to the US global positioning system (GPS).[64] This development levels the technological playing field in the military navigation game. Brady also notes that the further development by China and Russia of satellite ground stations on Antarctica may help both rival competitors in their efforts to improve military capabilities and power projection around the world.[65]

Russia, too, has eyed Antarctica as a satellite receiving station location for its own GPS analog to that of the US. Its global navigation satellite system went fully operational in 2011, coinciding with Russia's release of its Antarctic strategy. The strategy lists "ensuring space activities of the Russian Federation" in terms of the satellite system as one of its priority tasks for Antarctic activities, owing to the necessity of southern satellite receiving stations for full global coverage.[66] Russia identified the need for "expediency of creating such a network at the Russian Antarctic stations" and plans to "install . . . stations for collecting differential correction and monitoring measurements."[67] Additionally, the Russian Antarctic strategy notes the importance of Antarctica for "ground support of space activities," to include remote sensing and observations.[68]

The strategic value of Antarctica for space is unlike any other region on Earth. As the space domain evolves into having greater relevance, Antarctica's strategic stock value will likewise rise. Countries with active space programs and global force projection requirements need satellite-based communications and navigation to best enable effective global power projection. The polar regions are vital links to global communications and navigation ability, to include weapons system tracking and employment.

The Arctic and Antarctic are vital nodes for enabling communication with satellites and other space-based platforms.[69] This means that the future of US Space Force primacy will be dependent on infrastructure and accessible relays near the North and South Poles. In this vein, US space strategy should acknowledge such terrestrial constraints on space operations—and take actions to promote and defend polar access. And if the United States pursues these objectives for these reasons, we have to assume that near-peer rivals like Russia and China, with similar ambition and understanding of the polar imperative for space accessibility and force enabling, will likewise pursue their own agendas in the polar regions through competitive posturing that will, with enough confrontation, lead to conflict.

PUTTING IT ALL TOGETHER

When *National Geographic* magazine declared in its August 2019 issue that "the Arctic is heating up," it raised attention to what was then a relatively obscure observation. *National Geographic* presented the facts of the Arctic relative to increasing militarization, changing geography and climates, and increased commodities interests. But one particular quote stood out as concerning. When author Neil Shea embedded with Canadian Rangers conducting Arctic training for his story "The New Cold War," he captured this exchange between two Canadian Rangers:

> RANGER 1: Man, look at this. What would anyone do up here? Tanks driving around, soldiers, planes? Whaddya say, Marv? You ready to fight the Russians?
>
> RANGER 2: Too much hassle.
>
> RANGER 1: From a military standpoint, it doesn't make much sense, eh? You've seen how much time we spend out here just doing basic shit. You've seen how often our stuff breaks down, how much work it takes just to survive. Ain't no war comin' up here.[70]

To a growing scholarly voice that acknowledges the evolving realities of the polar regions, this exchange is both apathetic and deliberately dismissive—precisely the reason why we should care. Russia is counting on apathy to prevail in the Arctic; China is counting on it in Antarctica. They assume nobody wants to compete in the polar regions because they are vast, cold, dark, remote regions irrelevant to the rest of the world. Russia and China are leveraging international apathy to promote their own polar power. Iran has indicated its interest in and intent to build on Antarctica. Turkey, India, and Pakistan have also expressed their interests under the guise, perhaps, of science.[71] And the list continues to grow.

The polar regions are not the desolate, irrelevant regions many hold them to be, even today. Each has a long and rich history of significance and relevance to international security. Knowledge promotes interest, and interest motivates countries toward the poles. The logical extension of this is increased presence vying for resources and resulting competition. Competition, we have seen, will breed confrontation, and continued confrontation will—inevitably—breed conflict.

For the United States, the competition-to-conflict spectrum is narrowing in the Arctic. Already Russia is blurring the lines between peaceful activity and offensive military maneuvering. Given the geographic proximity of the Arctic at the northern doorstep of the United States, this is an issue that cannot be dismissed. For the United States and Russia, competition for the Arctic will soon rival the strain between southern countries and their interests in Antarctica. Chile, Argentina, Australia, and New Zealand all have vested interest in Antarctica given the proximity. Though it is difficult to imagine conflict arising in its current form, as China and Russia encroach on Antarctica and disrupt the existing order we will see increasing tensions and eventual conflict over claims and resources. With China and Russia both vying for Arctic influence and presence as well, it is an equally concerning dynamic for the United States in the High North as it is for the likes of Australia and New Zealand in the south.

Globalization is both a threat and an opportunity to international security. As the world becomes smaller and more connected, places like the polar regions—once thought of as distant and irrelevant—are becoming both accessible and relevant. Improving technology and transportation capabilities brings these regions closer to the conversation than ever before.

There have been military operations in the poles for nearly a hundred years, even without the knowledge of resource riches. Today's capabilities are orders of magnitude more sophisticated and motivations more sinister. From competition over commodities to considerations of communities, the polar Cs integrate each into a broader and inclusive lens through which to consider the future of these regions in terms of international security. To this end, we can also consider *compression* among the Cs of consideration, as more activity in the regions will inevitably compress the future battlespace and act as nodes for both remote control of weapons systems, but also critical hubs for space communications and improved battlespace connectivity and communications. In short, the polar regions are now, and again, part of the international security conversation. Accepting this argument requires a closer look at the polar players. In acknowledging the new reality, the next question is: Which countries matter for the evolving polar region dynamic? Who are the polar players? And within this lens, which are the peripherals versus the actual powers?

Notes

1. US Senate Security Subcommittee of the Committee on Commerce, Science, and Transportation, testimony of Mike Sfraga, "Expanding Opportunities, Challenges, and Threats in the Arctic: A Focus on the USCG Arctic Strategic Outlook,"

Washington, DC, December 12, 2019, https://www.commerce.senate.gov/services/files/5BC4FD83-53B8-49D1-B6E1864F71110ADD#:~:text=To%20re%2Dconceptualize%20the%20realities,Cooperation%2C%20and%207)%20Competition.

2. "Global Governance and Governance of the Global Commons in the Global Partnership for Development Beyond 2015," January 2013, p. 3, https://www.un.org/en/development/desa/policy/untaskteam_undf/thinkpieces/24_thinkpiece_global_governance.pdf.
3. Posen, "Command of the Commons."
4. Ibid.
5. Ibid.
6. Wolfers, *Discord and Collaboration,* chap. 5.
7. Cohen, *The Big Stick.*
8. Russia continues to mandate a Russian captain be aboard all passing foreign vessels using the disputed Northern Sea Route through the Arctic. The route is an international maritime throughway, though Russia claims that it follows along the continental shelf extension of its territorial boundaries. China continues to build artificial islands in the South China Sea and claim the region as an extension of its territorial waters.
9. Cohen, *The Big Stick,* p. 193.
10. Ibid.
11. Posen, "Command of the Commons."
12. Parker, *The Thirty Years' War.*
13. Ibid.
14. McDermott, "Brothers Disunited."
15. Sherwin and Bishop, "The Trillion-Dollar Reason."
16. *Partial Revised Submission of the Russian Federation to the Commission on the Limits of the Continental Shelf in Respect of the Continental Shelf in the Area of the Lomonosov Ridge, Alpha Ridge, Mendeleev Rise, Amundsen and Makarov Basins, and the Canadian Basin,* executive summary (Moscow: Russian Federation, 2021).
17. Axe, "Russia Is Sending S-400 Air Defense Systems to the Arctic."
18. United Nations, *United Nations Convention on Laws of the Sea,* pt. 2, *Territorial Sea and Contiguous Zones,* sec. 2, art. 3, https://nsidc.org/cryosphere/seaice/characteristics/difference.html.
19. "Exclusive Economic Zones," March 4, 2003, https://stats.oecd.org/glossary/detail.asp?ID=884.
20. 43 US Code § 1312 stipulates that the seaward boundary of each coastal US state as the "line three geographical miles from the coastline."
21. *United Nations Convention on the Law of the Sea,* art. 76, https://www.un.org/depts/los/convention_agreements/texts/unclos/unclos_e.pdf.
22. "Partial Revised Submission of the Russian Federation To the Commission on the Limits o fthe Continental Shelf in Respect of the Contintental Shelf of the Russian Federation in the Arctic Ocean – Executive Summary 2015," August 8, 2015, https://www.un.org/Depts/los/clcs_new/submissions_files/rus01_rev15/2015_08_03_Exec_Summary_English.pdf.
23. *Partial Revised Submission of the Russian Federation,* p. 6.; Tranter, "'You Cannot Claim Any More.'"
24. Leapman, "Denmark Joins Race to Claim North Pole."
25. There are numerous references detailing the long history of competing Arctic territorial claims. Many cover the same material. For example, see "Evolution of Arctic Territorial Claims and Agreements: A Timeline (1903–Present)," September

15, 2013, https://www.stimson.org/2013/evolution-arctic-territorial-claims-and-agreements-timeline-1903-present.

26. Barrett, "Department of the Air Force Arctic Strategy," p. 2.
27. Chernov, "New Port Planned."
28. Shea and Palu, "A Thawing Arctic."
29. Rogan-Finnemore, "What Bioprospecting Means," p. 204.
30. US Department of State, "Antarctic Treaty," January 20, 2009–January 20, 2017, https://2009-2017.state.gov/t/avc/trty/193967.htm#narrative.
31. Vicuna, "Antarctic Conflict and International Cooperation," p. 55.
32. Armed conflict has been fought over uninhabited territory in a Salt Marsh in India as well as in the Western Sahara in Africa. The argument that Antarctica is somehow too isolated to see human conflict ignores history.
33. Watts, "The Antarctic Treaty as a Conflict Resolution Mechanism," p. 65.
34. Fogarty, *Antarctica*.
35. MacDonald, "Coal, Oil, and Gas," p. 268.
36. Antarctic and Southern Ocean Coalition, *The Antarctic Oil Myth*.
37. MercoPress, "Oil and Gas in Antarctica: El Dorado Complex, According to British Scientist," May 21, 2012, https://en.mercopress.com/2012/05/21/oil-and-gas-in-antarctica-el-dorado-complex-according-to-british-scientist.
38. *The Antarctic Treaty*, Conference on Antarctica, Washington, DC, October 15, 1959, art. 4.
39. "The Arctic Council: A Backgrounder," September 13, 2018, http://arctic-council.org/index.php/en/about-us.
40. US State Department, "Agreement Between the Government of the United States of America and the Government of the Union of Soviet Socialist Republics on the Prevention of Incidents on and over the High Seas," January 20, 2009–20, 2017, https://2009-2017.state.gov/t/isn/4791.htm; United Nations, "Union of Soviet Socialist Republics and United States of America: Agreement on the Prevention of Dangerous Military Activities," June 12, 1989, https://www.un-ilibrary.org/content/books/9789210594875s002-c017; Western Pacific Naval Symposium, "Code for Unplanned Encounters at Sea," ver. 1.0, April 22, 2014, https://news.usni.org/2014/06/17/document-conduct-unplanned-encounters-sea.
41. Arctic Coast Guard Forum, https://www.arcticcoastguardforum.com.
42. "International Code for Ships Operating in Polar Waters (Polar Code)," https://www.imo.org/en/OurWork/Safety/Pages/polar-code.aspx.
43. Bouffard, Buchanan, and Young, "Arctic Security and Dialogue."
44. There is much debate concerning Jan Mayen's status as a stand-alone island or inclusive of and within the Svalbard archipelago. The International Organization for Standardization as well as the United Nations group both Svalbard and Jan Mayen under the same country code: ISO 3166-2:SJ. Spitsbergen is the largest island in the Svalbard archipelago, prompting many to refer to it simply as Svalbard.
45. "About Svalbard," http://en.visitsvalbard.com/visitor-information/about-svalbard.
46. "Status of Spitsbergen (Svalbard), 9 February 1920," art. 9, http://www.loc.gov/law/help/us-treaties/bevans/m-ust000002-0269.pdf.
47. Wither, "Svalbard."
48. Gosnell and Hildenbrand, "Emerging Challenges in Arctic Security."
49. Humpert, "China Looking to Expand Satellite Coverage;" Hurt, "Russia Continues to Test Western Resolve."
50. Woody, "The US Air Force Is Fixing Up a Remote Base."
51. Ibid.

52. Vicuna, "Antarctic Conflict and International Cooperation," p. 60.
53. Teller, "Why Do So Many Nations Want a Piece of Antarctica?"
54. *China's Arctic Policy* (Beijing: State Council Information Office of the People's Republic of China, 2018).
55. From 2015 to 2020, and though permissible in accordance with Article 7 of the Antarctic Treaty, China repeatedly restricted various base inspection efforts from visual observations of particular facilities and locations. In 2020 a US Coast Guard inspection team was permitted access to and inspected China's newest (and fifth to date) Antarctic base on Inexpressible Island. The US team made physical inspections of the facilities under construction and had nothing strange to report. The report also notes this was the fifteenth US inspection since 1961 and the first since 2012. "United States Antarctic Inspection February 2020: Report of Inspections Under Article VII of the Antarctic Treaty and Article 14 of the Protocol on Environmental Protection," September 2020, https://www.state.gov/wp-content/uploads/2020/09/United-States-Antarctic-Inspection-2020-508.pdf.
56. Brady, "China's Expanding Antarctic Interests," p. 6.
57. US Space Force, "Mission," https://www.spaceforce.mil/About-Us/About-Space-Force/Mission/#:~:text=The%20USSF%20is%20a%20military,capabilities%20to%20the%20joint%20force.
58. "821st Air Base Group," https://www.peterson.spaceforce.mil/About-Us/About-Peterson-SFB/.
59. Bertuca, "NORTHCOM Lists Underfunded Needs."
60. US House Armed Services Committee, "National Security Challenges and U.S. Military Activity in North and South America," March 11, 2020, https://armedservices.house.gov/hearings?ID=8313A04A-DB88-4037-9811-925864674E14.
61. Teller, "Why Do So Many Nations Want a Piece of Antarctica?"
62. Patten, "Soldier Pierces Through Snow."
63. "Defense Satellite Communications System (DSCS)," https://www.usap.gov/technology/4298.
64. "APPLICATIONS-Transport," http://en.beidou.gov.cn.
65. "Antarctic China's New Frontier?" https://www.theaustralian.com.au/subscribe/news/1/?sourceCode=TAWEB_WRE170_a&dest=https%3A%2F%2Fwww.theaustralian.com.au%2Fnational-affairs%2Fforeign-affairs%2Ffears-antarctic-is-the-new-frontier-for-chinas-military%2Fnews-story%2F2edba5f56a0cd1f4b849329c1829f393&memtype=anonymous&mode=premium.
66. "Antarctic Site," March 3, 2011, https://rg.ru/2011/03/31/antarktika-site-dok.html.
67. Ibid.
68. Ibid.
69. Mani et al., "Challenges in Operations and Maintenance"; Byers, "Cold, Dark, and Dangerous."
70. Shea and Palu, "A Thawing Arctic Is Heating Up a new Cold War."
71. Teller, "Why Do So Many Nations Want a Piece of Antarctica?"

4

Polar Peer Powers: China and Russia

A GREAT POWER IS A STATE POSSESSING THE NECESSARY combination of capability and intent to influence international affairs. We think of great powers as those states simultaneously strong in economic, political, and military domains—the states most able to combine their instruments of power to advance a national agenda and generate desirable effects on the global stage.[1] Today there is a seminal narrative warning of renewed great power competition with Russia and China. But is it accurate? Do Russia and China meet the rather subjective criteria of great power status? Answering this risks engaging in circular arguments on the basis of conjecture and extrapolation and also inclines toward dismissing the necessary relative value comparison between supposed rival competitors. Rather than engaging in the broad and ill-defined debate as to whether Russia and China are worthy of great power designation, let us instead focus on the polar regions and the power dynamics at play at the extreme ends of the Earth. Which states are the most capable in these regions? What is their intent?

A Power by Another Name

Russia is not a great power, at least not by economic standards. At $1.7 trillion, Russia's gross domestic product (GPD) is eleventh in the world, between Canada and South Korea.[2] It is a massive country by geography, an influential actor in world politics, and a formidable force militarily, but Russia's population is in decline and its economy is no more impressive than South Korea's, a country roughly the geographic size of the US state of Indiana. Without an expanding economic model to enable and sustain improved quality of life and the tax base necessary for military expansion, Russia risks succumbing to the same fate of the Soviet Union preceding its dissolution: economic collapse.

Fortunately for Russia, the Arctic's treasure trove of untapped natural and biological resources is set for extraction. As well, the Arctic's value in providing alternative routes for international commerce is a widely known, but to date a largely unrealized possibility due to historically impassable conditions. Since the end of the Cold War, the Arctic has been comparably irrelevant, rendering the High North a figment of the imagination for sea-weary freight captains longing for a shorter route between Asia and Europe. That is changing. The Arctic's evolving economic value proposition coupled with Russia's proximal advantage and declining economy motivate Moscow's Arctic exploitation agenda. Putin saw this opportunity coming in 2000, and has since led Russia on an ambitious Arctic scheme toward regional power status, some of which has extended into Antarctica as well. To the north, Russia's geography and northern coast make it—by proximity and posture alone—an Arctic force. Its military presence and policy commitment to the High North make it an Arctic power. To the south, its research activity and ability to deploy personnel and assets to Antarctica, coupled with its policy prescriptions for Antarctic influence, also make it an Antarctic power. Russia has both the capability and the intent to influence polar affairs such that Moscow is not a great power but a polar power. China is different.

With the world's second largest economy, a massive military, and expanding economic partnerships across the globe, China is a rising great power of impressive capabilities fueled by ambitious, and occasionally aggressive, intent. By way of GDP, China's economy is second only to the United States, and its population continues to rise along with its global influence. Despite its closest border being nearly a thousand miles from the Arctic Circle, China is a self-proclaimed "near-Arctic state" and a polar great power.[3] What China lacks in Arctic proximity it makes up for in posture, presence, power projection, and policies. Its Arctic intent is clear and efforts toward these goals are unmistakable. As a whole, China's polar region capabilities and intent are significant such that it is, like Russia, a polar power.

Relative to Russia and China, the United States is a polar power in that it has some presence in each polar region; it does project power to both; and it has some policies on its polar approach, though, to date, the US orientation to the polar regions assumes a scientific rather than security flavor. What it has in terms of proximal advantage with an Arctic coastline, it lacks in general presence relative to Russia and policy relative to China. The same can be said for Antarctica. In terms of national interest and intent, the United States maintains capable and regular Antarctic power projection and research presence but lacks substantive Antarctic security policy rivaling Russian and Chinese agendas. Relative to other polar-oriented states, Russia and China are most postured toward future polar region influence. The United States can catch up, but it will take commitment.

POLAR STATES VS. POLAR POWERS

Anne-Marie Brady defines polar states as "those few countries who are powerful at the Arctic and the Antarctic . . . global giants strong in economic, scientific, and military power" and strong at both poles.[4] Few countries meet Brady's definition of polar state criteria such that we can assume the term *polar state* to be synonymous with the term *polar great power*. Credited to Chinese President Xi Jinping in a 2014 speech in Hobart, Australia, Brady defines polar great power as a state that has "significant presence in the polar regions; high levels of polar scientific capacity and scientific research funding; significant polar economic, military, political, and diplomatic capacity; and a high level of participation in international governance relating to the polar regions."[5]

Brady's definition of polar great power extends from her definition of polar state, emphasizing scientific and economic capacity in the polar regions complemented by polar presence and participation in polar governance. Despite the myriad states with polar ambition, presence, and even influence, if we accept Brady's definition of polar great power, only three states meet the standard: the United States, Russia, and China. Whereas Brady's definition of polar state adds the "global giant" qualifier, her polar great power definition does not. Can a country be a polar state but not a polar great power, or vice versa? Are there other categories to consider relative to polar actors who do not rise to the level of meeting polar state or polar power criteria?

If Brady omitted global giants from her definition, others could satisfy polar state attributes. Norway is both active and influential in the polar regions. Between its mainland and archipelagic claims to Svalbard and Jan Mayen, Norway has sovereign territory in the Arctic Circle, making it an Arctic state by geographical standards. It also maintains maritime claims to portions of the Arctic Ocean and regularly engages in North Atlantic Treaty Organization (NATO) military exercises in the Arctic. To this end, Elizabeth Buchanan refers to Norway and other Arctic-border NATO member states as the "Arctic rim powers."[6] As another label, Buchanan suggests that Norway is a regional power in the Arctic. But even Norway, as the only state with a claim to both the Arctic and Antarctica, lacks the necessary attributes to be considered among the few states wielding simultaneous influence—by way of military power—at both poles.

In the south, Norway is one of seven states that laid claim to Antarctica prior to the Antarctic Treaty. Its 1939 claim to Queen Maud Land covers nearly 17 percent of the Antarctic continent, making it among the largest territorial claims of any country.[7] As the only country with territorial claims to both the Arctic and Antarctica, Norway is—by virtue of these claims, its status as an original signatory to the Antarctic Treaty, its status as an Arctic Council member state, and the long-standing presence in both regions—an active and influential participant in polar region affairs. In other words, Norway is simultaneously interested, present, and invested at both poles. But with a 2019 GDP just over $434 billion, Norway's economy is just greater than half of the US defense budget and ranks thirty-first in the world. Lacking the economic might, Norway as either a polar state or a polar great power, per Brady's definitions, is a tough sell. So where does it sit on the spectrum of polar states? And what do we call it? Using Norway as an analog, we extend the same questions to Canada, Denmark, and others in the Arctic, as well as Chile, Argentina, New Zealand, Australia, and others proximal to Antarctica. We need a better way of categorizing polar actors and their potential for influence in polar affairs.

A Polar Typology

To date, there is no existing heuristic for polar region actors within the international security scope. The definitions that we do have are ambiguous and exclusive, disregarding the preponderance of polar actors and their influence in polar affairs. While the conversation will ultimately gravitate toward the big three, other polar actors influence the polar regions. To be included in the polar region international security discussion, a state need not be a great economic, scientific, or military power. The ambiguity in current definitions requires more descriptive precision. For this, I offer a polar typology (see Figure 4.1) using two axes of analysis and four categorical labels to define polar actors relative to each other.

Figure 4.1 Polar Typology

	Polar Perceivers	Polar Powers
Intent *(posture + policy)*	Argentina Japan Australia New Zealand Chile Sweden Denmark Finland	China Russia United States
	Polar Peripherals	Polar Players
	Belgium Iceland South Africa	Canada France Norway United Kingdom

Capability

(presence + power)

It is helpful to anchor the analysis to known international security paradigms. Military capabilities and stated (or assumed) political intent define and determine the nature of polar actor labels. In this way, strategic studies use the canon equation of *capabilities + intent = threat*. I use the same paradigm for the polar typology, but note that a state's presence alone on the typology does not suggest it is a threat. We should consider the typology a means to assess relative polar region influence (those with the greatest attributes demonstrated via objective measures in the proceeding discussion have the most influence).

The polar typology deliberately excludes Arctic indigenous peoples and the organizations representing them as permanent participants of the Arctic Council. The typology likewise excludes similar nonstate organizations and groups, affiliated or unaffiliated with external bodies in either region. While unpopular with some, contradictory to their narrative, and difficult to accept as reality, these nonstate groups, peoples, and organizations do not command enough influence in the regions in terms of international security dynamics. Heads of state can—and often do—pander to these organizations, presenting them as influential voices in polar affairs. This may be the case for a host of matters relative to international polar institutions, but in terms of future polar defense, security, and military matters, and especially in the incidence of state conflict, nonstate actors at the poles will not be on the periphery of the conversation with substantive influence. Lending voice to nonstate actors is a privilege of peacetime. In the event of conflict, indigenous peoples are the low on the list of state concerns. In excluding nonstate actors, I consider polar actors as those states with presence, power, polices, and postures toward the polar regions and most able to summon their country's resources toward advancing polar region interests. Therefore, the proposed polar typology serves as an analytical tool in ongoing polar region discussions.

X-Axis: Capability

A state's capability is generally agreed to refer to its physical (and increasingly psychological) means to perform an action and achieve effects. Capabilities account for physical assets (bases, weapons, means of transportation, etc.) and their employment (including a state's budgeted commitment toward these ends). I host capability on the x-axis of the typology as it is more static and takes longer to change. Therefore, if a state has greater capability and capacity to effect change in the polar regions but lacks the intent, it can sooner change its intent than it can its capability, thereby progressing into mature levels of the polar typology more quickly than a state with the intent but lacking the capability and capacity to influence change. Whereas intent can change in a matter of hours because policies can be written in Tweets or made by speeches, it takes time to develop capabilities. For these purposes, I focus on a state's polar capabilities, or its means of achieving a desired effect in the polar regions via its combination of (or capacity for) acquiring, projecting, and sustaining military presence and power in the polar regions. In this way, presence and power are the anchoring attributes that define capability.

PRESENCE. Polar presence is a state's active existence—be it enduring or intermittent—within the Arctic and Antarctic. Presence indicators include permanent basing or research stations and infrastructure within the geographic bounds of either polar circle, as well as active scientific research at the poles, and military activity including support to scientific research or routine training and exercise maneuvers. Given the isolation, distance, and conditions, polar presence, or simply "being there," is a strong indication of a state's military power. The relative advantage of proximity to either polar region does not guarantee a state's ability to project military power at the poles. To be present in the polar regions requires the ability to distribute and sustain—or to get there and stay there.

POWER. Indications of polar military power include dedicated polar military capabilities and military support to scientific research commitments in the regions. Polar power projection capabilities are unique and offer limited multi-use value beyond specified polar applications, thus necessitating deliberate polar commitment to justify the procurement time and cost coupled with the use of the assets. The principal example of tangible polar power is the icebreaker.

Icebreakers are the most visible commitments to polar power projection and enabling complementary presence. They are expensive and tailored to the polar environment, offering little utility beyond polar-specific operations. As a result, few states maintain an active icebreaker fleet. Those that do have an advantage in polar access, navigation, and power projection. It follows that those without icebreakers but with polar ambition must rely on those with icebreakers, thereby furthering the power dynamics and favoring those in possession of icebreakers. Other indicators of polar power include polar-dedicated aircraft, polar military commands and units, as well as participation in polar training, exercises, or conduct of polar military maneuvers and operations. Indications of polar military power alone, however, are insufficient to raise a polar actor's profile within the typology. We also consider those actors with demonstrated intent to affect polar region dynamics, as signaled in national orientation to the polar regions through policies and posturing.

Y-AXIS: INTENT

A state's intent implies its resolve and commitment to execute an action. In this way, intent can be both described and prescribed. Descriptive and prescriptive mechanisms for state agendas come in the form of policy and posture, respectively. Indicators of polar actor intent are those mechanisms developed and executed by the state with specific orientation toward polar security and defense matters. As with the capability axis, the analysis of intent has two anchoring attributes: polar policy and polar posture.

POLICY. Polar policy is the state's codification of its interests, philosophies, and framework for prescribed actions in the polar regions.

Indicators are the existence of polar policies in the binary form. But again, to qualify for inclusion in a state's polar policy library, the documents must be relevant to the broader defense and security frame of analysis. Polar policies describing a state's polar agenda, with an eye toward security and defense matters, establish the basis for a state's polar posture as the second indicator of intent.

POSTURE. Polar posture, or the state's position on and actions in polar affairs, in terms of both philosophy and strategy, is the executed form of the state's polar policies. Posture can include diplomatic, informational, military, or economic activities. Some states have polar policies, guided by philosophies informing strategies, but lack the will to act on the prescriptions. Accepting Dahl's premise that "there is no action at a distance," the mere existence of policy alone forms only half of the intent equation.[8] To rise in the polar typology, a state must show evidence of polar posturing—be it diplomatic, military, informational, or economic—commensurate with its stated polar policies. Posture, as the resulting action of policy, is an indication of intent married to a state's capabilities. A state can have both policies and postures, and thus a high degree of intent, but lack the necessary capabilities in terms of power and presence to achieve its desired effect in the polar regions.

* * *

Therefore, we cannot think of policy, posture, presence, or power as mutually exclusive but rather as mutually supporting concepts informing placement of polar actors within the polar typology. The intersections of these attributes form the dimensions for categorizing the polar actors and serve as a frame for polar region security and defense analysis.

CORE DIMENSIONS AND VARIABLES

The determinants of polar actor influence in polar affairs are capability and intent with the specific attributes (presence, power, posture, policy) embedded within each. These dimensions and their relational attributes form the basis of a fourfold polar typology. Each quadrant in the typology represents a different categorical description of polar actors based on the assessed score of sixteen variables indicative of the polar attributes. The sixteen variables indicating a state's overall polar orientation and capacity for influence are (with point values in parentheses):[9]

1. Arctic Council: member (2); observer (1).
2. Antarctic Treaty: original signatory (2); post-accession consultative status (1).
3. United Nations Security Council: permanent member (2); elected member (1).
4. Gross domestic product (rank): 1–10 (3); 11–20 (2); 21–30 (3).
5. Nuclear weapons state: yes (1); no (0).
6. Regional proximity (to either polar region): border (2); within 1,500 miles (1).
7. Arctic territorial claim: yes (1); no (0).
8. Antarctica territorial claim: yes (1); no (0).
9. Airfields within region: four or more (3); two to three (2); one (1).
10. Deepwater ports within region: four or more (2); one to three (1).
11. Icebreakers: six or more (3); three to five (2); one to two (1).
12. Dedicated polar aircraft: yes (1); no (0).
13. Exclusive polar units/commands: yes (1); no (0).
14. Polar military exercises/maneuvers: Arctic *and* Antarctica (2); Arctic *or* Antarctica (1).
15. Scientific research presence/activity: yes (1); no (0).
16. Polar defense/security policies: Arctic *and* Antarctic (2); Arctic *or* Antarctic (1).

For simplicity, I have elected to bound the initial polar typology to only those states that are signatories on the Antarctic Treaty and/or Arctic Council member states, with one obvious exception: China. Each variable aligns to observable indicators based on publicly available data and absent subjective input. States receive the score relative to the objective evidence meeting the preceding variable criteria. A state's combined variable score (maximum of 32) produces its polar condition, or status relative to other polar actors. A polar actor's descriptive condition (score) relative to the variables produces its outcome and placement within one of the typology's four dimensions. The four dimensions describing polar actors, based on relative value scores, are polar peripherals, polar perceivers, polar players, and polar powers.

Polar Peripherals

Polar peripherals occur on the periphery of polar region dynamics. They are states with comparably little to no military presence in or posture toward the poles, coupled with limited polar capabilities and policy commitment or intent. Polar peripherals lack the economic and military capacity to influence world affairs, much less polar affairs, and do not demonstrate via policy or posture the intent to improve their position in the regional discussion. In short, polar peripherals possess neither the robust polar presence and power nor posture and policy to effect change in polar region security dynamics. They are not irrelevant, but given their positions relative to others, polar peripherals are mostly along for the ride. The polar peripherals, particularly in the case of Iceland, are most valuable in the polar influence spectrum through their geographic proximity on the periphery of the polar regions and the potential arrangements they can make with more influential polar actors seeking to benefit from basing rights. The polar peripherals (and scores out of 32) are: Belgium (8), South Africa (8), and Iceland (7).

POLAR PERCEIVERS

Polar perceivers are states that have both greater posture toward the polar regions and demonstrated intent by way of policy prescriptions outlining interests and approaches to polar region affairs. However, where their intent is ambitious, and in some cases aggressive, polar perceivers lack the robust capabilities necessary to leverage their postural—and for some proximal—advantage and policy interests toward regional influence approaching more influential status. Polar perceivers benefit from proximity and are active in polar advocacy. They are regularly present at one, but typically not both, poles, thus limiting their polar influence to either the north or the south. Their comparably unimpressive GDPs stymie any geographic advantage and any well-meaning advocacy, further limiting their capabilities to both produce and project polar power sufficient to influence polar affairs in the event of a militarized dispute. More often than not, the polar perceivers' chief attribute, or point of polar leverage, is in their geography, like the polar peripherals. The polar perceivers are: Denmark (14), Finland (13), Chile (13), Argentina (13), Sweden (12), Australia (12), New Zealand (11), and Japan (11).

POLAR PLAYERS

Polar Players are at the relational point of increased polar capabilities and influence by way of general presence, position in international polar institutions, and military power, but at a lower point of intent indicated by absent or superficial polar postures and policy prescriptions. The polar players have the capabilities and proximal advantage to exercise polar influence but tend to lack the aggressive hegemonic ambition of the polar powers. They are the states most able to enhance their polar influence through evolving policy interests and expanded posturing, but lack the intent to do so. The polar players are critical to polar region dynamics and, especially in the Arctic, have strategically relevant geography and military support apparatus. The polar players will be instrumental in the evolving polar region power balance such that the polar powers will leverage relations with each to further their own agendas. The polar players are: the United Kingdom (21), France (20), Canada (19), and Norway (16).

POLAR POWERS

Polar powers are at the highest levels of polar capability and intent. They have demonstrated and dedicated polar capabilities, inclusive of presence and ability to project power at both poles, complemented by polar intent, and inclusive of military posturing and defense policies oriented specific to the polar regions. Polar powers are the states most capable of influencing polar region affairs and standing to gain most from polar region influence, for which their presence is critical. Polar powers are those states most likely to determine the future of the polar regions—whether they remain peaceful or conflicted—in the twenty-first century.

It is the polar powers that will drive the future polar region international security conversation. This is not to say that other polar actors are irrelevant; rather, they lack the necessary combination of international influence, military power, capability, and intent to be considered within the polar power conversation. Polar actors bring value to the discussion and will play key roles in the evolving polar region security scape, but they will do so in a support role via geography, infrastructure, alliances, and partnerships. The relationships Russia, China, and the United States have or will develop and maintain with polar actors is a significant predictor of future polar region influence. The polar powers are the primary drivers of the polar region international security discourse. The polar powers are: Russia (30), the United States (27), and China (24).

The typology is inclusive of both polar regions. Running a similar analysis for one pole or the other while retaining the same dimensional categories or types would yield different results given the disparate regional orientation and geographies of each pole and its proximal actors. The takeaway is that few states possess the necessary capabilities and intent to be simultaneously influential in both the Arctic and Antarctica—to be polar powers (see Tables 4.1–4.4).

Table 4.1 Polar Powers

Polar Typology Category	Russia	United States	China
Arctic Council member/observer	2	2	1
Antarctic Treaty original signatory/post-accession (2/1)	2	2	1
UN Security Council permanent/elected member (2/1)	2	2	2
Arctic claim (1)	1	1	0
Antarctic claim (1)	0	0	0
Gross domestic product rank (3/2/1)	2	3	3
Airfields (3/2/1)	3	3	3
Deepwater ports (2/1)	2	1	1
Exercises/maneuvers (2/1)	2	2	2
Icebreakers (3/2/1)	3	1	2
Polar planes (1)	1	1	1
Polar commands (1)	1	0	0
Nuclear weapon state (3)	3	3	3
Polar policies (2/1)	2	2	2
Scientific research presence (2/1)	2	2	2
Proximity (2/1)	2	2	1
Total score	30	27	24

Note: Total score possible = 32; polar power = 24–32.

Table 4.2 Polar Players

Polar Typology Category	United Kingdom	France	Canada	Norway
Arctic Council member/observer	1	1	2	2
Antarctic Treaty original signatory/post-accession (2/1)	2	2	0	2
UN Security Council permanent/elected member (2/1)	2	2	0	0
Arctic claim (1)	0	0	1	1
Antarctic claim (1)	1	1	0	1
Gross domestic product rank (3/2/1)	3	3	3	0
Airfields (3/2/1)	3	2	1	1
Deepwater ports (2/1)	0	0	2	1
Exercises/maneuvers (2/1)	1	1	1	1
Icebreakers (3/2/1)	1	0	3	1
Polar planes (1)	0	0	1	0
Polar commands (1)	0	0	1	0
Nuclear weapon state (3)	3	3	0	0
Polar policies (2/1)	2	2	1	2
Scientific research presence (2/1)	1	2	1	2
Proximity (2/1)	1	1	2	2
Total score	21	20	19	16

Note: Total score possible = 32; polar player = 16–23.

Table 4.3 Polar Perceivers

Polar Typology Category	Denmark	Finland	Chile	Argentina	Sweden	Australia	New Zealand	Japan
Arctic Council member/observer	2	2	0	0	2	0	0	1
Antarctic Treaty original signatory/post-accession (2/1)	0	0	2	2	0	2	2	2
UN Security Council permanent/elected member (2/1)	0	0	0	0	0	0	0	0
Arctic claim (1)	1	0	0	0	0	0	0	0
Antarctic claim (1)	0	0	1	1	0	1	1	0
Gross domestic product rank (3/2/1)	0	0	0	1	1	2	0	3
Airfields (3/2/1)	2	2	2	2	0	3	3	2
Deepwater ports (2/1)	2	0	0	0	0	0	0	0
Exercises/maneuvers (2/1)	2	1	1	1	1	1	1	0
Icebreakers (3/2/1)	0	3	1	1	3	0	0	1
Polar planes (1)	1	0	1	1	1	1	1	0
Polar commands (1)	0	1	1	0	0	0	0	0
Nuclear weapon state (3)	0	0	0	0	0	0	0	0
Polar policies (2/1)	1	1	1	1	1	1	1	1
Scientific research presence (2/1)	1	1	2	1	1	1	1	1
Proximity (2/1)	2	2	1	2	2	0	1	0
Total score	14	13	13	13	12	12	11	11

Note: Total score possible = 32; polar perceiver = 9–15.

Table 4.4 Polar Peripherals

Polar Typology Category	Belgium	South Africa	Iceland
Arctic Council member/observer	0	0	2
Antarctic Treaty original signatory/post-accession (2/1)	2	2	0
UN Security Council permanent/elected member (2/1)	1	1	0
Arctic claim (1)	0	0	0
Antarctic claim (1)	0	0	0
Gross domestic product rank (3/2/1)	1	0	0
Airfields (3/2/1)	1	1	0
Deepwater ports (2/1)	0	0	0
Exercises/maneuvers (2/1)	0	1	1
Icebreakers (3/2/1)	0	1	0
Polar planes (1)	0	0	0
Polar commands (1)	0	0	0
Nuclear weapon state (3)	0	0	0
Polar policies (2/1)	1	1	1
Scientific research presence (2/1)	1	1	1
Proximity (2/1)	1	0	2
Total score	8	8	7

Note: Total score possible = 32; polar peripheral = 0–8.

EXAMINING THE POLAR POWERS

In the continued use of the polar typology's framework, I next discuss Russian and Chinese presence and military power in the polar regions (within the capabilities spectrum) as well as their current polar policies and postures (as part of the intent spectrum). The resulting overview indicates potentially formidable threats posed by both Russia and China in the polar regions that raise the potential for future polar region conflict. Let's examine why.

RUSSIA AS A POLAR PEER POWER

Those referring to Russia as a US peer power may not be seeing the whole picture. Moscow and Washington are not peers. Moscow realizes its current limitations and is working aggressively toward a strengthened position by way of the Arctic. The ambitious economic expansion is enabled by an increasingly deterrent military posture in the Arctic that Moscow hopes will prove sufficient to dissuade likeminded competitors. As it commits resources to Arctic posturing, Russia exemplifies ways to overcome logistical limitations to operating in the High North. In the austerity of polar operations, Russia is the exemplar for the rest of the world and enjoys proximal and technical advantage relative to the United States.

Russia is inoculating the rest of the world to its Arctic presence. To similar economic ends, Russia is extending its reach and influence toward Antarctica as indicated both in its research presence on the continent and in its Antarctic policies. Russia sees the polar regions as the equalizers where the United States is at a comparative disadvantage, and its policies reflect this push toward advancing polar influence in the absence of comparable US intent.

RUSSIAN ARCTIC POLICIES. Moscow has a history of polar interest. Following the collapse of the Soviet Union, Moscow sought internal opportunities for economic growth and influence to serve as the platform for the twenty-first-century Russian power resurgence. Owing to the Arctic's proximity and its relevance as a strategic corridor during the Cold War, Moscow reoriented its focus north. Moscow's 2000 policy on the fundamentals of the Russian Federation's agenda in the Arctic serves as the basis for Russia's twenty-first-century Arctic push and resulting military modernization. The policy designates the Arctic as an "independent object of state policy" due to Moscow's "special interests" in the region specific to "the needs of the country's economy."[10] Moscow, then, just like today, viewed the Arctic as a vital national interest and further stipulated in the policy that, with consideration given to the economic significance of the region, the "Arctic is of exceptional military-strategic importance."[11] Noting "problems that pose a threat to national security," the 2000 policy stated Russia's primary interests in the Arctic as follows:[12]

- There should be an atmosphere of persistent peace and cooperation in the region such that the differences between countries do not lead to tension and conflict.
- The Arctic countries, which bear a special responsibility for the preservation of the natural environment and the sustainable development of the Arctic, have preferential rights in the region in these areas in comparison with non-Arctic countries.
- Development of the Arctic and other activities are to be preserved and strengthened.

The policy prescriptions are curious. In 2000 there were few conflicts and those that were active were confined to areas with limited global implications. So why, in 2000, did Moscow list as its first policy priority to maintain the Arctic as a peaceful and cooperative domain avoidant of international tension and conflict? This signaled Moscow's intent. With the benefit of hindsight and subsequent Arctic policies to review, Russia saw the Arctic as an important geostrategic domain from the outset of the twenty-first century.

In 2000, Moscow set its Arctic agenda with the policy. In 2001 it set the policy in motion with the first United Nations (UN) lobby for extended continental shelf recognition in the Arctic. Though unsuccessful, this effort legitimized Moscow's intent and reinforced its commitment to the Arctic as a vital national interest. The UN rejected the extended claims in 2007, prompting the 2007 Russian flag-planting on the North Pole seabed as a demonstration of Russian Arctic orientation. In September 2008, Russia released an updated Arctic policy, covering fundamentals for the period up to 2020 and beyond, which established the frame for Russian Arctic orientation today.

The 2008 policy outlined four principles for the Russian Federation's Arctic lens. It referred to the Arctic as a "strategic resource base" that can provide "solutions" to the economic and social "problems" of the country.[13] Moscow saw the Arctic as a critical domain for the country's survival, a vital resource area linked to national interests. The concept of the Arctic as a resource base is not unique to this document, however. The Soviet Union, dating back to the 1950s, saw the Arctic as an economic opportunity with High North tundra aeration programs.[14] Similar efforts to extract resources from the Arctic occurred throughout the latter half of the Soviet twentieth and Russian early twenty-first centuries such that the Russian view of the Arctic as an economic resource is anything but a revelation. The three proceeding principles are more telling—the ones that hinted toward evolving Russian Arctic posturing we see today.

The second of the four principles in the 2008 Russian Arctic policy stipulates Russian intent to maintain the Arctic as a region of peace and cooperation.[15] Taken at face value, this is a statement of peaceful intent. But Vladimir Putin is a master manipulator of public discourse. This principle is pure propaganda. By stating in 2008 that it insisted on maintaining the Arctic as a peaceful and cooperative domain, Russia fostered similar sentiment among other Arctic-interested states by promoting an "if Russia wants peace, then so should we" narrative. The reality: Russia wanted then and still wants today to control its portion of the Arctic, and it wants more of the Arctic than the rest. By publishing a statement of peaceful intent, Russia sought to breed Arctic apathy among perceived

Arctic competitors. In doing so, others turned their attention elsewhere—on the premise that the Arctic is a peaceful domain, and "even Russia says so." While the other Arctic states operated on this assumption and all but ignored Arctic defense and security matters, Moscow began maneuvering to secure its Arctic posture and influence.

Russian Arctic military infrastructure development increased tenfold from 2008 to 2014. Russia built hundreds of new military facilities, airfields, satellite stations, and ports within its Arctic territory while simultaneously refurbishing and repurposing Soviet-era Arctic installations.[16] For a state intent on maintaining peace and cooperation in the Arctic, Russian actions pointed toward tension-fueled aggression, or insecurity. In a classic disinformation campaign, Putin and Moscow convinced the rest of the world that the Arctic did not matter in the security lens.

Continuing the 2008 policy review, Russia expressed interest in preserving Arctic ecosystems and its desire to monetize the Northern Sea Route as a primary transportation corridor. Today, Russia challenges international maritime law in asserting its unrecognized control and exclusivity over the Northern Sea Route. Moscow requires foreign vessels transiting the route to host a Russian pilot during the transit.[17] With these controlling claims, Putin has quipped that the Northern Sea Route will be the new Suez Canal.[18] Though the route is a long way from supplanting the Suez (thirty-seven ships transited the Northern Sea Route in all of 2019 compared to up to seventy-one ships in a single day in the Suez), Putin's Arctic emphasis speaks volumes about its future significance for Russian ambition and influence.[19] When we consider the 2008 policy platforms with the knowledge of today, Russia tipped its hat toward its true Arctic intent, and did so masterfully, complemented by a disinformation campaign meant to distract others while Moscow moved toward its High North objectives for 2020.

In grading performance toward its stated ends, Russia gets a B+. Today, Moscow uses the Northern Sea Route as a strategic corridor and takes active measures toward preserving and maintaining the Arctic ecosystems. By Russia's measure, the Arctic is a strategic resource base that contributes upward of 20 percent of its economic strength by way of access to and extraction of natural and biological resources. For these lines of effort, Russia has succeeded. In maintaining the Arctic as a region of peace and cooperation, Russia loses points.

The Russian military's Arctic expansion since 2008 has generated international attention. The Ice Curtain is a formidable military posture backed by policy commitments to the Arctic that the world should have seen coming.[20] In 2013, Russia released an Arctic national security–focused policy as a follow-on to its 2008 fundamentals policy, stipulating Putin's intent to militarize and defend Russian Arctic interests.[21] This policy vectored the Arctic as a Russian strategic priority linked to national security interests. It notes Russian security concerns in the Arctic, including the significance of declining Arctic population coupled with inadequate infrastructure to support the maintenance of the existing population. It also points to Russia's concerns relative to the Svalbard Treaty and Norway's aims to revise portions of the treaty limiting Russian commercial activities in the vicinity. The policy redirects attention toward expanding NATO exercises in the Arctic, couching them as a threat to Russian interests. Moscow sought to label NATO member states as Arctic aggressors instead. The incongruity is that NATO increased Arctic military activities in response to Russia's Arctic expansion.

Intentionally or not, Russia's military orientation to and within the Arctic generated a northern security dilemma, prompting increased NATO Arctic military presence and resulting tensions in what was ostensibly to be a common zone of peace and cooperation. While there still is an exceptional level of cooperation, the Arctic is seeing evolving competition and increasing confrontation. For its supposed intent to maintain the Arctic as a zone of peace and cooperation, Moscow's Arctic militarization has had an opposite effect. Owing to the changing Arctic dynamic, the 2020 version of the Russian Arctic fundamentals policy advances toward an even more assertive narrative.

Russia's policy covering the period up to 2035 is the second installment in the series, following the 2008–2020 policy outlining Moscow's Arctic goals. The 2020–2035 policy emphasizes continued Arctic commitment as a strategic resource, but hosts more assertive rhetoric toward Russian Arctic intent. In particular, the 2020–2035 policy states Moscow's intent "to ensure Russia's sovereignty and territorial integrity."[22] In 2008, Russia did not perceive a threat to its territory or sovereignty sufficient to include this Arctic priority; in 2020 things were different. This points to Russia's intent to further its defensive militarization of the Arctic, and to assert an aggressive posture to ensure its Arctic interests. The document elaborates, describing Moscow's desire to deter aggression militarily and to improve its Arctic military capabilities and infrastructure. Whereas the 2008–2020 principles focused almost exclusively on economic interests, the 2020–2035 principles indicate a shift toward security priorities in the Arctic, in some ways more overt, in others more subtle.

Among the notable changes from 2008 to 2020 is the Russian view of the Arctic, at least in terms of stated policy. Russia sought, in 2008, to maintain the Arctic as a region of "peace and cooperation." In 2020, Russia now seeks to "preserve" the Arctic as a region of peace, "with stable and mutually beneficial partnerships."[23] In removing the term "cooperation" in favor of "partnerships," Moscow opened the door for competition. A state committed to cooperation is unlikely to compete or raise conflict. A state committed to "mutually beneficial partnerships" is not, by default, also committed to cooperation. To cooperate is to work together or jointly toward the same end. To partner is simply to engage in similar activities.

Arctic cooperation implies working together with other Arctic states toward shared international interests. Arctic partnerships imply Russia working with like-minded states sharing similar interests, either consistent with or independent of the interests of other Arctic states. The nuance is superficially subtle but scrupulously significant. In this way, Moscow absolves itself of its commitment to international cooperation from the 2008 policy and extends its "strategic partnership" with Beijing to the Arctic and toward shared interests independent of other Arctic states' interests. This is made more curious by the timing of the policy release relative to Russia's assumption of the Arctic Council chairmanship in 2021.

The Russian policy emphasizes Moscow's commitment to ensuring the Arctic Council is the "key regional institution coordinating the international cooperation in the Arctic."[24] By one interpretation, Russia's commitment to the Arctic Council as a cooperative body indicates Moscow's intent to maintain cooperation. But the 2020 policy deliberately removed cooperation in favor of partnerships. Considering Moscow's Arctic Council role in 2021, Russia seems to be establishing the means to embolden the Arctic Council beyond a purveyor of peace and into a more authoritative institution in international Arctic affairs. In assuming the chair role in concert with a stronger and more influential council, Russia will be in the advantageous position to leverage its influence and power toward its Arctic goals.

The 2020 Russian policy cohort builds from its previous national security policy and seeks to "guarantee high living standards and prosperity" for the Russian Arctic peoples.[25] The 2020 policy also maintains Moscow's commitment to the Arctic as a "strategic resource," but instead of using the Arctic as a base of solutions for Russian problems, as stated in the 2008 policy, the 2020 policy promises that the Arctic will be used to "speed up national economic growth," furthering the narrative of Russian Arctic aggression toward national ends.[26] The 2020 policy also insists that the Northern Sea Route will be a "globally competitive" corridor, with Russia seeking to "protect the Arctic" as its "primordial homeland."[27] The policy rhetoric is a marked shift from 2008 and complemented by the second installment of the corresponding Russian Arctic national security policy to 2035 (see Table 4.5).

Complementing the 2008 plan, Russia's strategy for development of the Arctic zone and provision of national security for the period to 2035 is the second in the similar "basic principles" series of the same years. Developed by the Russian National Security Council, this policy is the blueprint for Russian Arctic ambition. In concert with the State Arms Plan to 2027, the Russian National Security Strategy, and a strategy for socioeconomic development of the federation's Arctic zone, the 2020 Arctic national security policy underscores the significance of the Arctic to Russian interests. The Arctic features prominently as a steady and recurring priority in Russian policy. And while some say that "conflict is bad for business," for Russia in the Arctic, Moscow seems intent on securing its Arctic interest through any means necessary, including open competition and conflict.[28]

Building from these documents, in April 2021 Russia released an Arctic action plan outlining specific measures to implement the policy prescriptions outlined in its fundamentals and strategy documents.[29] This latest installment outlines 268 "events" the Russian Federation intends to pursue to advance its Arctic agenda. Among these are activities to ensure "the military security of the Russian Federation in the

Table 4.5 Russian Arctic Policies, 2020 vs. 2035

Russian Arctic Policy 2020	Russian Arctic Policy 2035
Use Arctic as strategic resource base for country's social and economic challenges	Ensure Russian sovereignty and territorial integrity
Maintain Arctic as a region of peace and cooperation	Preserve Arctic as peaceful region with stable and mutually beneficial partnerships
Preserve unique ecology of Arctic	Guarantee high living standards for Russian Arctic people
Use Northern Sea Route as primary transport route	Develop Northern Sea Route as globally competitive national transport corridor
	Protect Arctic as primordial homeland

Source: Adapted from Klimenko, "Russia's New Arctic Policy Document."

Arctic."[30] Russia plans to continue improving its military force composition stationed in the Arctic; its weapons formations and military units; and its military infrastructure to facilitate further "basing of troops" in the Arctic zone.[31] Taken alone, the Russian drive toward Arctic influence is neither surprising nor independently concerning. Coupled with Moscow's policy rhetoric toward Antarctica, however, we see an emerging pattern of ambition aimed at the polar regions as prize targets for economic expansion and influence.

RUSSIAN ANTARCTIC POLICIES. The international community credits a Russian expedition with discovering (read: seeing) Antarctica in 1820.[32] Fast-forwarding to the mid–twentieth century, the Soviet Union was an original signatory on the Antarctic Treaty and active on the continent in the years following World War II until its collapse. The dissolution of the Soviet Union forced Antarctic base closures in the 1990s and the shuttering of active Antarctic programs. Russia renewed its interest in Antarctica with Putin's rise to power. As a complement to its Arctic ambition, Moscow sees Antarctica as a similar value proposition. Former Russian prime minister and now deputy chairman of the Russian Security Council Dmitry Medvedev declared Russia as occupying a "leading place" in Antarctic studies.[33] Russia's activities on Antarctica and its policy posture seem to support this assertion.

Russia's capstone Antarctic policy, the strategy for development activities on Antarctica up to 2020 and beyond, makes no reservations about its intent. Published in March 2011, it stipulates the Russian assessment of "enormous resource potential" in Antarctica. Among the pools of Russian interest are the "aquatic biological resources" that are "many times greater" than those available in the entirety of the Russian exclusive economic zones.[34] Here the policy claims that Russian access to and extraction of these and other resources "will be able to ensure a sustainable long-term growth" and production capacity of the Russian Federation fishing fleet.[35] Clear economic interests in Antarctica compel Russian presence. Though the document states Russia's commitment to "maintaining peace and stability in Antarctica," it calls for a systematic "increase of influential presence" consistent with the "place and role of Russia in the international community."[36] Russia views itself as a global superpower and sees Antarctic presence as a means to demonstrate power and achieve influence. The 2011 Antarctic policy extends this logic through strategic objectives.

In addition to its intent to strengthen its economy and international prestige via Antarctic presence and activities, Russia saw potential for international conflict on Antarctica years ago. Of the stated objectives, its top priority is the "prevention of possible threats to national interests in Antarctica" and "preventing the possible emergences of hotbeds of international tension."[37] To achieve this, the document outlines a series of tasks. A common thread is the "modernization and reorganization" of Antarctic infrastructure. At the time, Russia was intent on creating or restoring expeditionary "field bases," choosing this term versus "research stations." Complementing field base restoration or construction, Russia set its sights on useable snow and ice runways, improved trails for tracked vehicles, and the development of expeditionary ships and aircraft suitable for polar operations.[38]

Its expectation from all of this was the "development of Russian fisheries in Antarctic waters." Since, Russia has made progress toward each of these goals, though Russian political leaders have expressed frustrations over arduous approval processes for Antarctic activities, leading some to believe that Moscow is growing tired of compliance with international institutions seen as obstacles in the way of economic ambition for the continent.[39] The question is: What is Russia likely to do next? And with whom might Moscow align toward this end? The logical answer is China.

CHINA AS A POLAR PEER POWER

Unlike Russia, the prevailing view of the Chinese economy is one of strength and expansion. China is the leading contender to supplant the United States as the global economic leader.[40] Using GDP as the sole power metric falls short, however. China's economic growth is slowing when we account for productive and consumptive values. China's GDP is impressive, but so is its consumption. With approximately 1.5 billion people, China accounts for nearly 20 percent of the global population. In a pure numbers sense, China is four times the size of the United States. But this massive population is both a producer and a consumer. GDP is a gross indicator, a measure of total production independent of consumption and costs of production. In failing to account for consumption rates and production costs, GDP fails to produce a reliable or accurate power metric without consideration for other factors. It is a useful metric in gross comparisons in these senses, but does fall short in some areas.

Not accounting for production, welfare, and security costs risks overinflating a state's relative power.[41] Typically, states like China with the largest populations have the highest costs for doing business (production costs) and have massive outlays of welfare and security costs to support the population. The GDP metric does not account for high-consumer states like China with its net resource profile, or what is "left over" after accounting for gross production rates relative to costs and consumption. In this way, China's impressive GDP, as a gross production indicator, is weaker when accounting for its net resources after subtracting consumption and the cost outlays required to sustain its enormous population. China's available resources for producing and projecting power are far less than its GDP indicates.

With this, Beckley argues for a power-as-resources approach emphasizing a state's net resources rather than gross production as a better frame of analysis.[42] He argues that China is not the great power threat most believe. Beijing knows this. So what does China do to fuel its global hegemonic ambition while recognizing its consumption rates and increasing resource needs? It seeks to increase net resources to increase relative power. Seeking a bigger net resource portfolio, China is pursuing economic interests beyond its borders. This is why China has its eye toward the polar regions in addition to dozens of other strategically valuable locations around the world.

Naval strategist Alfred Mahan long advocated that rising powers should expand their navies, target global markets, establish colonies, and secure access to resources by extension.[43] China's Belt and Road Initiative is a play out of Mahan's playbook. The initiative's emphasis on expanding infrastructure projects aims to improve Beijing's diplomatic and economic relations globally. Started in 2013 under President Xi Jinping, the Belt and Road Initiative has resulted in the establishment of economic relations with dozens of countries, including several economic and military partners and allies of the United States.[44] China's controversial "debt-trap diplomacy" tactics have enabled Beijing to secure port access in Africa, the Indian Ocean, and the South Pacific, among other locales.[45] But even more telling about the scope of China's intent under the Belt and Road Initiative is its policy orientations informing its approach toward both poles.

From curious public statements about Antarctica to overt attempts at diplomatic partnerships in the Arctic, Beijing continues to situate the polar regions in the crosshairs of its economic plan, though each presents unique opportunities for Beijing to advance its agenda and satisfy its thirst for resources. Based on the policy language, China sees the polar regions as among the critical regions to "draw the resources to become a global power."[46] The polar regions are key nodes in China's ambitious grand strategy to assert global influence. In the Arctic, China's primary focus centers on accessibility and resource opportunity.

CHINESE ARCTIC POLICIES. China's Arctic policy orientation dates from its 1925 signing of the Spitsbergen (Svalbard) Treaty to its involvement in the International Arctic Science Committee and subsequent scientific research in the 1990s. China led its twenty-first-century Arctic interests with the establishment of the Yellow River research station on Svalbard in 2004, which serves as the primary hub for Chinese Arctic research activities.[47] Beijing's more recent Arctic policy interests date to 2011 and the release of the twelfth five-year plan.

The 2011 installment specified Chinese interests in the Arctic as primarily economic in nature, but marked the first time the Arctic was identified as a strategic inflection point in Chinese Communist Party policy.[48] Following China's 2013 designation as an Arctic Council observer, the 2016 version of the five-year plan furthered the narrative and stipulated China's intent to be a player in shaping Arctic norms and behaviors.[49] In 2017, Beijing unveiled its vision for maritime cooperation under the Belt and Road Initiative, identifying Arctic shipping lanes as "blue economic passages" and stressing the need to "promote the concept of common maritime security for mutual benefits."[50] The document also stipulates China's intent to "actively participate" in Arctic international relations, despite its geographic separation from the region.[51]

Where the aforementioned policy document outlined China's vision for the Arctic as a viable and valuable economic corridor, Beijing's 2018 Polar Silk Road policy detailed a more assertive tone in its intent to leverage shorter shipping routes from Beijing to Europe and increase Chinese Arctic presence and influence (see Figure 4.2). To this end, Chinese interests extend to Norway and Greenland. China's resource needs are staggering, but so is its ambition. The Belt and Road Initiative along with the Polar Silk Road policy seeks to further China's influence in the Arctic as a region of opportunity for Beijing's grand strategy, but some contend the economic flavor of Beijing's Arctic policies gives no credence to the narrative that China intends to militarize the Arctic in pursuit of economic goals.

To this camp, Chinese Arctic militarization amounts to little more than unfounded alarmism. Beijing's policies do not indicate an intent to militarize the Arctic now or at any point in the future. Some go so far as to insist that Arctic conflict between Russia and the United States or NATO may even undermine Chinese economic interests.[52] Elizabeth Buchanan's quip that "conflict is bad for business" (for Russia) is echoed in her argument that there is no "Arctic axis" or alliance between Russia and China. China has too much at stake economically in the Arctic to advance toward a conflict that would threaten its interests

Figure 4.2 Northern Sea Route vs. Suez Canal

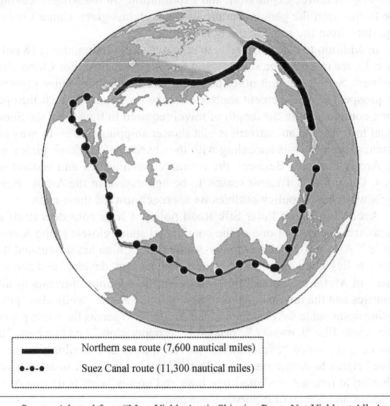

Source: Adapted from "Most Viable Arctic Shipping Route Not Viable at All: Arctic Institute," *Turkey Sea News,* March 3, 2014.

and access to resources.[53] Arctic shipping exploration and expansion coupled with the potential to partner with Moscow over liquid natural gas investment and extraction are potential boons to the Chinese economy that are sufficient motivations for Beijing to stay out of the Arctic conflict continuum.[54] Still, some are not convinced.

In a 2019 speech in Finland, then–US secretary of state Mike Pompeo said that "China's words and actions raise doubts about its intentions in the Arctic" and that the region "has become an arena for great power competition."[55] Whereas the Polar Silk Road policy promises Chinese support for international institutions, this is the ultimate contradiction given Chinese actions in the South China Sea. The Polar Silk Road policy curiously cites treaties such as the United Nations Convention on the

Law of the Sea (UNCLOS) and general international law as the basis for rights of "resource exploration and exploitation" in the Arctic, leaving one to question the genuine nature of these claims given China's overt departure from the same in the South China Sea.[56]

In addition to claiming rights to resource exploitation, the 2018 policy calls for more Arctic security and better governance. For China, the Northern Sea Route and other potential Arctic shipping lanes present the prospect of a 30 percent shorter distance for goods to reach Europe when compared with the length of travel required to transit via the Suez Canal today.[57] The attractiveness of a shorter shipping route—by way of distance, not time—is appealing with the absence of maritime piracy in the Arctic Ocean.[58] Between the resource possibilities and economic boon, China has sufficient reason to be aggressive in the Arctic. Beijing's white paper policy outlines its approach toward these ends.

According to the Polar Silk Road policy, China considers itself a "near-Arctic state," or one of the continental states closest to the Arctic Circle.[59] As a self-proclaimed near-Arctic state, China has articulated its Arctic policy goals as follows: "understand, protect, develop, and participate" in Arctic governance to "safeguard the common interests of all countries and the international community in the Arctic" while also "promoting sustainable development of the Arctic."[60] Whereas the white paper uses words like "harmony," "peaceful," "cooperation," and "respect," it also uses the word "exploitation" (seven times) in describing its perceived rights to Arctic resources. With China's continued insistence on adhering to international maritime laws and norms, what is its true Arctic intent and how will it pursue these aims?

The Polar Silk Road policy outlines five lines of effort toward executing Beijing's intent. It provides the illusion of Chinese cooperative interests—the written policy for the world to see what Beijing has to say. The problem is that what Beijing says by way of policy can be inconsistent with its true intent and resulting actions. Consider President Xi Jinping's many statements indicating his desire to see China as the leading global superpower. For all the Chinese rhetoric in the Polar Silk Road policy about cooperation and harmony, Xi's statements considered in the aggregate contradict the policy message. A resource-hungry state intent on securing its status as the global hegemon, and one that also requires unfettered access to the Arctic to sustain its economic and hegemonic ambition, is more likely to contest than cooperate in a competitive domain. To contest, a state must possess the requisite military capability and presence in the region to project power and generate influence. With this in mind, consider China's five policies and positions on Arctic affairs:[61]

1. Deepening the exploration and understanding of the Arctic.
2. Protecting the eco-environment of the Arctic and addressing climate change.
3. Utilizing Arctic resources in a lawful and rational manner.
4. Participating actively in Arctic governance and international cooperation.
5. Promoting peace and stability in the Arctic.

Accepting Chinese lines of effort is as ignorant as it is wishful. Whereas China may dedicate effort and resources toward its objectives, the alternative suggesting a more subtle approach toward nefarious ends is equally plausible. So we should consider the intent and its possible alternative meanings.

China is not a credible Arctic actor. Aside from its distance, China has limited infrastructure and therefore even less Arctic influence. China's goal is to frame the Arctic as vulnerable to international tensions and in need of an outside actor to right the ship. The policy focus on research, environmental protection, adherence to international law, cooperation, and peace attempts to create a narrative of sound intent benefiting the international community.

In terms of deepening Arctic exploration and understanding, China intends to expand its research presence in the region for myriad reasons. China's Svalbard-based research station compelled the US Department of Defense to warn in its annual report to Congress on China's military and security developments that Beijing's "civilian research could support a strengthened Chinese military presence in the Arctic Ocean, which could include deploying submarines to the region as a deterrent against nuclear attacks."[62] Why would the Department of Defense make this assertion?

China's Arctic agenda is disingenuous and self-serving. How does a country nearly a thousand miles removed from the Arctic Circle at its northernmost and relatively uninhabited point expect to reasonably protect the Arctic's eco-environment? Answer: through partnerships with Iceland and Greenland (Denmark), and soon Norway as well. Though China's development efforts in Iceland stalled, Beijing's investment in Greenland is larger than in any other country, at approximately 11 percent of its total GDP.[63] In recent years, China has sought both to develop an airstrip on Greenland and attempted to purchase an old US military installation for its own use.[64] Limited success of these arrangements prompted Beijing and its private investors to turn their attention to Norway as their next potential northern infrastructure partner.

Beijing's Arctic rhetoric claims it to be a steward of combating climate change and protecting the Arctic. Legitimizing these efforts in the international eye requires presence to be effective—presence that China does not currently have. This explains, at least in part, why China is fixated on the Arctic—not for climate change advocacy and protrection, but rather because Beijing seeks to exploit the Arctic for its resources. As it seeks greater access to valuable natural resources to fuel its ravenous consumption and grow its economy, China requires Arctic access. China's continued efforts toward building and fostering diplomatic relations with Arctic states are a necessity for the geographically challenged "near-Arctic state."

Through business partnerships with Arctic states, China sees opportunity to advance its economic posture while building optics of static Arctic presence and activity. Being present enables China to inoculate other Arctic actors to its activities over time as "normal" while its research efforts provide the curtain for the resource exploitation clearly written in its Arctic policies. Regular Arctic activity gives China the visual presence of a committed Arctic actor. This commitment serves to improve China's credibility gap in the Arctic, leading toward its next goal of active participation in Arctic governance.

An Arctic observer since 2013, China remains on the periphery of Arctic influence. Its policies indicate intent to shift the Arctic governance landscape through power diffusion. In couching the Arctic as a region of rising tensions and instability, as well as opportunity, China's policies subvert the Arctic Council's legitimacy as an effective institution. By asserting its diplomatic, economic, and research presence in the Arctic, China carves its way into Arctic governance through multilateralism, where even non-Arctic states have a say in Arctic affairs. Emphasizing international cooperation, China will cite the nature of the Arctic as an international commons to explore and benefit from (or in Beijing speak: exploit). In its advocacy for a multilateral approach to Arctic affairs, China seeks the diffusion of power away from the Arctic Council and the Arctic eight. To Beijing, the more diffuse the power structure becomes, the greater the opportunity for China to increase its influence. Ultimately, with greater influence China can advance its objective of promoting a public narrative of Arctic peace and stability and thus Arctic apathy, while simultaneously exploiting the Arctic's resources for its own gain in an increasingly competitive and resource-strapped global environment.

To these ends, there is a logical progression from China's stated policy goals to its current activities and to its predicted approach in the

Arctic. Continued infrastructure development and Arctic partnerships under the guise of research will yield dual-use facilities serving both scientific and military purposes. Dismissing this ignores the realities of subversive Chinese actions in other areas of the world. It also ignores the realities of Chinese military research, training, and development of specific polar capabilities and technologies aimed at advancing Beijing's Arctic policy agenda. China remains committed to developing polar military technologies and training military units in extreme cold weather. China is well on its way toward realizing its ambitious Arctic agenda. In 2017, Anne-Marie Brady told us that "China's polar strategy is an undeclared foreign policy."[65] In 2018, China declared its Arctic policy to the world in the Polar Silk Road white paper. Whereas its Arctic strategy took some years to develop and release, Beijing's Antarctic strategy has been brewing in Chinese public narrative for years.

CHINESE ANTARCTIC POLICIES. China wants to colonize Antarctica and, like the Arctic, exploit its resource pool for national gain. China does not project its policies and intent to a global audience as a predictor of future action. Rather, China acts first toward a goal and outlines a policy consistent with its actions later. This is a subtle and effective method of advancing toward national ends under the international radar rather than announcing its plans to the world and inviting challenge. This strategy enables China to quietly build momentum toward a strategic goal, leaving the international community to observe and react. So while China errs on the side of subtlety rather than prescriptive policy, it does signal its intent via public engagements, speeches, and attention-drawing activities that can help us put the puzzle together and better predict its future approach.

In 2015, Chinese filmmaker Fang Li, in collaboration with the Polar Research Institute of China, released a film titled *Antarctica 2049*. The film and its collaboration with and endorsement from the Chinese Communist Party are telling and point to China's eye toward an opportunity to relax restrictive elements of the Antarctic Treaty's Madrid Protocol in 2048, when its current provisions on maintaining Antarctica as a region dedicated to peace and science enter a period for renegotiation.[66] The example of this film is anecdotal to Beijing's national narrative on Antarctica. Examining Chinese Antarctic policies and rhetoric reveals a clear conclusion: Antarctica is a Chinese political, economic, and even military priority for the twenty-first century.

Antarctica has been featured in China's national narrative for decades. Beijing's Antarctic policy platform is informative to its strategic interests and its resulting approaches. Looking to Brady's contributions and assessments of Chinese Antarctic interests, we see three common threads within their policy documents to date: security, resources, and science and technology.[67] According to Brady, China's Antarctic security interests focus on the continent's "unresolved sovereignty" as an opportunity for exploitation.[68] Beijing sees Antarctic governance as an opportunity and a threat. Its economic interests in Antarctica are opportunistic in that securing access to mineral mining, fishing, and other resources carries the potential for a windfall of riches necessary to meet China's consumption demands and global economic agenda. However, securing access requires careful navigation of Antarctic geopolitical affairs *and* robust polar power projection capabilities. Chinese activities to secure access to the continent may be seen as a threat that must be overcome, or at least disguised.

Whereas China may not be militarily interested in the Arctic (yet), it is interested in projecting military power to Antarctica to fuel its security interests and access resources. Beijing is keen on Antarctica's assumed and untapped wealth. Access to mineral mining and hydrocarbons is a significant economic incentive for a host of energy needs. The unique marine ecosystem provides attractive fisheries for China's fleets, whereas the luster of the frozen continent compels a steadily increasing tourism industry, both of which are key elements of China's national economy and reliant on improving science and technology capabilities, not the least of which points to space.

Antarctica is an essential location for China's BeiDou navigation system as a competitor to the US-delivered global positioning system. China requires Antarctic access as a critical node for its space programs and weather-forecasting efforts.[69] Between its security, resource, and science interests on Antarctica, China requires significant polar capabilities to meet these demands.

With four research stations (and a fifth under construction), three airfields, two field bases, polar planes, and icebreakers, China outspends the United States and every other state on Antarctic infrastructure and capabilities. To this end, China has the second largest number of people living, working, and visiting Antarctica on an annual basis, behind only the United States.[70] While most of China's infrastructure lies within eastern Antarctica and the Australian Antarctic territory, its newest research station in the Ross Sea region is located close to the US McMurdo Research Station on Ross Island, signaling a potential strategic counterbalance to US Antarctic presence.

Like the US Antarctic Program's partnership with the Department of Defense and Department of Homeland Security via the US Coast

Guard for Antarctic support, the Chinese Antarctic research program has a full complement of air, land, and sea platforms and continues to expand. According to Brady, China in 2017 proposed to designate an area surrounding its Kunlun Base as an Antarctic "special managed area," intended as an environmental protection zone and thus subject to more restrictive access protocols. Due to their designations as protected zones, such areas exclude regular traffic in and through the space. For China, its subsequent petition to the Antarctic Treaty consultative meeting included designating its snow road, known as China Boulevard, as part of the proposed special managed area. China Boulevard is an analog to the US-operated South Pole Highway connecting Phoenix Airfield to McMurdo Station. As the only state besides the United States to maintain a dedicated snow road on Antarctica, achieving the status of special managed area for the road and area around Kunlun Base would ensure no foreign presence within the zone and thereby function as Chinese sovereign territory without the official status. What special managed areas lack in the form of sovereignty they gain in function. This is a form of "soft presence for states that want to seize control over territory in Antarctica."[71]

To date, the Antarctic Treaty consultative meetings have not approved China's proposal for a special managed area. Continued failed proposals will lead China toward a more assertive posture that advances this claim in function despite the resistance of the international approving body. The question is: Why does China desire a special managed area around one of its Antarctic bases? China has restricted site access to multinational inspectors, despite the Antarctic Treaty's provision that Antarctic sites are to be open and accessible at all times. Then–Pacific Air Forces commander and current Air Force chief of staff General C. Q. Brown in 2019 publicly questioned a Chinese icebreaker's return to China from Antarctica rather than its sailing to the closest available repair port in New Zealand following unspecified mechanical problems.[72] There are enough Chinese actions in Antarctica to cause question of its intent relative to maintaining a peaceful dynamic on the continent. But unlike the Arctic, where China insists its interests are focused on peace and stability, Beijing's Antarctic policies tell a different story.

Chinese Antarctic activities date to the 1980s. Its more substantive policy prescriptions can be traced to the late 1990s. Beijing's strategic research vision for Antarctica prioritized the region as the "main area of operations in Antarctica" in 1998 and built the policy foundation for Antarctic orientation for the next two decades.[73] Today, China sees Antarctic presence as a demonstration of status as a global power.[74]

Considering its evolving activities and national narrative, Beijing is progressing toward a territorial claim.[75] Public comments from Chinese officials, including President Xi, advance this narrative. In a 2014 visit to the Chinese icebreaker *Snow Dragon* at port in Hobart, Australia, President Xi was quoted saying: "The Chinese side stands ready to continuously work with Australia and the international community to better understand, protect, and *exploit* the Antarctic."[76] However, as Brady recounts, there was much manipulation of Xi's speech in Chinese media accounts, with the word "exploit" replaced with "explore." This is more than a semantic argument. Words mean things.

Antarctica is collectively governed and ostensibly peaceful. To "exploit" this peaceful continent conjures a significantly more aggressive message than to "explore." Other Chinese officials doubled down on the same. In 2017, China's deputy director of the State Oceanic Administration said that China has "no immediate plans to exploit Antarctic resources" but that it does worry about Antarctica's changing environment and the prospect of competition on the continent.[77] As "exploit" continues to populate Chinese narrative, consider the possibility, if not the probability, that China has malign intent for Antarctica. For its broader polar ambition, the explore/exploit debate was silenced with the release of the Polar Silk Road policy for the Arctic and its repeated use of "exploit" and "exploitation" throughout. In context, Xi's terminology for the Antarctic seems deliberate and calculated. Accepting China's intent to exploit Antarctica in the twenty-first century, the international community should look to how it will execute its plan.

China's thirteenth five-year plan, for 2016–2020, specified its intent to engage in polar region research. Looking back on China's approach relative to its stated Antarctic policy in this and other documents, we see evidence of advancement toward and even achievement of several objectives. But for all of Beijing's investment and rhetoric toward Antarctica, it still falls short on proximity.

With this limitation, China continues to pursue expanded relationships with Antarctic gateway countries like Australia and New Zealand. Whether Beijing is engaging in debt-trap diplomacy or predatory economics, or simply being "neighborly," is up for debate. Regardless, the end state is clear: China sees both Australia and New Zealand as points of leverage for Antarctic influence critical to its national narrative and desire to foster perception as a prestigious global power influential at the ends of the planet. Improving relations with both countries is seen as a necessary effort toward furthering Beijing's ambition. In Australia, China sees another exploitation opportunity and has been pursuing it for years.

According to some experts, Australia is nearing financial ruin. Australia has put itself into a precarious financial position that will necessitate desperate measures to reverse. As Australia nears a point of strategic immobility brought by economic turmoil, China sees an opportunity for exploitation and advancement of its long-term strategy. Australia is the leader in Antarctic advocacy—a default Antarctic protector by way of proximity. As the global Covid-19 pandemic persists, Australia continues to scale back Antarctic operations and retrench due to limited resources relative to other competing commitments. Australia is the largest Antarctic stakeholder but may soon cede its influence to China, as Beijing is better positioned to pursue and facilitate for mutually beneficial and multinational strategic partnerships. In this scenario, Australia gains economic support from China. In return, China gains southern infrastructure and access to one of its most coveted prizes: Antarctica. But few see it this way.

To many, China is interested in Antarctica because of its scientific curiosity, the same as it is interested in Australia as an additional node for its global Belt and Road Initiative. Arguing that Antarctica can be the subject of malign actor intent is ludicrous to this camp. The naysayers in Australia and around the world cling to the insistence that international interests, peace, and stability in Antarctica are protected by the Antarctic Treaty System. That a state can or would deviate or depart from the treaty is unfathomable to this group. This is ignorant, or what Brady refers to as the "bare bum strategy," when a state is "well-dressed to the north" by way of policy and orientation but comparably naked to the south.[78]

Holding to the idea that China or any other country will adhere to the provisions of the Antarctic Treaty System simply because it exists increases the likelihood of, to extend the bare-bum metaphor, getting caught with one's pants down. Chinese policies and national narrative are a metaphorical blueprint for forceful and contested Antarctic annexation. The further it progresses south, the closer China comes to realizing its goal of becoming an actual polar power not only by typology measure of its capability and intent, but by proximity and influence as well.

As the only other polar power, the United States is the only state capable of deterring malign intent in Antarctica. Chinese and Russia polar policies surpass US polar policies in both substance and intent. Whereas Russia and China have long seen the polar regions as opportunistic hotbeds for material gain, economic advancement, and international prestige, the United States is decades behind in terms of comparable security and defense policy commitment to the polar regions as burgeoning geostrategic and geopolitical flashpoints.

Notes

1. Waltz, "The Emerging Structure of International Politics."
2. World Bank, "GDP per Capita (current US $)," 2019, https://data.worldbank.org/indicator/NY.GDP.MKTP.CD?most_recent_value_desc=true&year_high_desc=true.
3. Hobard speech by author, November 20, 2014, http://www.oceanol.com/redian/shipping//2014-11-25/38013.html.
4. Brady, "China's Expanding Antarctic Interests," p. 7.
5. Brady, *China as a Polar Great Power,* p. 137.
6. Buchanan, "West Must Cooperate with Russia in the Arctic."
7. "Norway in Antarctica: The History and Activity of Norwegians in Antarctica," https://www.coolantarctica.com/Antarctica%20fact%20file/activity_of_Norway_in_antarctica.php.
8. Dahl, "The Concept of Power," p. 204.
9. See Table 4.1 for a summary of the data and individual country scores in table form.
10. President of the Russian Federation, "Osnovy gosudarstvennoy politiki Rossiyskoy Federatsii v Arktike" (Fundamentals of the State Policy of the Russian Federation in the Arctic) (Moscow: Government of the Russian Federation, 2001), http://www.sci.aha.ru/econ/A111c.htm.
11. Ibid.
12. Ibid. Translated.
13. Russian Federation, "The Foundations of Russian Federation Policy in the Arctic Until 2020 and Beyond," September 18, 2008, http://www.arctic.or.kr/files/pdf/m4/rusia_eng.pdf.
14. Conversation with former US intelligence official in the Soviet Union, September 2020.
15. Russian Federation, 2020 Arctic policy.
16. Aliyev, "Russia's Military Capabilities in the Arctic."
17. Congressional Research Service, "Changes in the Arctic: Background and Issues for Congress" (Washington, DC, August 2020).
18. Katya Golubkova and Gleb Stolyarov, "Rosatom Sees Northern Sea Route Costs at 735 billion Roubles, Russian Budget to Provide a Third," *Reuters,* June 24, 2019, https://www.reuters.com/article/us-russia-rosatom-arctic/rosatom-sees-northern-sea-route-costs-at-735-billion-roubles-russian-budget-to-provide-a-third-idUSKCN1TP1LB.
19. Charles Digges, "Putin Unveils More Plans to Boost Northern Sea Route," March 7, 2020, https://www.maritime-executive.com/editorials/putin-unveils-more-plans-to-boost-northern-sea-route; "Suez Canal Makes All-Time Record on Wednesday," *Egypt Independent,* January 23, 2019, https://egyptindependent.com/suez-canal-makes-all-time-record-on-wednesday.
20. Conley and Rohloff, *The New Ice Curtain.*
21. Buchanan, "The Overhaul of Russian Strategic Planning."
22. Russian Federation, "The Foundations of the State Policy of the Russian Federation in the Arctic for the Period up to 2035," March 5, 2020, http://static.kremlin.ru/media/events/files/ru/f8ZpjhpAaQ0WB1zjywN04OgKiI1mAvaM.pdf.
23. Ibid.
24. Ibid.

25. Ibid.
26. Ibid.
27. Ibid.
28. Buchanan, "The Overhaul of Russian Strategic Planning."
29. Russian Federation, "One Plan: Measures to Implement the Fundamentals of State Policy of the Russian Federation in the Arctic for the Period up to 2035 and the Development Strategy of the Arctic Zone of the Russian Federation and Ensuring National Security for the Period up to 2035," April 15, 2021, http://static.government.ru/media/files/p8DfCI0Pr1XZnAk08G7J3jUXUuDvswHr.pdf.
30. Ibid., p. 41.
31. Ibid.
32. Blakemore, "Who Really Discovered Antarctica?"
33. "Medvedev Spoke About Russia's Strategic Interests in Antarctica," January 29, 2020, https://ria.ru/20200129/1564025091.html.
34. Russian Federation, "Strategy for the Development of the Activities of the Russian Federation in Antarctica for the Period up to 2020 and for the More Distant Future," March 31, 2011, https://rg.ru/2011/03/31/antarktika-site-dok.html.
35. Ibid.
36. Ibid.
37. Ibid.
38. Ibid.
39. Russian Federation, "The Antarctic Treaty in the Changing World," submission to the Antarctic Treaty consultative meeting, May 5, 2019, https://cdn.theatlantic.com/assets/media/files/the_antarctic_treaty_in_the_changing_world_(1).pdf.
40. Pew Research Center, "Global Indicators Database" (Washington, DC, 2017), http://www.pewglobal.org/database.
41. Beckley, "The Power of Nations."
42. Ibid.
43. Mahan, *The Influence of Seapower on History.*
44. Chatzky and McBridge, "China's Massive Belt and Road Initiative."
45. Green, "China's Debt Diplomacy."
46. Brady, "China's Expanding Antarctic Interests," p. 1.
47. Embassy of the People's Republic of China, "China Opens 1st Research Station in Arctic Area."
48. Havnes and Seland, "The Increasing Security Focus in China's Arctic Policy."
49. National Development and Reform Commission, "The 13th Five-Year Plan for Economic and Social Development of the People's Republic of China (2016–2020)," 2016.
50. "Vision for Maritime Cooperation Under the Belt and Road Initiative," June 20, 2017, http://www.xinhuanet.com/english/2017-06/20/c_136380414.htm.
51. China released its fourteenth five-year plan in March 2021. Unlike previous iterations, early translations of the fourteenth plan exclude any specific mentions of the Arctic or Antarctica (or polar regions broadly).
52. F. Liu and D. Liu, "Security of the North Pole and China's National Security Interests from the Perspective of the New National Security Law" (Beijing: State Council Information Office of the People's Republic of China, 2018).
53. Buchanan, "There Is No Arctic Axis."
54. Staalesen, "Putin Steps Up Talks with Beijing."
55. Pompeo. "Looking North."
56. People's Republic of China, "China's Arctic Policy," January 2018, http://www.scio.gov.cn/zfbps/32832/Document/1618243/1618243.htm.

57. US Coast Guard, "Arctic Strategic Outlook," https://www.globalsecurity.org/military/library/policy/navy/uscg-arctic_strategic_outlook_20190422.pdf; Lino, "Understanding China's Arctic Activities."

58. Though the route is shorter by mileage, many estimates claim that transiting the Arctic as an alternative to the Suez Canal may take just as long by way of time, as the seas are more challenging and the ice is unpredictable, necessitating slower speeds and more deliberate navigation.

59. "China's Arctic Policy" (Beijing: State Council Information Office of the People's Republic of China, 2018).

60. Ibid.

61. Ibid.

62. US Department of Defense, *Annual Report to Congress: Military and Security Developments Involving the People's Republic of China, 2019* (Washington, DC, 2019).

63. Rosen and Thuringer, *Unconstrained Foreign Direct Investment.*

64. Thompson-Jones, "Why America Should Lose Sleep over Greenland."

65. Brady, *China as a Polar Great Power*, p. 35.

66. Ibid., pp. 33–59.

67. Brady, "China's Expanding Antarctic Interests."

68. Brady, "China's Undeclared Foreign Policy at the Poles."

69. Brady, "China's Expanding Antarctic Interests," p. 12.

70. Brady, "China's Undeclared Foreign Policy at the Poles."

71. Ibid.

72. Pawlyk, "More US Military Power Needed in Antarctic."

73. Ibid., p. 10.

74. Brady, "China's Expanding Antarctic Interests," p. 9.

75. Ibid., p. 2.

76. Ministry of Foreign Affairs of the People's Republic of China, "Xi Jinping Visits Chinese and Australian Antarctic Scientific Researchers and Inspects Chinese Research Vessel 'Snow Dragon,'" November 18, 2014, https://www.fmprc.gov.cn/mfa_eng/topics_665678/xjpzxcxesgjtldrdjcfhdadlyxxlfjjxgsfwbttpyjjdgldrhw/t1212943.shtml.

77. Brady, "China's Undeclared Foreign Policy at the Poles."

78. Brady, *China as a Polar Great Power.*

5

US Polar Policy and Strategy

HAVING GAINED FOUNDATIONAL KNOWLEDGE ON THE importance, complexity, and evolving security environment of the polar regions in the twenty-first century, one would logically conclude that a global hegemon like the United States would have a robust polar policy posture informing its approach toward achieving strategic ends. It does not—at least not in comparison to the other polar powers. In reviewing US polar policies with an eye toward defense and security issues, we see a remarkable gap in substance relative to policies informing US approaches to other global hotspots. But just because the polar regions are cold in no way means they are not also heating up, at least by way of international security tensions. This general lack of US policy orientation toward the polar regions through the years created an avenue of approach that great power competitors Russia and China exploited with their own polar policies and pivots. As a result, the United States has increased its polar policy substance since 2019, but in a reactive rather than proactive manner.

The relative absence of polar policy—inclusive of both the Arctic and Antarctica—to inform US national interests and strategy development will continue leading the United States toward a strategic imbalance in the polar regions that will produce spillover effects in global great power competition with Russia and China. The United States can no longer assume global primacy as a default condition of its military strength, as it did for much of the twentieth century. There are rising threats to the US-led world order and hegemony in the twenty-first century, and they present uniquely in the polar regions.

How Did We Get Here?

Compared with Russia and China, the United States arguably has a more robust polar policy platform in terms of time. For instance, given Cold War tensions and proximity with the Soviet Union in the Arctic, in 1971 Richard Nixon first directed the National Security Council to develop an Arctic policy, a trend that has continued in every administration since.[1] To this point, the United States has a long-standing tradition of at least including the Arctic in national security dialogue. But to what end and degree of substance?

As the Cold War ended and the Soviet Union collapsed, so did the perceived "over-the-Arctic threat." With the creation of the Arctic Council in 1996 and the United States as the world's only superpower of the time, the Arctic policies continued, but the region's importance waned the more the United States found itself meddling in other regions in the late twentieth and early twenty-first centuries. In Antarctica since the mid–twentieth century and owing to the creation of the US-led Antarctic Treaty, US policy posture has been almost exclusively devoted to scientific research and absent substantive security dialogue. This reflects the US assumption of the treaty as a legitimate international intuition sufficient to dissuade malign activity on Antarctica. To date, this has been a good gamble and largely due to regular international presence on Antarctica and productive engagement complemented by twentieth-century US hegemony. In short, nobody had the capability or intent to cross the United States or challenge its position.

As the global hegemon in the twentieth century, the United States did not require an Antarctic security policy; its presence and engagement in Antarctic affairs sufficiently promoted and ensured stability. Over time, however, complacency set in. The United States generally turned what little attention it did have on the polar regions elsewhere, leaving the door open for China and Russia to bolster their own polar policies and national security narratives while assuming a position of increasing influence that, in Russia's case in the Arctic, is now a strategic advantage.

In viewing the polar regions as international commons, and with a long-standing tradition of ensuring freedom of navigation, the United States set and enforced the rules in the polar regions in the twentieth century. It did so mostly by way of projecting worldwide presence—including in both polar regions—and maintaining the premier military force on the planet sufficient to deter aggression. Freedom of the commons was thus intact; US-led covenants provided additional structure ensuring a rules-based order; claims were either uncontested or unchanged as a result of the structure; and the prospect of the cosmos and space war-fighting had yet to enter into the international security dialogue in any influential manner.

In the twenty-first century, however, and after twenty years of sustained conflict in Iraq and Afghanistan, the United States has lost its way and no longer enjoys the same global influence it did in the twentieth century. Or, as Cooley and Nexon tell us, the United States is "exiting from hegemony."[2] Through continued orientation to assumed threats to national security in the Middle East, Asia, and North Africa, the United States has entered into a time of what Conley and Melino refer as "policy stagnation" when it comes to the polar regions.[3] Today, the polar regions present as geographic hotspots of increasing international competition stemming from philosophical divergence among how Russia and China view the Arctic and Antarctica relative to the commons, covenants, claims, and cosmos. Now, with increased attention toward the polar regions from Beijing and Moscow, Washington is reacting. Until recently, the United States had all but forgotten about the polar regions and their importance to the global balance of power. US policy and strategy through the years only affirms this position.

POLAR POLICIES THROUGH THE YEARS

US presidents since Harry S. Truman have had polar policies touching on defense, security, or military affairs, broadly. President Truman commissioned Antarctica's Operation High Jump in 1946 and supported expanded Antarctic research programs. To the north, Truman's offer to purchase Greenland from Denmark, also in 1946, was seen as an inflection point on the geostrategic significance of the Arctic in the postwar era.[4] As the Cold War evolved, so too did the Arctic's relevance to the national security conversation. The Nixon administration's 1971 National Security Decision Memorandum (NSDM-144), seen as the first substantive US Arctic security policy document, directed the development of the Arctic Policy Group as a reporting entity to the National Security Council (NSC). Signed by Henry Kissinger and directed by President Nixon, NSDM-144 directed that the United States would support "sound and rational development of the Arctic" promoted by "international cooperation," "protection of essential security interests," and "preservation of the principle of freedom of the seas and superjacent airspace."[5] This 1971 approach doubled down on the idea of US liberal hegemony and command of the commons while also establishing the basis of future US Arctic policies for the rest of the twentieth century.

Presidential Policies

In 1983 the Reagan administration released its own US Arctic policy in the form of a National Security Decision Directive (NSDD). Of the 325 NSDDs released during Reagan's presidency, from February 1981 to January 1989, the 1983 Arctic policy (NSDD 90) was the only national security document pertaining to either polar region, at least by way of title (containing the words "Arctic policy"). For comparison, the administration released fifteen NSDDs pertaining to the Soviet Union during this time: ten with "terror" or "terrorism" in the title; three with Iraq; and two with Afghanistan. As a standalone document, NSDD 90 contained significant language outlining US Arctic interests. Specifically, the document stipulated that the United States has "unique and critical interests in the Arctic region related directly to national defense" sufficiently establishing the Arctic as a region that "warrants priority attention."[6]

With this, the Reagan administration reinforced Nixon's 1971 NSDM proclamation and insisted that the United States continue "preservation of the principle of freedom of the seas and superjacent airspace" in the Arctic.[7] Mikhail Gorbachev's Murmansk Initiative speech in 1987 seemed to advance this narrative, claiming the Soviet Union no longer wished to view the Arctic as a battlefield, even if only in terms of military posturing.[8] The dissolution of the Soviet Union a short time later defused any remaining Arctic tensions between Washington and Moscow. A rebuilding and cash-poor Russia in the early 1990s was forced to shutter research programs in the Arctic and Antarctica. As the only competing polar power of the time, the reduced presence of the Soviets/Russians in both poles in the late 1980s and early 1990s allowed for equally reduced US policy attention on the polar regions during the George H. W. Bush administration through 1992.

In 1994 the Clinton administration released a Presidential Decision Directive titled "United States Policy on the Arctic and Antarctic Regions" (PDD-26). Unique among past administration policy documents, PDD-26 included Antarctica in the mix. For its stance on the Arctic, PPD-26 again emphasized basic "national security and defense interests." In a curious departure from past administrations' Arctic stance, rather than declaring an intent to continue to preserve freedom of the seas and airspace, as did Reagan and Nixon before, Clinton's Arctic policy stated only the US intent to be able to "move ships and aircraft freely under the principles of customary law reflected in the 1982 Law of the Sea Convention."[9]

Past administrations' promises to preserve freedom of navigation are consistent with the long-standing US tradition of "command of the commons." The Clinton administration's decision to omit this phrase in its Arctic policy in favor of a more US-focused approach sent a message of budding US Arctic apathy to others reflective of the lack of Arctic competition at the time. As an additional departure from past policies, Clinton's directive removed references to either polar region as a matter of national priority. In this way, Clinton laid the foundation for a receding US Arctic policy platform that may well have motivated Russia to move on Arctic advancement with similar implications for Antarctica in later years. Of the four pages of policy substance in PDD-26, three are Arctic-focused, with the final page discussing the administration's commitment to preserving Antarctica's "unspoiled environment." The document adds one sentence reinforcing the US commitment to the Antarctic Treaty and its intent to promote and maintain international cooperation and peaceful use of Antarctica. Generally, though, the document lacked expanded discussion detailing the US approach toward these ends.[10] In this way, Clinton's polar policy document may have set the stage for further US Arctic departures and opportunities for others to assume positions of influence in future years.

Fifteen years later and building on Clinton's PPD-26, the George W. Bush administration, just prior to its transition to the Obama administration, signed National Security Presidential Directive (NSPD) 66 and Homeland Security Presidential Directive (HSPD) 25 on Arctic region policy. In the national security lens, these 2009 documents were the first updated polar policy since PPD-26 in 1994. Notably maintaining PPD-26's guidance for Antarctic policy, NSPD-66/HSPD-25 established fresh Arctic policy, particularly labeling the United States as an "Arctic nation."[11] Though it appears to relegate Antarctica to irrelevance in international security with a broad adoption and continuation of 1994 policy (something to discuss later), the Bush administration's stance on Arctic defense and security was arguably the first US polar policy with metaphorical teeth. Signed less than two years removed from Russia's infamous North Pole flag-planting spectacle, the Bush Arctic policy actually brought a needed sense of importance, if not urgency, to US Arctic interests.

In defining US national and homeland security interests in the Arctic—which it referred to as "broad and fundamental"—NSPD-66/HSPD-25 made clear the US intent to act "either independently or in conjunction with other states" to safeguard the Arctic and US homeland.[12] In a remarkable shift from past administrations' policies and undoubtedly recognizing expanding Russian Arctic presence and influence, Bush's policy was the first of its kind to stipulate military interests and activities beyond the soft implication of past policies to conduct naval activity to ensure freedom of navigation. In particular, the policy outlined the administration's Arctic priorities, including:[13]

- Missile defense and early warning.
- Deployment of sea and air systems for strategic sealift, strategic deterrence, maritime presence, and maritime security operations.
- Ensuring freedom of navigation and overflight.

In addition to outlining other concerns related to preventing terrorism (a cornerstone of the Bush administration's foreign policy, apparently even in the Arctic), the document further clarified the US commitment to Arctic law and order, as well as Washington's intent to ensure sovereignty of its Arctic territories and extended zones. Like past Arctic policies, NSPD-66/HSPD-25 left nothing to question regarding the US pledge to maintain "freedom of the seas," noting that such was a "top national priority."[14] The document further labeled the evolving Arctic maritime channels (Northwest Passage and Northern Sea Route) as international "strategic straits"—an important classification of the Arctic as both economically and militarily relevant in the twenty-first century while also rejecting Canadian and Russian claims to sovereignty over each, respectively. With this, the Bush administration charged the Department of Defense and Department of Homeland Security to develop greater capabilities and capacities; increase domain awareness; preserve global mobility; project sovereign presence; and encourage peaceful resolution of disputes in the Arctic.[15] The Obama administration followed shortly after with a similar take on the evolving Arctic situation.

In May 2010 the Obama administration's National Security Strategy (NSS), like NSPD-66/HSPD-25 a year before, reinforced that the "United States is an Arctic Nation" with associated national security "needs" in the Arctic.[16] Labeling the Arctic among the "key global challenges" within the 2010 NSS, the administration established the basis for further policy substance in subsequent years. In May 2013 the White

House released the first-of-its-kind National Strategy for the Arctic Region (NSAR), outlining three lines of effort:[17]

1. Advance US security interests.
2. Pursue responsible Arctic region stewardship.
3. Strengthen international cooperation.

Additionally, the 2013 NSAR insisted that the United States would support and preserve freedom of navigation and overflight to maintain the Arctic as an "area free of conflict."[18] While acknowledging the changing Arctic conditions and increasing global interest in the High North, the NSAR mentioned freedom of navigation and freedom of the seas several times throughout as a lynchpin of the US strategic approach to maintaining Arctic peace and stability despite increasing and unregulated activities. Here we begin to see the emergence of the assumed importance of the polar regions as potentially contested commons governed by international covenants. This language in the NSAR tacitly referred to increasingly contested claims in the Arctic and its presentation likely saw the developing reality of the Arctic as an enabler of increased space capabilities for a twenty-first-century competitive advantage. The NSAR, with its continued emphasis on the long-standing tradition of US command of the commons and freedom of navigation, served as the basis for the November 2013 Department of Defense Arctic strategy.

DEFENSE POLICIES

The 2013 Department of Defense Arctic strategy expanded on the NSAR, establishing the department's Arctic end-state as "a secure and stable region where U.S. national interests are safeguarded, the U.S. homeland is protected, and nations work cooperatively to address challenges."[19] To meet this intent, the strategy outlined a series of Department of Defense-specific tasks furthering the narrative of Arctic significance to twenty-first-century security priorities. Notably, the Arctic strategy designated US Northern Command (NORTHCOM) as the official "Arctic advocate" for the department. In doing so, this created a curious operational and command dynamic, to be discussed later.

With an Arctic advocate in NORTHCOM that is also responsible for homeland defense, the strategy revisits the need to protect the US homeland and preserve freedom of the seas in the Arctic. An unwavering bedrock principle for US Arctic interests since Nixon, freedom of the seas and of navigation continued among US Arctic priorities—in terms of policy language—throughout the Obama administration. With increased attention on the Arctic domain, the Arctic strategy did recognize the fiscal realities of the 2013 sequestration. Without budgeted intent to make good on its many promises, few came to fruition. Still, continued policy attention through the end of the Obama administration in 2016 and toward the Arctic indicated an evolving US defense interest in and commitment to the region as a twenty-first-century security concern that even made its way into the most prominent annual defense policy of the United States.

Section 1068 of the 2016 National Defense Authorization Act (NDAA) required the Department of Defense to submit a report updating "military strategy for the protection of United States national security interests in the Arctic region."[20] The NDAA required the report to include discussions on operational plans and military requirements for, among other things, freedom of navigation in the Arctic. It also required an assessment of operational seams, capabilities, and gaps, and of the overall Arctic security environment as necessitating greater US attention. In December 2016, the Department of Defense released its strategy report answering the NDAA's requirements.

The 2016 Arctic strategy built on the many prior policies and defense strategies in its framing of the Arctic's situation. In addition to again emphasizing preservation of freedom of the seas in the Arctic, the strategy affirmed the Bush administration's 2009 Arctic region policy interests and specified how the Department of Defense would pursue these objectives in the future. The strategy noted the operational seams of responsibility unique to the Arctic in that two US geographic combatant commands share responsibility for the Arctic: NORTHCOM and EUCOM (US European Command). It also identified the increased tensions and disagreements about the Arctic commons relative to both Russian and Canadian claims as potential future "friction points."[21]

Owing to these and other noted issues throughout the strategy, the 2016 strategy encouraged the Department of Defense to enhance Arctic capabilities to defend the homeland; strengthen deterrence as well as alliances and partnerships; preserve freedom of the seas; improve domain awareness through more robust engagement; evolve Arctic infrastructure; support civil authorities; partner with others in support of safety; and support international institutions and the rule of law.[22] In sum, the 2016 Arctic strategy provided a robust overview of Department of Defense interests in the Arctic relative to its status as a commons; concerns about claims tensions; and its reliance on international covenants and institutions to ensure a rules-based order. The document was a blueprint to executing lines of effort toward US interests in the region. However, there was no mention of great power competition at any point in the 2016 strategy, or in any previous Arctic document for that matter.

Meanwhile, Antarctica remained absent the national security rhetoric as well, with its last cursory policy mention in Bush's 2009 strategy harking back to Clinton's 1994 policy. We saw a marked shift in national security policy priorities with the Trump administration in 2017, but, ironically, little polar attention given the new emphasis toward great power competition in the national narrative.

POLAR POLICIES IN THE ERA OF GREAT POWER COMPETITION

The Trump administration's 2017 NSS mentions the Arctic once, among a list of "common domains" where international institutions play a role in keeping them "open and free."[23] There is no mention of Antarctica. President Trump's 2017 NSS did little to promote focus on "great power competition" by way of terminology, mentioning the phrase only once, but it did firmly establish Russia and China as "revisionist powers" dissatisfied with the world order and intent on establishing a multipolar dynamic as a principal challenge to US interests.[24] However, the NSS prioritized homeland defense and, within this sphere, missile defense, though the discussion focused on North Korea and Iran and did not mention Russia's development of hypersonic missiles or the Arctic as a northern approach. In this way, we can think of the Arctic in 2017 as a strategic blind spot to the north—a forgotten border despite the NSS's insistence on the need to strengthen borders and enhance border security.[25] Subsequent policy documents would equally fail to capture the significance of the Arctic challenges despite the continued shift of great power attention to the same.

The 2018 National Defense Strategy (NDS), under then–secretary of defense James Mattis, followed the 2017 NSS with even more emphasis on long-term, or interstate, "strategic competition," labeling Russia and China as "strategic competitors" challenging the international rules-based order.[26] The 2018 NDS noted that the United States was in a period of "strategic atrophy" necessitating a return to lethality and reliance on allies and partners.[27] It specified China's perceived economic and military "ascendance" and Russia's continued efforts to undermine international institutions to its favor.[28] To this point, the NDS raised concern over the "weakening" post–World War II international order and Russia's and China's efforts to change it.[29] In this context, the

NDS also made the revelation that "the homeland is no longer a sanctuary," and that "we cannot expect the same success fighting tomorrow's conflicts with yesterday's weapons or equipment."[30]

For all of this, though, there was no mention of the Arctic, despite the irony that—at the time of its release—Russia was ten years into its Arctic modernization efforts and three years removed from the creation of its Northern Fleet Joint Strategic Command in the Arctic. As well, China had announced its plans for an Arctic policy, though Beijing released the official Polar Silk Road paper about a week after the 2018 NDS was published. The intent indicators were there, but the Department of Defense, it appeared, was not paying attention with this or subsequent policy documents.

Building on the NDS, the 2018 National Military Strategy (NMS) did little more than summarize the NDS priorities, with its only notable addition being the specific mention of the reemergence of great power competition and its associated challenges as a strategic focus. We did not see the first substantive Trump administration policy look at the Arctic until the release of the fiscal year 2019 NDAA. Section 1071 of the 2019 NDAA required a "report on an updated Arctic strategy to improve and enhance joint operations," which the Department of Defense soon produced.[31]

As required by the NDAA, the June 2019 Department of Defense Arctic strategy's end-state remained unchanged from its 2016 predecessor. Its three priorities did, however, take a more direct approach than the 2016 version in establishing the necessity of advancing and securing US interests. To do so, the strategy required the United States to undertake efforts toward building Arctic awareness; enhancing Arctic operations; and strengthening the rules-based order in the Arctic.[32] Whereas the 2016 Department of Defense Arctic strategy mentioned China only once in the context of being an Arctic observer, the 2019 strategy, eighteen months removed from Beijing's Polar Silk Road white paper, mentioned China eighteen times in the context of Beijing's challenges to rules-based order in the Arctic, strategic competition, Arctic governance, economic exploitation, and other matters. Here the United States acknowledged Chinese icebreaker operations in the Arctic and the potential for future submarine deployments under the guise of evolving civilian research efforts. As well, the strategy made no reservations in its assessment of Russia's increasing Arctic posturing and Arctic strength, noting specifically the creation of the Northern Fleet Joint Strategic Command; expanded and refurbished Arctic infrastructure; and Moscow's "concerted effort to establish a network of air defense and coastal missile systems" among other polar capabilities.[33] With these indicators, the 2019 strategy presented a decidedly different Arctic tone than its predecessors.

Owing to the new Arctic dynamic, Department of Defense listed the region as "strategic terrain," a "corridor for strategic competition," and even as a "potential vector for an attack on the U.S. homeland."[34] This, together with the inclusion of sections discussing increased military activity and altering Arctic governance, presented a categorically more dramatic tone than in 2016. Though the strategy granted that the "immediate prospect of conflict in the Arctic is low," the latest Arctic defense blueprint advanced the United States toward a more aggressive Arctic posture.[35] It warned of "strategic spillover" effects from tensions elsewhere and the resulting need for a "collective deterrent" among the United States and its allies and partners to balance against the great power competitors Russia and China.[36] To this end, the strategy outlined three Arctic objectives to guide future defense activities: defend the homeland, compete when necessary, and ensure common domains remain free and open.[37] Curiously, though, the 2019 strategy noted that "Russia views itself as a polar great power" even though Russia had not, in any public record, used such a term to describe itself, whereas China had—repeatedly—used this exact phrase since 2014 in self-assessing its polar status. From a military standpoint, this indicated the Department of Defense's apparent disregard for China as a military competitor in the Arctic, though China was acknowledged as an economic challenger in the region with assumed military interests. Instead, in using China's self-described term for its description of Russia, the United States pointed the scope directly at Russian Arctic military aggression as the principal challenge to US Arctic interests and set the stage for further policy action in the 2020 and 2021 iterations of the NDAA.

Compared with past NDAAs, the 2020 and 2021 laws are both saturated with Arctic references (55 in 2020; 108 in 2021). Signed into law six months after the release of the Department of Defense's 2019 Arctic strategy, the fiscal year 2020 NDAA unambiguously builds the US case and requirements for greater Arctic orientation, noting in particular that "it is the sense of Congress that the Arctic is a region of strategic importance to the national security interests of the United States."[38] The NDAA further requires the United States to "better align" military posture, presence, and capabilities to this "emerging strategic choke point of future great power competition."[39] To meet current and future Arctic challenges, the NDAA mandates an evaluation of several requirements, but few more significant than the "designation of strategic Arctic ports."[40] Such language shows necessary US commitment to Arctic power projection to balance against rapid increases in Russian presence and to potentially deter continued Chinese infrastructure investment in competing locations, which is significant enough to warrant a dedicated section in the NDAA.

Section 1260E of the 2020 NDAA addresses Chinese foreign direct investment in countries of the Arctic region. The section directs the Department of Defense to commission a study examining myriad aspects of Beijing's Arctic interests, activities, and ambition. It paints a clear picture that the United States views Chinese Arctic ambition as both aggressive and subversive to international institutions and norms. The requested study examines transparency in Chinese foreign direct investment in the Arctic and, notably, the "extent to which Chinese research activities in the Arctic region are a front for economic activities, including illegal economic espionage, intelligence gathering, and support for future Chinese military activities in the region."[41] These and other reporting requirements will be part of a larger study to be released in early 2022 and will have decided effects on future US defense policies and strategies for the Arctic. The 2021 NDAA takes these requirements and adds more.

In addition to various Arctic reporting requirements, the 2021 NDAA requires the Department of Defense to assign responsibility for the Arctic region to a deputy assistant secretary of defense position. This is a significant requirement stipulating the Arctic as a domain of specific importance, rather than one traditionally relegated to a peripheral concern within the homeland defense realm of the Pentagon. The 2021 defense law also requires the establishment of an Arctic Security Center and several complementary efforts designed to better understand the evolving military, defense, and security challenges presenting in the Arctic.[42]

With all of this emphasis on the Arctic, however, there is, again and still, no mention of Antarctica anywhere in this or any other twenty-first-century NDAA, which makes the June 2020 White House memo on safeguarding US national interests in the Arctic and Antarctic regions even more interesting.

THE 2020 POLAR MEMO

The presidential "polar memo" released on June 9, 2020, is the first US presidential memorandum in the twenty-first century to specify Antarctica within the scope of national security and defense interests.[43] Though its four pages focus mostly on the need to develop and deploy a "ready, capable, and available fleet of polar security icebreakers" by 2029, the memo's inclusion of Antarctica as a national security and defense matter is significant. Whereas the host of past policies and strategies exclusively attended to Arctic matters, this polar memo hints at increasing US orientation to and acknowledgment of the emerging Antarctic situation relative to international security and global interest. This comes after a series of articles in late 2019 and early 2020 raised attention to Antarctica as another arena for future great power competition.[44]

The first of its kind, the memo charges provision of a "persistent United States presence in the Antarctic region," accelerating polar region security interests and, by including Antarctica, creating an avenue of interest and dialogue for an entirely new area, literally, of military strategy and defense policy.[45] Further, the memo directs the Department of Homeland Security, through the US Coast Guard and in consultation with the Department of Defense, to study and provide recommendations on the development of polar-class security cutters "appropriately outfitted" to meet the memo's objectives. What constitutes an "appropriate outfit" for a twenty-first-century polar icebreaker according to the Trump administration and relative to US national security interests?

The wording is subtle, but to the keen policy eye the inference is significant. The memo directs the US Coast Guard to produce an assessment of operational capabilities needed for modern icebreakers to "support national security objectives" through the use of "systems" related to unmanned aviation, surface, and undersea; space; maritime domain awareness; command and control; secure communications and data transfer; and intelligence collection. In addition to these systems requirements, the memo specifically requires an evaluation of "defensive armament adequate to defend against threats by near-peer competitors" for inclusion in the new icebreaker designs.[46]

"Defensive armament," in blunt military speak, means guns. Most commonly associated with World War II and the dog-fighting era, defensive armament on military aircraft often took the form of machine guns and cannons. For instance, through the 1970s the B-52 strategic bomber's "defensive armament" referred to its complement of .50-caliber machine guns and 20-millimeter rotary cannons. A largely antiquated term in the twenty-first century makes its use in the polar memo relative to polar-class security cutter design even more curious.

As another layer of complexity, let us recall the Antarctic Treaty's prohibition on military maneuvers. With Russian military activity in the Arctic compounded by the so-called icebreaker gap, the presence of modern icebreakers with military capabilities in the Arctic leaves little to question relative to need. But what are the national security interests of the United States in Antarctica sufficient to compel the design, development, and eventual deployment of weaponized icebreakers to the southernmost anti-militarized continent? As a prediction, if the United States at some point in the future deploys weaponized icebreakers to Antarctica, this will mark the beginning of the end of the Antarctic Treaty as we know it, and it will not be long before China, followed shortly after by Russia, will begin military maneuvers and active deployments of military force south of the Antarctic Circle. If we reach that point, military confrontation in Antarctica is inevitable. Likewise, the more aggressive the US stance becomes toward the Arctic, the closer the great powers come to open conflict. Following the release of the polar memo, the US military services each started jumping into the polar policy and strategy game—but chose only the Arctic to address.

US MILITARY ARCTIC STRATEGIES

The US Air Force became the first of the US military services to release an Arctic strategy. The July 2020 release of the Department of the Air Force's Arctic strategy follows the aforementioned White House polar memo. The Arctic strategy details the service's objectives toward a stable Arctic through four lines of effort: vigilance, power projection, cooperation, and preparation.[47] Repeating much of the 2019 Department of Defense's Arctic strategy, the US Air Force's Arctic strategy outlines the Arctic's unique geography and regional intersections between three geographic combatant commands: NORTHCOM, EUCOM, INDO-PACOM (US Indo-Pacific Command) (by including the Aleutian Island chain's link to the Arctic) and claims its "capacity as a strategic buffer is eroding," thereby creating a threat to the US homeland relative to Chinese and Russian advancements.[48] Labeling the Arctic as a "cornerstone of the nation's defense" and a "region of immense geostrategic significance," the US Air Force's Arctic strategy borders on hyperbolic rhetoric, especially in comparison to past Arctic strategies prior to the reemergence of great power competition. Not to be outdone, the US Navy released its own Arctic strategy soon thereafter.

In its "Blue Arctic," the navy outlines a strategic blueprint for the Arctic, highlighting the need to enhance presence in the High North.[49] The problem? The navy does not have icebreakers or ice-hardened hulls on its ships to enable sustained Arctic surface presence like it intends. Shortly after the navy's release and curious statements about its desire to be present in the Arctic despite lacking the requisite capabilities, the

US Army released its own version of an Arctic strategy, which it curiously titled "Regaining Arctic Dominance."

On January 19, 2021, two weeks removed from the navy's Arctic strategy, the army's analog went to press. Beyond the obvious head-scratching title implying the US Army once enjoyed Arctic dominance (it did not), the strategy is also riddled with strange statements that leaves one questioning the motivations behind the writing and whether the army can actually accomplish some of its intended lines of effort anytime in the next century. Beyond improving Arctic capabilities, competing in the Arctic, and conducting mutlidomain operations, one has to wonder how—absent even a single Arctic base anywhere on Earth—the US Army expects to "defend the far north in crisis and conflict" or "project power across the Arctic."[50] The last statement is made even stranger when one considers that the Arctic region is greater than 70 percent water. Of the remaining 30 percent of the Arctic in the land domain, where the army would operate, nearly half of this available space is Russian territory. In effect, the army intends to dominate an Arctic region where it can realistically operate in only about 15 percent of its available space—and even that estimate is exaggerated given the utter lack of suitable infrastructure from which to support and execute sustained land operations.

The Department of Defense operates on a joint force model, yet the army, navy, and air force have developed independent Arctic strategies. With this newfound and "immense" significance of the Arctic, we should expect to see corresponding narratives in future iterations of the NSS, NDS, and NMS. Until we see such corresponding language in primary-source national security and defense policies that compel budgetary commitment and tangible investments toward meeting these and other polar policy objectives discussed, all of this amounts to little more than a good idea; policies and strategies are merely words absent action. In the absence of awareness leading to advocacy to compel US action, Russia will widen the Arctic power gap while China creeps closer to a position of advantage in the High North. Meanwhile, in Antarctica, China will continue its unfettered expansion on the southern continent under the auspices of science and absent international oversight that might otherwise reveal military intentions. Russia, too, will follow China's lead in Antarctic expansion. With this, the United States must put action behind these policies and strategies.

The United States needs to view the polar regions as both providers and potential disruptors—providers in opportunity for strengthened relations with international partners and allies; providers in economic opportunity; and providers of strategic opportunities to assert US global leadership and influence. The polar regions also prove the US opportunity to establish greater capabilities in the cosmos as a critical domain to twenty-first-century security capabilities. However, the polar regions can—and will—serve as disruptors to the same absent US commitment and leadership—disruptors to international relations broadly and the strength of once firm institutions or covenants; disruptors to the global economy through malign actor influence and control of strategic throughways, commons, and resource pools; and disruptors to the global balance of power via competing claims sufficient to shift in favor of revisionist states set on supplanting Western values and asserting authoritarian models. With this in mind, let us next consider the potential realities of what great power competition in the polar regions will look like depending on US action.

Problematizing the Poles

It is a useful exercise to problematize the situation—to assess and question the factors shaping the current polar region dynamics and predict how these factors will transform the environment. The polar Cs (commons, claims, covenants, cosmos) encompass the relatively static geopolitical and environmental elements of the polar regions and provide a comparative anchor of independent variables. Returning to the polar Cs as our constant frame of analysis, there are three variable polar region outcomes depending on how states perceive and act relative to the polar Cs in the renewed great power competition: treaty-oriented stability, transactional balancing, conflict.

Treaty-Oriented Stability

Our first potential polar outcome most reflects the current environment of cooperative governance promoted through various covenants presided over by legitimized international institutions sufficient to compel compliance. Treaty-oriented stability is a status quo outcome: the continuation of applied liberal intergovernmentalism favoring "multilateral treaties and agreements, international organizations, and institutions that make rules and norms, monitor compliance with those rules and norms, resolve disputes, and provide for public, private, and club goods."[51] This model assumes the maintenance of the current world order in the polar regions absent actor deviation that would otherwise threaten regional stability. In this model, both the Arctic Council and the Antarctic Treaty, as the premier international polar institutions stipulating the rules, remain intact and legitimate. This outcome assumes each party or member state is content with the current order produced at each pole by the existence of these institutions.

In assumed satisfaction, a status quo treaty-oriented stability model further assumes continued state compliance with the established norms and written provisions of the myriad polar agreements. Under treaty-oriented stability, the polar powers in particular collectively agree that the polar regions shall remain global commons available for all to transit and benefit. The polar powers also agree to comply with the decisions, provisions, and decrees of the United Nations and other international bodies relative to matters of competing or contested territorial claims within the polar circles, despite what their policies and rhetoric imply. Moreover, under the status quo outcome, polar covenants like the Arctic Council and Antarctic Treaty remain in force, legitimately recognized by all party members. Finally, in its assumption of state compliance with the notions of global commons, claims recognition, and international covenants in the polar regions, the status quo model portends celestial stability by extension.

The cosmos is a common domain becoming more accessible. Space is now congested and competitive; it will soon be contested. The polar regions are critical to enhanced space capabilities such that they present opportunistic areas for ambitious countries to expand and improve their space power. Despite the enticing clarity of the southern skies over Antarctica for space power projection, a system of assumed treaty-oriented stability assumes polar actors will elect to voluntarily restrict their space activities and comply with the Antarctic Treaty, for instance, and refrain from using the continent as a base of military operations.

With this, the status quo outcome assumes international liberalism will prevail. It is rooted in the idea, or the hope, that multilateral agreements, institutional compliance, and international norms are sufficient to elevate the collective interests of all states above the self-interest of one. This position also assumes that global power rationality will thus ensure that self-governance prevails in the polar regions. In other words, the status quo model holds that global powers are not interested in setting the world on fire while competing for an ice bath in the north or an ice cube in the south.

There are inherent flaws in this argument that seem to disregard the behaviors and advancing rhetoric coming from Moscow and Beijing, directed at the polar regions and elsewhere. Both Russia and China, for years now, have engaged in deliberate sharp power campaigns designed to delegitimize international institutions. From Russian meddling in foreign elections to Chinese censorship of narratives critical of the Chinese

Communist Party, both have unabashedly engaged in attempts to manipulate messages and degrade the integrity of otherwise credible institutions around the world.[52] In addition to seeking to undermine confidence in institutions, Russia and China have demonstrated their disregard for international law as well as state sovereignty in other areas of the world, namely Crimea and the South China Sea, respectively. To assume either is willing to self-govern and comply with the bounding conditions of any international body again dismisses the realities of their actions and rhetoric elsewhere.

Those countering this argument cite rational actor theories and insist that even Moscow and Beijing can calculate the risks associated with departing from international institutions—the risks to their economies and diplomatic positions in particular, and thus their standing on the global power stage. Critics say that bucking the trends in this way will further alienate and decrease Beijing's and Moscow's economic power sufficient to compel compliance. As a counter to this counter, it is equally feasible to suggest Russia and China have weighed the risks and deemed the economic proposition of the polar regions greater than the potential loss of international capital stemming from their departure from international norms and laws. The idea that Moscow and Beijing will accept the continuation of a US-led unipolar movement is also flawed and inconsistent with China's and Russia's ambition toward a multipolar world order.

The status quo model leaves the United States as the team captain, so to speak, in both poles, and Russia and China as subordinate players. Russia seeks a polycentric world order whereby multiple powers seek and claim leadership in spheres of influence. China, on the other hand, makes no reservation about expressing its desire toward global hegemony. Either way, assuming Beijing's and Moscow's continued acceptance of and compliance with the status quo model is difficult, absent an aggressive shift in US rhetoric and action to compel compliance—and at this rate, Washington has demonstrated neither the capability or inclination to execute such a prescription. In the absence of US leadership and compulsion toward treaty-oriented stability, China and Russia are more likely to seek their own interests and are therefore unlikely to continue voluntary compliance with international norms, laws, treaties, or agreements in the polar regions. This is not to say, however, that this will inevitably result in conflict. Conflict is a possibility, but there is opportunity for balancing behavior to stem tension and avoid conflict, if Washington is willing to consider such an approach with what it continues to insist are adversarial actors.

Transactional Balancing

If we adopt the assumption that the first outcome of liberalist-inspired treaty-oriented stability is currently in jeopardy and thus unlikely to sustain as the dominant polar region model of governance, then the logical question is: What happens next? Given the national rhetoric to date from the three polar powers (though only the United States is a global hegemon), a second plausible outcome is a situation of transactional balancing in the polar regions. Under this system, there is a polar balance of power kept in check by a series of transaction-based agreements of shared interests. The system assumes, at best, the maintenance of the covenants like the Arctic Council and Antarctic Treaty in form, but their dissolution in actual function as effective governance mechanisms. In this way, existing treaties and councils are seen as formalities and suggestions rather than credible international institutions compelling compliance. At worst, it assumes the actual dissolution of each in both form and function, resulting in the polar regions transitioning from quasi-governed to ungoverned contested commons.

As the polar regions are contested commons with significant economic opportunity, militarization within claimed areas and aggressive resource extraction are both likely sub-outcomes. Without credible international institutions able to motivate behavioral boundaries, this will see increased military presence with nothing and nobody to prevent it. Increased militarization by one or more polar actors will inevitably motivate militarization by others. With more military posturing, the resulting dynamic will be a system of balancing whereby Russia, China, and the United States seek military presence to check against the other and ensure the security of their respective interests. Achieving a balance of power in the polar commons will necessitate transactional balancing among the various polar actors.

The dissolution of international covenants stemming from likely Russian and Chinese deviations will raise international condemnation, but finger-wagging alone will be insufficient under this model to devolve into open conflict. Transactional balancing, in this case as the product of institutional degradation, will yield complementary partnerships to existing institutions like the North Atlantic Treaty Organization (NATO). In this case, the United Nations will serve as the lead international institution in polar governance. In the interim period where the United Nations seeks to establish regional bylaws and conduct standards beyond the United Nations Convention on the Law of the Sea and the International Polar Code, allied and partner states will align capabilities toward their mutual polar interests, much as they do now but independent of the perceived shackles—or reinforcements depending on perspective—of the polar covenants.[53]

Given the potential economic gain from polar presence, interests will advance principally on transactional arrangements toward the mutual benefit of the transacting parties. These alignments will galvanize some relationships and fracture others. The contours of transactional balancing in the polar regions will determine future international relations fault lines that will undoubtedly test NATO's durability to evolving and competing international pressures, as well as its relevance to the North Atlantic region as its namesake. China's continued bilateral economic development projects with Norway and Denmark already serves as an example of transactional balancing that will strain each country's position relative to their NATO commitments. This will, in turn, force both to weigh NATO's collective security proposition relative to economic opportunity and, in some ways, improved quality of life. What Norway and Denmark decide relative to these relationships will have certain effects on the Arctic balance of power, and China is betting on and investing in it.

Another product of this system will be the marking of claims and territory via geographic boundaries enforced through military presence. Absent functioning international covenants establishing behavior boundaries, states will claim sovereignty over previously contested or unrecognized maritime regions and will ensure access to and protection of these claims through military presence and power projection. Logic holds that those states with more powerful militaries will prevail, absent conflict and on the basis of power perception and deterrence, where claims compete. The transactional-balancing model will encourage even adversarial states to engage in partnerships enabling mutual access to claimed territories, and potential resource extraction for states without claims but with other access interests.

Of course, the risk to the transactional-balancing outcome is malign states seeking expanded power and influence absent an institutional body or agreement to appease. In this way, we may see even greater Arctic presence by Russia to assert its extensive claims over the Lomonosov and Mendeleev Ridges, claims contested by Canada and Denmark. In asserting these claims, we should expect Moscow to impose taxes on transiting vessels while permitting Danish and Canadian activities in the contested zones and taxing their extractions. This will function as a transaction of mutual benefit whereby Russia receives a bounty for access to its claim and whereby Canada and Denmark maintain access to potential resources and avoid conflict with a militarily superior Russia. In Antarctica, we will likely see new Chinese claims to areas along and within the unclaimed West Antarctic Ice Sheet as a means of preventing the US projection. Beijing will likely leverage its expanding economic ties with Australia to pursue additional claims within Australia's Antarctic territory. With more infrastructure on newly claimed territory, we can expect to see Chinese military assets deployed to Antarctica under the transactional-balancing model in due time to secure rights to access and to impose restrictions or even fees on state activity within China's claims.

In effect, transactional balancing in the polar regions becomes a system of opportunistic bilateral transactionalism adhering to continually evolving norms and assumed rational behaviors seeking to avoid conflict. It is not reliant on international institutions to establish order, security, and stability and instead assumes state self-interest will generate transactional relationships toward these ends. Moreover, transactional balancing assumes a bilateral dynamic devoid of ideological restraint enabling states to interact and transact on the basis of mutual interests alone, rather than avoid beneficial partnerships solely on the basis of labeling conventions.

Some states, weighing their perceived economic gain relative to the perceived anarchy of such a model, will elect to retreat from the regions or refrain from entry. Others will cautiously wade into the fray, hoping to transact with others toward mutual gain that carries the potential benefit of both an economic boon and an alternative security blanket. The ensuing partnerships based on mutual interests within this model will undoubtedly strain NATO's legitimacy, and may, in time, even be the catalyst for its own dissolution. Under transactional balancing, factions of commonly interested states will emerge and transact on the basis of voluntary agreements rather than engage in voluntary self-constraint by way of being party to signed treaties. In this form of self-governance, states operate in their self-interest first—as is their inherent nature—but with the presumption of shared interests leading to mutually beneficial relational dynamics sufficient to, in time, produce normative structures that will eventually set the behavioral bounds and expectations for polar region activities.

I discuss the notion of transactional balancing as a workable theoretical construct in greater detail in Chapter 7. For now, transactional balancing in the polar regions has the potential to fundamentally alter global alliance and partner networks and create spillover effects in other regions. It is not inconceivable to imagine a successful model in this vein that establishes strong Euro-Asian partnerships promoted by Chinese connections to and with Norway, France, and the United Kingdom as influencers in the region. Russo-Sino relations may also blossom from a fractious "strategic partnership" to something more established and stable under such a model. Other dynamics such as Russian-Norwegian relations may improve, just as likely as they may strain. It is entirely speculative, but also not entirely implausible.

In theory, this model is attractive for a host of reasons, but principally because it assumes a system of advancing reciprocal relations based on mutual interests by way of informal but normative transactions enabled via laissez-faire approaches allowing the system to define itself and its expectations. Though such an outcome is, at least for a brief period, conceivable, it assumes that the regional balance of power can and will be maintained better by government abstention from polar region geopolitics. While this may be the case for a time, the notion of a sustained power balance is inconsistent with history. In reality, the balance of power is a historical anomaly such that we cannot and should not rely on a system of laissez-faire-inspired transactional balancing to be successful in the polar regions.[54]

Polar Region Conflict

The third potential outcome for future polar region affairs is increasing competition leading to confrontation eventually resulting in military conflict. This assumes the failure first of formal institutions presiding over and maintaining the status quo at the poles. It assumes as well that the polar peer powers, among others, are unhappy with the restrictive models imposed by the polar institutions sufficient to justify their departures from each, either formally via decree or informally via deviation. Progressing from this, the conflict model further assumes that the resulting transactional-balancing construct proves insufficient to indefinitely satisfy sustained interests opening the door to conflict.

The transactional model has some flaws in that it assumes that the polar powers, left unchecked by formal institutions, will elect to pursue mutually beneficial transactions on the calculation that aggression will lead to conflict and loss, whereas avoiding conflict through state-to-state agreements would otherwise produce gains. A transactional model may work between some states, particularly those with existing partnerships or mutual interests, such as those among the NATO structure. However, it assumes that a balance of power dynamic will prevail in which the biggest and most powerful states will make and enforce the rules in the poles without so much as a challenge from weaker, less powerful states. For example, despite competing territorial claims to the Arctic, the transactional model assumes Russia might partner and transact with Canada and Norway, and that Canada and Norway—being the weaker in the relationship, will accept a subordinate and therefore less prosperous outcome as more advantageous than entering into protracted alliance-supported conflict to achieve a marginally more desirable outcome. Maybe this will be the case; but maybe it will not.

To the south, the model also assumes that the Antarctic will eventually be militarized and parts will be claimed by China, followed shortly after by Russia, and soon the United States and other states seeking to militarize and secure economic interests in the absence of a functioning treaty system. This outcome, in assuming Antarctic militarization as a future norm, holds that military presence will produce stability of known behavioral bounds sufficient to compel distance and balance on the southernmost continent. It further assumes transactions will occur that see the likes of Australia and New Zealand, among others, partnering with China in Antarctic exploration and expanded resource extraction as the preferred alternative to protesting and possibly prosecuting a war. Russia, too, as a likely state to militarize Antarctica following China's lead, will pursue opportunities to side with potential economic partners. We do not know, however, the extent to which Moscow will align with Beijing, especially given the latest tensions between the two powers surrounding Russia's joint offshore exploration efforts with Vietnam in the South China Sea.

In July 2020, Beijing successfully pressured Hanoi into terminating its collaborative extractive venture with Russia in the South China sea, thereby effectively blocking a Russian economic opportunity and further adding tension to already uncertain Russo-Sino relations.[55] It may be that with continued strife with Beijing, Russia seeks alterative economic alignment with European states in both polar regions, and possibly even the United States in that Russia's economic position is far more fragile than China's. Moscow requires promising economic partnerships more than does China and will seek opportunities to advance its position regardless of ideological orientation. This is the essence of the transactional model.

Regardless of the economic relationships that may or may not transpire, transactional balancing assumes that the United States accepts treaty deviations and polar militarization, but deems such actions innocuous enough not to confront and challenge, or less costly than confrontation and eventual conflict. Under the Trump administration, this outcome was more plausible. Under the Biden administration's renewed policy rhetoric reinforcing the need for adherence to "sacred" international institutions, the transactional outcome is less likely.[56]

The economic proposition coupled with the potential impact to geopolitical relations resulting from transactional balancing presents significant departures from the current US-led world order. This model challenges US global leadership in assuming the dissolution of covenants that the United States once led the establishment of, thereby challenging US legitimacy and standing in the world. Assuming fractured covenants no longer regulating behaviors in the global commons, this model also raises the specter of newly restrictive maritime commons subject to great power taxation, particularly within the Arctic's increasingly accessible shipping routes and the Southern Ocean's Drake Passage. Moreover, the model increases the likelihood of competition and confrontation on the basis of contested claims in both polar regions.

As discussed, contested territorial claims repeatedly serve as the basis for conflict throughout history. We should not assume anything different with the poles. With the additional prospect and allure of improving space capabilities through expanded polar claims, the cosmos factors into the equation as an additional element compelling increased tensions in the polar regions. Considering the tensions resulting from the potential for collapsed international covenants, restricted global commons, and increasingly contested territorial claims, conflict is not only plausible, but also likely. The major detractor to this argument is the presence of nuclear weapons among a handful of the involved states. Nuclear weapons make major conflict unlikely for fear of escalation, but not improbable, especially considering the unique prospects of influence present in the polar regions for those interested in securing them first.

The prospect for polar conflict continues to evolve. The Covid-19 pandemic has only exacerbated the problem and injected more tension into the increasingly tenuous status of international institutions. With annual meetings canceled or suspended during the pandemic, states that once came together for productive international discourse resorted to attempting diplomatic dialogue from behind a computer, or elected not to participate at all. The June 2020 Antarctic Treaty consultative meeting was canceled due to Covid and replaced by an online forum.[57] The resulting effects, if any, of the alternative meetings have yet to materialize. However, similar cancelations or adjustments to diplomatic meetings, while not in and of themselves a catalyst for conflict, are certainly not helping to defuse mounting tensions in either region. Historical precedent and tradition are now in peril.

For the Arctic Council, its founding occurred in a unipolar world led by the United States and absent a near-peer great power competitor. There was no choice at the time but to comply with US stipulations. At this time, it was easy to include indigenous groups in Canada and Alaska as influential voices in Arctic affairs. Canadian Inuit, in particular, made a transition to quasi-sovereignty under the council's creation and enjoyed then as they do now recognition as a standing international body with a heard voice in Arctic affairs. Across the Atlantic, the domestic politics and interests of the European Arctic states were satisfied by the council's charter. With the ongoing transition to an increasingly multipolar world, the international situation is far less defined and predictable.

As the polar environments continue changing and the economic proposition evolves, it is hard to imagine a situation whereby states, especially rising powers like Russia and China, continue to bind future basing, transit, and trade decisions to the indigenous voice represented within the frame of an increasingly weakened international institution in the Arctic Council.[58] Canada bestowed sovereignty upon the local indigenous in the Canadian Arctic at a time when the Arctic was not the focus of international commerce and competition—rather when the United States was the lone global hegemon and supported Canada absent a geographic rival. But respecting the voice of a nonstate actor is a privilege of peacetime. In the event of conflict, the indigenous voice may matter less. Canada is the principal voice of the indigenous communities and does have an ongoing rift with the United States in the Arctic that may render Canada's support for the indigenous weaker, though few want to discuss it.

Citing a long history of Inuit activities, Canada claims the Northwest Passage as territorial waters. The United States, like China and others, disputes the Canadian position, instead claiming the Northwest Passage as an international strait.[59] In the renewed great power competition and especially as Northwest Passage tensions mount, Ottawa will cling to the tethers of the NATO security blanket (as long as it exists) and the bilateral defense agreement of the North American Aerospace Defense Command (NORAD) between the United States and Canada. Despite the Inuit presence and Canada's claim to sovereignty, the Northwest Passage is one among many points of likely future tension that may spill into conflict. When that time comes, Canada is poised to reestablish governing control over the areas under likely NATO pressure. This is one of many scenarios preceding potential conflict that we must acknowledge as increasingly likely rather than continue to insist as implausible. Increasing Russian-US confrontation in the Arctic, as well, sets the stage for potential escalation.

In the midst of a growing pandemic and toilet paper battles at American big box stores in March 2020, US and Canadian fighters intercepted Russian reconnaissance planes flying near Alaskan airspace.[60] Two Russian Tupolev Tu-142 maritime reconnaissance aircraft flew within 60 nautical miles of the Alaskan coastline, breaching the Alaskan Air Defense Identification Zone barrier and triggering US and Canadian fighters to scramble to intercept the Russian aircraft. Now-retired air force general Terrance O'Shaughnessy, then commander of NORAD/NORTHCOM, testified to the House Armed Services Committee that same month that the Russian planes loitered for four hours even with US and Canadian fighters on their tails, and at about 2,500 feet above an active US naval exercise in the Arctic.[61] That US and Canadian fighters intercepted Russian aircraft near Alaskan airspace is not new. In fact, this was the second such occurrence at that point in 2020 and one of dozens of similar incidents to occur since Russia resumed long-range Arctic reconnaissance sorties in 2007.

The relative frequency of these incidents over the Arctic leads many to dismiss Russian activity as routine. In past years, perhaps this was an acceptable conclusion. Given recent developments in the Arctic, however, the United States can no longer afford to overlook continued Russian aggression in the High North. To this point, O'Shaughnessy's Arctic testimony in March 2020 was anything but passive. The general charged with defending the US homeland conveyed to lawmakers a straightforward message: that the Arctic is no longer a peaceful domain. Rather, he noted, the region is now the "principal avenue of approach we need to defend," and further referred to the Arctic as a "battlespace" and claimed that great power competition "has arrived" in the Arctic.[62] As Arctic confrontation increases, so too does the potential for miscalculation and resultant escalation. As well, further overseas operations in contested regions of the South China Sea and elsewhere risk strategic spillover into the Arctic and other regions of geostrategic significance and intersecting but currently peaceful operations such as in Antarctica.

With this, the time has passed for preventing tension in the polar regions; it is already here. It is now necessary to prepare for the reality of polar region competition, resulting confrontation, and potential conflict. The indications of conflict are mounting. We are in the midst of a US transition from hegemony and the rise of competing powers intent on changing the current world order. As Russia and China seek greater global influence and to undermine Western influence promoted via formal institutions, it is inevitable that they seek to exploit the most opportune regions—those regions where the United States currently lacks relative influence via sustained military presence to balance against and stifle rising powers. It is thus inevitable that the polar regions, in their isolation and opportunity, will become the focus of strategic competition and influence for rising great powers. In accepting this inevitability, we must next question what the future looks like relative to conflict in the polar regions and take steps necessary to manage these future challenges. Those states that anticipate change and are active in managing it will be the ones to successfully navigate and best shape the future environment toward their desired ends; those who wait and react will be caught in a trap and find themselves operating amid undesirable conditions.

Notes

1. Weingartner and Orttung. "US Arctic Policymaking under Trump and Obama."
2. Cooley and Nexon, *Exit from Hegemony*.
3. Conley and Melino, "The Implications of US Policy Stagnation."
4. Nelson, "Wanna Buy Greenland?"
5. National Security Decision Memorandum 144, "United States Arctic Policy and Arctic Policy Group," December 22, 1971, https://fas.org/irp/offdocs/nsdm-nixon/nsdm-144.pdf.
6. National Security Decision Directive 90, "United States Arctic Policy," April 14, 1983, https://fas.org/irp/offdocs/nsdd/23-2075t.gif.
7. Ibid.
8. Åtland, "Mikhail Gorbachev," p. 290.
9. Presidential Decision Directive 26, "United States Policy on the Arctic and Antarctic Regions," June 9, 1994, p. 2, https://fas.org/irp/offdocs/pdd/pdd-26.pdf.
10. Ibid., p. 5.
11. National Security Presidential Directive 66 / Homeland Security Presidential Directive 25, "Arctic Region Policy," January 9, 2009, https://fas.org/irp/offdocs/nspd/nspd-66.htm.
12. Ibid.
13. Ibid.
14. Ibid.
15. Ibid.
16. Barack Obama, *US National Security Strategy* (Washington, DC: US Government Printing Office, 2010).
17. White House, "National Strategy for the Arctic Region" (Washington, DC, 2013).
18. Ibid. p. 2.
19. US Department of Defense, "Arctic Strategy," November 2013, p. 2.
20. *National Defense Authorization Act for Fiscal Year 2016*, sec. 1068.
21. US Department of Defense, "Report to Congress on Strategy to Protect United States National Security Interests in the Arctic Region" (Washington, DC, December 2016), p. 6.

22. Ibid., pp 9–12.
23. Donald J. Trump, *National Security Strategy of the United States of America* (Washington, DC, Executive Office of the President, 2017), p. 40.
24. Ibid. p. 25.
25. Ibid.
26. Mattis, *Summary of the 2018 National Defense Strategy*, p. 1.
27. Ibid.
28. Ibid., p. 2.
29. Ibid.
30. Ibid., pp. 3, 6.
31. *National Defense Authorization Act for Fiscal Year 2020*.
32. US Department of Defense, "Report to Congress Department of Defense Arctic Strategy (Washington, DC, June 2019), p. 1.
33. Ibid., p. 4.
34. Ibid., p. 6.
35. Ibid., p. 3.
36. Ibid., pp. 6–7.
37. Ibid.
38. *National Defense Authorization Act for Fiscal Year 2020*, sec. 1752(a)(1).
39. Ibid., sec. 1753(a)(2).
40. Ibid., sec. 1753(c).
41. Ibid., sec. 1260E (b)(5)(d).
42. *National Defense Authorization Act for Fiscal Year 2021*.
43. Trump, "Memorandum on Safeguarding U.S. National Interests."
44. As noted in Chapter 4, during a public engagement in July 2019, then–US Pacific Air Forces commander General C. Q. Brown drew parallels between the Arctic and Antarctica in future great power competition, noting that "the Arctic is kind of a precursor to the way I look at the Antarctic." In October 2019, Lieutenant Colonel Jahara Matisek of the US Air Force and I published an article in the *Marine Corps University Journal* that outlines the strategic implications of Antarctica to great power competition and argues the need for an "American polar pivot," inclusive of military orientation to both polar regions. In December 2019 we published a follow-on piece with the Modern War Institute at West Point further amplifying our argument for greater Antarctic attention in national security and defense affairs. Since these publications in late 2019, there have been additional articles published in *The Atlantic, Center for Naval Analyses,* and other venues addressing Antarctica in the context of great power competition. The White House memo on the subject comes only months after the initial round of public discussion on the topic and indicates a path of expanding interest in the years to come.
45. Trump, "Memorandum on Safeguarding U.S. National Interests," p. 2.
46. Ibid.
47. Barrett, "Department of the Air Force Arctic Strategy."
48. Ibid., p. 2.
49. Braithwaite, "A Blue Arctic."
50. McCarthy, "Regaining Arctic Dominance."
51. Cooley and Nexon, *Exit from Hegemony*, p. 22.
52. Walker, Kalathil, and Ludwig, "Forget Hearts and Minds."
53. Joost Pauwelyn, Ramses Wessel, and Jan Wouters, "When Structures Become Shackles: Dynamics in International Lawmaking," *European Journal of International Law*, 25 (No. 3, 2014), pp. 733–763.
54. Kissinger, *Diplomacy*, pp. 21–22.

55. Clark, "Oil and Gas Fueling South China Sea Tensions."
56. Biden, "Why America Must Lead Again," p. 64.
57. Antarctic and Southern Ocean Coalition, "ATCM Week 2020," June 18, 2020, https://www.asoc.org/news-and-publications/latest-news/2018-atcm-2020. As of this writing, the June 2021 Arctic Treaty consultative meeting is also scheduled as a videoconference event rather than an in-person meeting.
58. Irrelevant in that the Arctic Council does not, by way of deliberate design, address defense and security issues within its forum. However, these are precisely the issues now driving much of the Arctic dialogue in the twenty-first century.
59. Burke, "The Northwest Passage Dispute."
60. Portions of the remainder of this chapter appeared previously published Burke, "Great-Power Competition."
61. US House Armed Services Committee, "National Security Challenges and U.S. Military Activity in North and South America," Washington, DC, March 11, 2020, https://armedservices.house.gov/hearings?ID=8313A04A-DB88-4037-9811-925864674E14.
62. Ibid.

6

The Polar Trap: Conditions for Conflict

OVER SEVENTY YEARS AFTER ADMIRAL CRUZEN WARNED IN 1948 of the pitfalls of confining "strategic thinking to the tropic and temperate zones," little strategic thinking or policy has been devoted to the polar regions.[1] Now the United States has a bipolar power problem in its unipolar world. The United States has demonstrated punctuations of polar interest through the years but, in the aggregate and relative to the myriad regions of sustained US presence and power projection, has been strategically apathetic toward the polar regions during most of the twentieth century and the first decades of the twenty-first.[2]

The polar regions are changing and their strategic value propositions are increasing.[3] Polar powers are orienting their policies, postures, and power projection to each region while the current international order is not an "order" at all. Absent military confrontation, the United States will not contain China. The post–World War II status quo is changing and observable effects are occurring in the polar regions. The resulting shift in polar affairs will create a system of transactional balancing as the new norm. However, if transactional balancing fails, conflict is likely.

As of this writing, the possibility of polar conflict between the United States, China, and Russia remains low due to continued emphasis on counterinsurgency, deterrence, and conventional war. However, the problem of tomorrow should be the debate of today, and tomorrow's problem increasingly looks like great power competition and potential limited conflict in the polar regions rather than the false premise of preparing for a conventional war.

Compared with Russian Arctic military posture and Chinese Antarctic orientation, the United States is behind. With recent Russian military and Chinese economic expansion, the Arctic is now *en vogue* for international security scholars and practitioners—and even a former US president.[4] In 2019, President Trump followed in Harry Truman's footsteps and quipped of his interest in purchasing Greenland. While the media mocked the president's comments at the time, they dismissed the historic precedent and strategic implications: Greenland has tremendous geopolitical and strategic value in shaping future polar dynamics in the twenty-first century and beyond.[5] And though the Department of Defense claims the "immediate prospect of conflict in the Arctic is low" and omits substantive discussion about Antarctica in its defense and security posture, the intrigue of polar conflict is generating discussion marked with passionate arguments either sounding the alarm or quieting the herd.[6]

The Polar Picture

Antarctica receives scant attention relative to the Arctic in contemporary security affairs. Unlike Antarctica, the cold Arctic is a hot topic lately. Arguments concerning potential Arctic conflict have adopted two competing positions. The first group presents what I have referred to in previous writings as an Arctic alarmist narrative of geopolitical and geostrategic interest warranting attention from the US defense establishment to thwart the potential for Arctic conflict.[7] The second group presents what I call an Arctic apologist narrative, dismissing claims of strategic competition in the High North and seemingly apologizing to the international community for the dangerous rhetoric. This group's argument borders on Arctic apathy—a belief that Arctic militarization is sensationalist rhetoric absent legitimate concern and that the United States should abstain from engaging in Arctic militarization to avoid conflict. Similar dynamics present when confronting the strategic competition descending on Antarctica. Given the divergence between the two intellectual camps and the influence each has on future polar affairs, it is prudent to consider their foundations and evolution. As we will see, each camp misses a critical commonality in their predictive end-states: regardless of whether the United States aggresses to or abstains from polar militarization, competition is happening such that confrontation is inevitable, and with confrontation comes conflict.

A Thawing Polar Debate?

In terms of potential polar conflict stemming from strategic competition, the Arctic takes center stage in the academic and policy debates of the day. The arc of the Arctic security literature swings from the bellicose alarmist viewpoint to the nonbelligerent apologist perspective, with the latter viewed as the leading collective position. The Arctic apologists suggest that the United States should not increase Arctic militarization and that any advocacy otherwise is fear-mongering and provocation, or "poking the bear."[8]

Arctic Apologists: Avoiding Confrontation

The Arctic apologist camp offers various reasons about why the United States should refrain from power projection in the Arctic, such as limited US icebreaker capabilities relative to China and Russia; overstated geopolitical significance of the Arctic; and unneeded Arctic economic resources that all collectively amount to nonintervention. Arctic apologists claim Arctic defense and security concerns to be unfounded melodrama and further accuse Arctic alarmists' claims for Arctic militarization as creating the caricature of a cold war with China and Russia over polar bears and seals.

Chapter 5's review of US Arctic policy showed an increasingly assertive tone largely in response to equally significant Russian and Chinese rhetoric. Despite the fact that US defense officials are gradually raising the Arctic profile, there is a disquieting narrative to US Arctic policy promoting a restrained approach. This camp contends that "there is no scramble for the Arctic" and that the United States must resist temptation to expand its Arctic military footprint—because doing so will provoke Russia.[9] This narrative paints the Arctic as a traditional "zone of peace" such that anything challenging it injects irrational fear.[10]

This narrative holds that Russian Arctic military expansion is innocuous and defensive, unworthy of international attention and hardly enough to compel US military posturing in response. It views Russian Arctic militarization as a means of protection and economic survival in the face of perceived rival great power expansionism in Russia's own back yard. However, apologists ignore the growing Russian military activity in the Arctic, resting their assumptions on the supposed notion of "exceptional" peace inherent in the region that somehow, by way of a fancy label, makes the region immune to conflict. Ironically, these apologists anchor their position of a peaceful Arctic to the debunked notion of Arctic exceptionalism.

In 2015, researchers at the Finnish Institute of International Affairs examined the notion of Arctic exceptionalism: a "political vision . . . as a 'zone of peace' and a 'territory of dialogue'" unlike any other region.[11] Though the Finnish scholars concluded Arctic exceptionalism to be misguided, the idea of the Arctic as a remote and peaceful domain devoid of conflict has become a dominating narrative—in part because it is true. Whereas some scholarly articles advanced this "peaceful" position in recent years, the Arctic apologist narrative has gained the most popularity in the twenty-first century.[12]

Arctic apologists have taken their arguments and filled the pages of online commentary, scholarly discourse, and even Twitter feeds. Public platforms are ripe with articles warning of the perils of Arctic militarization. Since 2015 alone, there have been dozens of pieces advancing this position. For instance, Pincus and Berbick believe that the Arctic is not a top US geopolitical priority, and encourage nonmilitarized strategic engagement.[13] Similarly, Robert Murray claimed "little to gain" for Russia if it were to engage in military conflict with North Atlantic Treaty Organization (NATO) allies in the Arctic.[14] He argued that Russian activities are a defensive effort to secure vital Arctic economic interests, and that ideas of confronting Russia only provoke tension. Stephanie Pezard echoed similar sentiments about the United States treading lightly in the Arctic to avoid unnecessary militarization and competition.[15] Pezard presented an apologist framework for avoiding Arctic competition and conflict, with a warning that "tit-for-tat dynamics (in the Arctic between U.S. and Russia) could lead to escalation."[16]

More recently, Rachael Gosnell contends that the Arctic Council has sufficiently neutralized Arctic tensions for years, as a stabilizing institutional body, although Russia's 2018 exclusion from the Arctic Security Forces Roundtable has raised the specter of hostility.[17] Dave Auerswald suggests the United States should "play the long game," contending that freedom-of-navigation operations in the Arctic with insufficient capabilities are a waste of time.[18] He contends that there would be a bigger payoff to creating a global public narrative that rejects Russia's Arctic actions rather than militarily confronting the Russian threat. To this end, others like Robert English warn of the costs of getting involved in an "Arctic arms race," arguing that doing so would be motivated by "threat inflation" and would likely amount to another of the past "foreign policy blunders" of the United States.[19]

This is not a comprehensive illustration of the commentary denouncing Arctic militarization; rather it is a mere sampling of the evolving position arguing for a passive approach to Arctic security that is—ironically—almost entirely reliant on the increasing fragility of international institutions, norms, and traditions to maintain Arctic stability. There is even an evolving phenomenon in which Arctic apologists mock Arctic alarmists through dismissive and satirical writing—a scholarly positional harrying seeking to discredit references to the Arctic as a potential geostrategic zone of competition and conflict.[20]

Dozens of pieces circulate with similar apologist positions advancing Arctic pacifism. Despite the Department of Defense's 2019 Arctic strategy (as well as the air force, army, and navy's strategies of the same tone) calling for increased Arctic awareness, enhanced Arctic operations, and rules-based order in the Arctic, the narrative has been mainstreamed as a default US Arctic policy position.[21] Whereas online commentary is littered with utopian arguments assuming geopolitical centrism and calling for a restrained approach to Arctic security reliant on institutional liberalism and diplomacy, there is comparably limited peer-reviewed academic scholarship during the similar period that does the same. Instead of the dominant position in online commentary viewing the Arctic as an insignificant, unwinnable, and low-threat region, others in both online and scholarly media argue the opposite and expect the Arctic—and its southern polar counterpart Antarctica—to be among the most important geopolitical and geostrategic hot spots shaping twenty-first-century great power competition and beyond.

Arctic Alarmists: Leverage Through Strength

Those arguing for greater US involvement in the Arctic note expanding Russian military infrastructure and Chinese economic interests for trade routes as ways the power balance can shift out of US favor absent corresponding orientation and posturing. According to this camp, Moscow's and Beijing's efforts indicate deliberate attempts to outmaneuver the United States in the Arctic. Russia, under Putin, counters the United States by engaging in political information warfare against the West. Moreover, US officials believe Russia is violating international treaties by testing low-yield nuclear weapons at an Arctic site in the Novaya Zemlya islands.[22] China, under Xi Jinping, is also undermining the United States and the West. Chinese nuclear icebreakers will likely support the clearing of maritime channels for an evolving Chinese commercial industry and trade routes. However, under the Chinese Communist Party, China will likely use its icebreakers in support of shrouded military objectives. Thus, future Chinese icebreaking and so-called commercial traffic might be a guise for positioning military assets in the Arctic, similar to the Chinese use of commercial fishing vessels in the South China Sea to veil actual military activity. With these and other activities in mind, Arctic alarmists point to the many significant geopolitical and geostrategic indicators discussed in their lobbying for Arctic importance.

Arctic security discourse tends toward climate discussions while pitting the Arctic as the pinnacle domain affected by anthropogenic changes to Earth's atmosphere. Since 2011, there have been four Arctic-focused edited volumes examining northern geopolitics, security, and climate change.[23] Though each book rebukes notions of Arctic tensions, the prevailing position contends that the Arctic is a complex domain of great power rivalry and competition spurred by environmental changes and increased access. Each text is layered with content discussing the precarious position of international laws, institutions, and norms as they seek to collectively bind Arctic actors to a codified list of acceptable activities in a unique global commons returning to relevancy in the twenty-first-century surge for resources. Whereas some, like Exner-Pirot, who notably wrote a 2018 Arctic security satire piece, outline the evolving nature of Arctic militarization as reality—despite the Arctic's long-enjoyed designation as an international "zone of peace"—they acknowledge the trends but stop short of advocating the same.[24] There are more pieces dotting the pages of scholarly journals acknowledging the same realities of renewing Arctic tensions, though few extend their arguments to suggest deliberate Arctic militarization.

Despite this prevailing hesitancy, scholars grapple with the observable realities leading to consensus conclusions that the Arctic is no longer exceptional nor is it a zone of peace. But just as they contend with Arctic security issues in myriad ways, they also—with some exceptions—hold a predominantly positive outlook advocating change and improvement to stave off future Arctic tensions and resulting conflict. Owing to their optimism, these scholars are better labeled Arctic advocates than alarmists, as they advance the dialogue in constructive ways but without blindly clinging to dated notions of Arctic stability while simultaneously seeking improvement and avoiding hyperbole.

Those who contribute to the discourse still look to great power economic interests and initiatives as conflict avoidance mechanisms, but acknowledge that these can just as easily be points of future contention if mismanaged.[25] They acknowledge the trillions of dollars of untapped Arctic natural resources ripe for exploitation by capable actors as a major motivator for further Arctic undertakings.[26] But where the Arctic advocates stop and separate from Arctic alarmists is in their perception of great power activities and underlying intent.

The Arctic alarmists perceive Russian Arctic expansionist indicators as displaying similar intent to the 2014 annexation of Crimea, while likewise extending China's actions in the South China Sea as a predictive analog for the latter's Arctic intent. Some scholars dispute the "South China Sea as a precursor to the Arctic" argument and further question the existence of a Russo-Sino alliance.[27] Noting the Russian-Chinese tensions, Arctic alarmists insist that Russia and China exhibit bandwagoning behaviors and seek to supplant the United States as the global hegemon, perceiving the Arctic as an opportunistic avenue to do so. For Arctic alarmists, establishing a military foothold now and consistent with the US Air Force's 2020 Arctic strategy calls for an expanded infrastructure base in addition to power projection, vigilance, deterrence through cooperation, and cold weather preparation.[28] Arctic alarmists remind us that Russia operates nuclear-powered submarines in the Arctic, has dozens of military facilities in its Arctic territory and a dedicated Arctic military command, and flies bomber sorties throughout the Arctic regularly. Russia is already years ahead of the United States in the Arctic.

To alarmists, Russian military efforts are a precursor for controlling the High North, challenging US command of the commons, asserting influence, and even holding the US homeland at risk. Already, Russia's military capabilities threaten the US homeland due to its "unstoppable" hypersonic ballistic missiles based in the Arctic.[29] In the words General Terrance O'Shaughnessy, former commander of US Northern Command (NORTHCOM): "the Homeland is not a sanctuary" the way it once was.[30]

Scholars will continue to debate whether the Arctic matters for the United States such that it should compel military involvement. There will continue to be disputes over Chinese and Russian Arctic ambition relative to US interests. These discussions will grapple with whether Russia aggressively seeks offensive expansion or merely defensive security for its northern territories. Others will contend with whether China—as a self-proclaimed "near-Arctic State"—actually desires Arctic influence via its Polar Silk Road (part of China's broader economic Belt and Road Initiative) or only seeks to advance its own economic position via access to Arctic resources and alternative shipping lanes connecting Asia and Europe.[31] We will continue reading about Russian icebreaker capability outnumbering that of the United States twenty to one, or even forty to one—the so-called icebreaker gap and what the United States should (or should not) do about such a capability imbalance.[32] Moreover, Arctic alarmists point to the continued Russian military buildup of Arctic infrastructure; the questionably legal control Russia claims over the Northern Sea Route; and the 2014 establishment of the Northern Fleet and its Arctic focus coupled with Moscow's planning and execution of thousands of Arctic exercises and infrastructure modernization efforts as points of attention for the evolving Arctic significance.[33]

For this side, Moscow's economic and military commitment to the Arctic indicates significant interest and intent such that the United States must not dismiss as irrelevant to future international security, especially considering that the United States is an Arctic state with a national coastline on Arctic shores. We must reject the false notion of Arctic exceptionalism as irrelevant in the twenty-first-century great power competition. Instead, we need to adopt a notion of Arctic essentialism that sees the Arctic for its value in the international security chess game, not for what we hope it will be.

Focusing the Arctic Debate on Harsh Realities of Military Power

The Arctic is the only coastal region of the United States with an active strategic competitor conducting regular military activity off the coast, and yet northern air defenses are obsolete. The North Warning System is a dated northern tier radar array spread across Alaska and Canada designed to identify incoming missile threats. The system relies on technology from the 1980s and needs to be replaced.[34] This twentieth-century system is incapable of providing sufficient warning to defend against modern Russian air- and sea-launched cruise missiles with standoff ranges able to strike North American targets from beyond the extent of existing radar coverage. The Russian hypersonic missile threat presents an objective capability that the United States cannot overcome.

Hypersonic missiles keep US planners up at night. These are dual-threat weapons combining the flightpath maneuverability of guided cruise missiles with the speed of ballistic missiles capable of suborbital trajectory. They can be used in two ways: as a hypersonic cruise missile propelled by a hydrogen propulsion air-breathing engine, or as a hypersonic glide vehicle launched via a rocket before detaching to glide to its target. Irrespective of delivery method, hypersonic projectiles can accelerate to several times faster than the speed of sound and are able to maneuver for thousands of miles in minutes, enabling them to defeat modern missile defense systems. Further compounding the threat, hypersonic missiles can be launched from land-based mobile rocket launchers or fighter aircraft, can carry conventional or nuclear warheads, and maintain precision strike accuracy to within 10 to 20 meters of their target (though Russia claims within 1 meter).[35] The United States has no publicly stated capability to reliably defend against hypersonic missiles. While some warn against "buying into the hypersonic hype" and argue instead that the threat is embellished, the United States cannot take that risk. As such, Russia's deployments of hypersonics to the Arctic should give US officials reason for concern.

In December 2019, Russia confirmed the deployment of the hypersonic Kinzhal (Russian for "dagger") air-launched ballistic missile to the Arctic.[36] The aptly-named Kinzhal can be launched from Russian fighter aircraft with a conventional or nuclear warhead traveling over 7,600 miles per hour and strike targets 1,200 miles away with precision accuracy. Another recently deployed Russian hypersonic weapon, the Avangard hypersonic glide vehicle, reportedly travels twenty to twenty-seven times the speed of sound, or 15,000 to 20,000 miles per hour, and can strike targets up to 3,700 miles away.[37] But Russia hardly needs this range to reach the United States.

Russia has an air and naval base on Wrangel Island, about 300 miles from the Alaskan coastline on the western edge of the Chukchi Sea.[38] However, such close proximity is almost irrelevant with maneuverable land- or air-launched hypersonic missiles capable of traversing the Arctic Ocean to strike their target with nuclear warheads from over 3,000 miles away in less than ten minutes. At these standoff ranges, much of Alaska is within range of the Russian Avangard if it were to be launched from any of the dozens of Russian military bases north of the Arctic Circle. These are—as Russia claims—"unstoppable" missiles that both Russia and China possess while the United States has neither a close analog nor the technology to sufficiently defend against them.

According to General O'Shaughnessy, Russian hypersonic missiles can "strike Alaska with little indication or warning."[39] The North Warning System is over thirty years old and incapable of effectively tracking and warning against modern hypersonic missiles. So, as the saying goes: the best offense is a good defense. To establish a good defense, the United States is pursuing answers to this tangible threat in the Arctic via its efforts to develop the Strategic Homeland Integrated Ecosystem Layered Defense (SHIELD), a system designed to detect and defeat threats to the United States. The problem is that, as a fanciful-sounding good defense, SHIELD is a long way from operational reality.[40] In the absence of a good defense against "advancing adversaries" in the Arctic, the United States needs a good offense in the surface domain to defend against these formidable systems. This problem is only compounded by the fact that the situation is no better in the maritime domain.

Beyond the inadequacy of the North Warning System relative to modern Russian surface strike capabilities, Russia's new submarines are quieter and more difficult for US undersea surveillance capabilities to reliably track and predict. Russian submarines can effectively maneuver undetected throughout the Arctic Ocean.[41] US naval presence in the Arctic provides a "fundamental security confidence" for US power projection, but even US naval capabilities are equally inadequate when it comes to polar operations relative to Russia and China.[42]

As Russian capabilities advance in both speed and distance, the vast Arctic—as a new "battlespace"—begins to compress.[43] Battlespace compression leads to reduced reactions times and—given US reliance on twentieth-century technology—an inability to defend the US homeland against a modernized Russian Arctic force capable of exploiting US complacency in future strategic competition. The Department of Defense insists that the 2019 Arctic strategy is rooted in and informed by the 2017 National Security Strategy (NSS) and 2018 National Defense Strategy (NDS). The first pillar of the 2017 NSS is to "protect the American people, the homeland, and the American way of life," and the first subpillar of this priority focus is to "secure US borders and territory." Despite this charge, the United States cannot meet this intent on its northern Arctic border given the current technological disparity. This is a critical vulnerability that Washington must address. In the words of O'Shaughnessy: "We cannot defend the Nation against 21st-century threats with 20th-century technology."[44]

Russian capabilities coupled with Chinese nuclear icebreakers and polar flying squadrons have collectively established a polar offset with greater polar military capabilities compared with those of the United States.[45] Measuring and understanding intent is difficult to quantify and interpret, so predicting future conflict is equally challenging. However, the Arctic alarmist argument looks at objective indicators of the polar power policies and activities in the poles, coupled with the changing geography and corresponding geopolitical environment, to inform its collective position that the Arctic is now—or soon will be—an arena for great power conflict. To this end, interpreting Arctic actions by strategic competitors is just as important as understanding their similar behavior patterns in Antarctica.

THE SOUTH POLE BLIND SPOT

Polar geopolitics with an eye toward defense and security affairs, inclusive of both the Arctic and Antarctica, is not a topic of regular debate among academics and practitioners. Few have questioned how the polar regions collectively will evolve as geopolitical and geostrategic inflexion points of strategic competition. What are the implications for Arctic competition relative to Antarctica?

Whereas Arctic security is now again a regular discussion point, Antarctic dialogue generally assumes that the Antarctic Treaty System will ensure indefinite peace.[46] The Antarctic Treaty of 1959—and its complementary agreements forming the treaty system—compose the primary regulatory framework for Antarctic activity. The Antarctic Treaty prohibits military maneuvers and specifies that military assets can be used only for assisting scientific research, logistics, and search-and-rescue missions. The Protocol on Environmental Protection to the Antarctic Treaty (or simply the Madrid Protocol), signed in 1991, designates Antarctica as a "natural reserve devoted to peace and science."[47] Thus Antarctica has been—save for a handful of singular incidents previously discussed—entirely demilitarized since the treaty entered into force in 1961.[48]

Despite the treaty's restrictions on Antarctic militarization, China's and Russia's actions elsewhere indicate their willingness to deviate from international laws, rules, and norms. Some scholars and policymakers remain committed to the assumption that China and Russia will respect international institutions, despite numerous contradictory actions.[49] Currently, Chinese actions in Antarctica blur the lines between military operations and research. Just as the Chinese expand their "civilian research presence" in the Arctic as an apparent veil for enabling future military presence tied to economic interests, they likewise appear to be pursuing a similar approach in Antarctica through expanding capabilities and infrastructure projects including research stations, airstrips, and a dedicated Antarctic air squadron in 2016.[50]

According to Anne-Marie Brady, China is "keeping other states guessing about its true intentions and interests" in Antarctica.[51] Brady and others perceive China's increased Antarctic activity—now totaling thirty-six Antarctic expeditions and counting—as posturing for exploitation after the Madrid Protocol enters a period for renegotiation in 2048, or perhaps earlier if the treaty is abandoned.[52] To this point, recall air force general Charles Brown's sentiments about questionable Chinese intent and activity in Antarctica. Speaking at the Mitchell Institute in 2019, General Brown recounted an incident in which a Chinese icebreaker experienced mechanical issues, and instead of traveling to New Zealand (the closest port of repair), it went direct to China. "Coincidence? Makes me a little suspect," General Brown stated.[53] In the context of strategic competition and the potential for future conflict, Chinese and Russian motives must be reexamined.

Chinese military ambition is global in nature. Beijing has invested (or attempted investments) in Greenland, Iceland, Canada, Nicaragua, sub-Saharan Africa, the South and East China Seas, Australia, New Zealand, Papa New Guinea, and other areas to form the linked network for the Chinese Belt and Road Initiative as the primary vehicle for advancing its global hegemonic ambitions.[54] Antarctica is no exception. Considering these and other Chinese actions, we should not be surprised that General Brown publicly states that the Antarctic is "just a number of years away" from a similar fate as the Arctic as the renewed focus of great power competition.[55]

Though Antarctica does not rival the Arctic in geographic relevance or economic importance to the United States, continued omission of Antarctica from the strategic competition narrative further enables Chinese exploitation of the ambiguities rooted in international agreements. The United States is not a near-Antarctic power by geographical standards, but by being a hegemon and defender of the commons, is a de facto near-Antarctic power.[56] There is too much at stake in the era of evolving great power competition and the evolution of space as a future conflict domain for Antarctica to remain Washington's strategic blind spot. The United States must strengthen its partnerships with New Zealand and Australia (and other near-Antarctic partners) as gateway countries for Antarctic access. The continued use of Christchurch International Airport to fly annual Operation Deep Freeze missions in support of the US Antarctic Program warrants bolstered support.[57] Scholars and policymakers must attend to Antarctica in future debates and include it in strategic discussions on polar defense and security.

Besides excluding Antarctica from the polar picture, the debate is superficial and devoid of historical context and theoretical considerations as predictors of future action. The discussion over true Russian and Chinese intent in the polar regions is ambiguous, and ambiguity begets speculation. With speculation saturating public commentary, the discourse continues to overlook the lessons of history. What about the evolving polar region dynamic parallels history, and what can we learn to offer a glimpse into the future of potential polar conflict? In terms of strategic competition and conflict, history must be included to form the predictive narrative influencing future policy and strategy. Policy that informs strategy toward particular ends is best informed by an understanding of the relevant history shaping the current environment. For the polar regions, history runs deep.

HISTORY AND CONTEXT

As discussed in Chapter 2, the United States and other states have conducted polar military operations and military-supported scientific expeditions since the early twentieth century. As more countries arrived in the polar regions, the need for international cooperation mechanisms grew. Both the Antarctic Treaty and the Arctic Council were designed as solutions to international tensions that make the polar regions a cornucopia of international relations theoretical case studies. Yet they are seldom discussed in such a manner within contemporary policy circles. Historical antecedents are often useful points of departure such that we cannot afford to continue overlooking relevant history and theory in our ongoing debate about the future strategic competition in the Arctic and Antarctica. History provides insights on how command of the commons is at stake in the polar regions, and how disagreement over who commands the commons is a reliable predictor of confrontation and eventual conflict.

From the seventeenth century to the early twentieth, the British controlled the maritime commons. Because they controlled the commons, they controlled the seas. Those who control a domain make—or at least most influence—the rules. China and Russia are attempting to establish polar dominance via their respective polar pivots. Polar presence will promote influence, which will lead to economic gain and increased global power sufficient to potentially destabilize the international system to the detriment of the West. Hegemonic stability theory holds that the world order is most stable under unipolarity with a single global hegemon. So a Chinese or Russian challenge to US command of the commons—via related challenges to or departures from the existing polar claims and international covenants—will have certain destabilizing effects.[58] Considering the tenets of long-cycle theory, since the fifteenth century, hegemonic power transitions have tended to occur, on average, every seventy-five years. It has been seventy-five years at the time of this writing since the United States assumed status as the world leader. If history is any indicator, the United States is primed for challenge to its hegemony.[59]

There are numerous warning signs of rising powers asserting regional hegemonic ambition in the Arctic and Antarctica. The budding Chinese and Russian "strategic partnership";[60] a revisionist Russia relapsing to Cold War–era aggression and rhetoric; and China's antagonistic global expansionism combined with known and demonstrated polar interests, activities, and investments demonstrate commitment to change. Revisionist states have explicitly undermined US interests in the past decade such that their ambitions cannot be dismissed as innocuous or inconsequential. The polar regions are opportunistic low-risk, high-payoff targets for China and Russia given the relative lack of US polar presence and policy commitment to the high latitudes.

Strategic competition is on the rise and the ingredients for international confrontation and eventual conflict are brewing. The polar regions, more than any other, pose the greatest threat to current US hegemony, with two rising powers challenging the current power. History again tells us, by way of Graham Allison's descriptive problem of the Thucydides Trap, that when these conditions present, the potential for conflict increases. In this way, there are indications suggesting that we are progressing toward the realization of a similar—albeit derivative—outcome that I call the polar trap.

The Polar Trap

Considering Chinese and Russian policies and actions, the polar regions are becoming easy power grabs. Whereas the United States stands as the current global hegemon, or the ruling power in historical narrative, increased activities by China and Russia in the polar regions—coupled with US strategic dithering elsewhere in the world—contribute to the necessary preconditions for realization of the Thucydides Trap. Coined by Graham Allison in 2015, the Thucydides Trap suggests that whenever the rise of an ambitious power threatens to dethrone the existence of a current hegemon, the likely result is war.[61]

According to Allison, twelve of the sixteen recorded cases of a rising power threatening a ruling one in the past 500 years resulted in war.[62] Some question Allison's assumptions, chiefly that his case-selection bias supports his theory *and* that the four cases where war did not result all occurred after 1945 where nuclear weapons changed the calculus great power wars. Still, there is empirical validity to the concept providing a template for understanding future polar power competition, and a potential polar trap under similar circumstances.[63]

The Thucydides Trap is illustrative of a security dilemma when a ruling power proactively confronts a rising power militarily, over a contested domain, thus leading to greater militarization and raising the potential for conflict. In each of Allison's cases, he identifies the period in which the conflict occurs, a ruling power, a rising power, a contested domain, and a binary outcome of war or no war. Using this framework, there are similarities to the evolving situation in the polar regions. Whereas the rise of Athens supposedly threatened Sparta and catalyzed war, continued tensions stemming from Russian and Chinese presence in the polar regions will likewise undermine US hegemony. Increased military activities by rival competitors will continue producing the conditions for confrontation.

CONDITIONS FOR THE POLAR TRAP

Allison's theory stems from his interpretation of Thucydides's writings in the *History of the Peloponnesian War*.[64] Here, Thucydides focused on the shift in the balance of power between Athens and Sparta as the basis for the eventual conflict. Allison argues that Thucydides specified two primary drivers of the dynamic leading to the trap: first, burgeoning entitlement, sense of importance, and demand for influence by the rising power, secondly coupled directly with the rising power's fear and insecurity.[65] When a rising power demonstrated each of these attributes, Allison and his research team found that they challenged—in some way—the ruling power of the time. Though Allison's team limited their study to sixteen cases, in 75 percent of the historical cases meeting these criteria, the result was war.[66] They further identified two cases in which the United States was the ruling power and was simultaneously threatened by at least one rising power: World War II and the Cold War.

In general, the international order maintains stability when states are satisfied with the order and thus adopt a status quo orientation. Threats to the international order tend to come from dissatisfied states seeking to gain more territory, better status, or different rules. Dissatisfied states, then, adopt revisionist agendas and increasingly "mount challenges against the hegemon and its order" whenever the hegemon fails to accommodate their interests or actively seeks to restrict them.[67] In this way, the circumstances of World War II are notably similar to twenty-first-century great power competition.

In World War II, the United States faced the Axis powers: a German, Italian, and Japanese alliance intent on upending Western democratic norms. In today's competitive environment, Russia and China demonstrate similar motivations. Is Russia or China baiting the United States toward conflict with one so that the other can rise to power? The nuclear tensions and military posturing of the Cold War are similar to today's contemporary security environment in that the presence of nuclear weapons alone seems to prevent large-scale military conflict for fear of irrecoverable escalation into nuclear warfare.

Whereas the existence of nuclear weapons continues to serve as a mutual deterrent, great power conflict is not a figment of twenty-first-century imagination. Rather, an emerging body of scholarship suggests that great power conflict can "unravel without anyone ever firing a shot."[68] History tells us that during periods of hegemonic transition, the hegemon

> faces increasing difficulties in maintaining its preferred international order; its relative decline encourages other states unhappy with that order to seek to renegotiate terms, build alternative arrangements of one kind or another, probe for weaknesses, and even directly challenge the dominant power or its allies. In the worst-case scenario, peaceful adjustment to the changing distribution of military and economic capabilities proves impossible; as it did in World War I and World War II, the system collapses into a devastating great-power war.[69]

After seventy-five years of hegemony, today the United States is facing difficulties against Russia and China as it seeks to maintain global leadership. History is not on Washington's side at the moment. Moscow and Beijing are working to build alternative structures that seek shifts in the global dynamic. Each continues prodding for US vulnerabilities, carried out via sharp power campaigns meant to undermine US domestic and US-led international institutions. China and Russia are actively pursuing military and economic influence efforts in the polar regions, as a perceived weakness to US primacy. Given this weakening status, Cooley and Nexon argue that US hegemony can fall via three main mechanisms, or pathways, of change: great power challenges, changing behaviors of small and weak states, and transnational contention.[70] There is evidence of each occurring in the contemporary international security environment.

Polar Pathways of Change

In terms of great power challenges (direct contestation from competing peer or near-peer states), the United States faces increasing challenges from Russia and China alike spanning economic, diplomatic, and informational strategies. Military challenges remain distanced and indirect, but confrontations between US, Chinese, and Russian forces are becoming more frequent in the Arctic and the South China Sea, respectively. China's ascent to international influence has also led to notable behavioral changes from small and weak states. As an example, eighteen of the thirty NATO member states currently have a signed memorandum of understanding to partner with China on its global Belt and Road Initiative.[71] NATO states with ties to the initiative are predominantly among those considered "weakest" within the NATO alliance, furthering Cooley and Nexon's notion of changing behaviors of small and weak states as a precursor to US hegemonic unraveling. What does China's Belt and Road Initiative and its connection to the weak states within the NATO alliance say about NATO's future stability?

According to Cooley and Nexon, transnationalism entails the destabilization of previously held norms and foreign policy frameworks. They further contend that rising powers wishing to contest the ruling power and the established order adopt "wedge" strategies to dissolve the fabric of the order and its structure.[72] Hegemons like the United States provide a collective security proposition to weaker states incentivizing allegiance absent a better alternative. This proposition provides a security blanket to small states lacking strong economies to build and maintain organically powerful militaries sufficient for their own security.

When economic powers like China enter the mix and offer financial incentives to small states, it can be a compelling and competing value proposition straining existing alliances. In a form of realpolitik, if a powerful state can offer sufficient incentive for a weaker state to question the value of its existing security blanket and ideologies, this threatens to unravel the threads of ideologically sewn alliances. That most NATO states are now, in one form or another, economically partnered with China—a country the United States now labels as its greatest potential adversary—raises question about NATO's legitimacy as an alliance durable enough to withstand Beijing's apparent economic wedge-driving.[73]

Consider as well that many of the current international institutions constituting the "connective tissue" of the contemporary international order were established during the US unipolar movement.[74] These long-standing US-led institutions are at risk of dissolving at worst, or repurposing and reorganizing at best. From 2017 to 2020, the Trump administration governed on an "America First" platform that openly denounced the value of and need for multilateralism, international organizations, alliances, and liberal values in general, viewing such arrangements as a "threat to American power."[75] As the United States backed further away from international institutions under the Trump administration, questioned alliances and partnerships, and generally condemned the international community for collectively "free-riding" on the back of the US economy, Washington gambled its hegemony to the point that it is now in peril, first and foremost by way of competition with China. Returning to Allison's indicators for rising powers challenging a ruling one and leading to war, the evidence speaks for itself.

CHINESE CONDITIONS

In developing his theory, Allison focused on China as a rising power intent on challenging the United States as the current ruling power. To this end, Allison notes that Lee Kuan Yew—whom Allison calls the "world's premier China watcher"—predicted that China's ambition is unquestionably global hegemony.[76] Adding to this, Chinese president Xi Jinping has stated—on numerous occasions—his unambiguous intent to change the world order by putting China on path to "global eminence."[77] China's growing sense of self-importance and global ambition is robust. Few doubt China's intentions of unseating the United States as the dominant global superpower. Worse, China has developed a "grievance-fueled sense of entitlement" as demonstrated in the ongoing territorial disputes in the South and East China Seas.[78]

We should consider China's behavior here and in other areas as an indicator of broadening—and largely unchecked—ambition. The United States is the only state capable of balancing alone against Beijing's ambition. However, China is leapfrogging US containment efforts and is on path to challenge US hegemony in renewed great power competition.[79] Whereas the United States maintains over 800 bases or installations worldwide, its polar region presence is comparably nonexistent.[80] Beijing knows this and is out to exploit this gap in US strategic oversight.

Absent military presence and strategic orientation to the north and south, the United States is unable to influence these areas the way it can elsewhere. Without a power to balance against at the ends of the planet, Beijing began its own polar pivot in 2017. China's self-proclaimed status as a "near-Arctic State" illustrates entitlement despite the fact that no such recognition exists.[81] A "near-Antarctic state" view is also fostered domestically in China by its sending the second largest number of tourists to Antarctica of any country, thereby familiarizing its citizens with the continent and providing a narrative of destiny for managing the future of Antarctic control.[82]

In further attempts to advance its polar influence, China's Polar Silk Road policy broadens its ambition to assert power and influence over the polar regions. China's Yellow River Research Station in Svalbard is among its most prized polar achievements. To the south, its newly developed Antarctic Air Squadron serves a research mission similar to that of the US Air Force in its logistics support of the National Science Foundation, yet questions remain about the nature of such activities due to China's ongoing efforts to conceal the extent of its Antarctic operations.[83]

Since Australia and New Zealand are members of the US-led "Five Eyes Alliance," Beijing knows in a crisis neither country would support Chinese operations in Antarctica. Hence, China appears to be laying the groundwork for supporting Antarctic operations via infrastructure projects in the South Pacific near New Zealand and Papa New Guinea. Beijing is building a port facility and—presumably—military infrastructure at Luganville Wharf in Vanuatu, a small underdeveloped island nation only a thousand miles north of New Zealand, to the concern of Australian leaders.[84] Similarly, China inked a deal with Papa New Guinea to build a "comprehensive multifunctional fishery industrial park" on Daru, a small island community just off the southern coast of Papa New Guinea and about 125 miles north of Australia.[85] This deal gives Beijing proximal access to northern Australia, and Port Darwin, where Beijing has a long-term port lease that has deterred the US Navy and Marine Corps from establishing their own infrastructure as a result.[86] The implications extend beyond Beijing's apparent attempts at driving a wedge between Australia and the US military's attempts at securing regional presence.

Daru Island sits about 4,100 miles south of China's Port of Shanghai—the world's largest container port—via maritime route. Hardly a coincidence, Daru Island sits about 4,000 miles north via maritime route of China's newest Antarctic research station, on Inexpressible Island in Terra Nova Bay in the Ross Sea, which is China's closest station to the US McMurdo Station on Ross Island.[87] In Daru Island, China gains likely dual-use (commercial and military) infrastructure at an equidistant location between its largest mainland port and its newest Antarctic research station, while also securing a location that puts it in close proximity to its Darwin port and the geographic focal point of the US Navy and Marine Corps in the region. Couple these geostrategic moves with US military commanders' concerns with China's unwillingness to allow unfettered consultative inspections of their five Antarctic research stations, per Article 7 of the Antarctic Treaty.[88] Continued Chinese secrecy in both Arctic and Antarctic activities lends further weight to the argument that Beijing's polar ambition extends beyond benign and into the malign.

Those who continue to dismiss the rise of China as a threat to the United States and international norms are not paying attention. The Chinese economy is expanding to outcompete the United States in numerous ways and depending on one's measure of economic strength.[89] In terms of gross domestic product (GDP), China's meteoric ascent since the 1980s shows no signs of leveling off. Yes, using GDP as the basis of assessing China's economic strength is unidimensional in that it only measures production and ignores costs or consumption rates, but it is nonetheless a global indicator of a state's economic productivity. Some will argue that China—due to its enormous population and consumption needs—is an inefficient economy in terms of its net indicators (or, more generally, its productivity minus its costs).[90] Whereas China's GDP makes it the second most powerful country in the world by that sole indicator, if we consider its net indicators inclusive of its productivity minus costs, Beijing's strength is far less impressive.

To this end, others contend that China is not a threat, because of its fragile economy—that the significance of its global influence is overstated on the basis of flawed logic ignorant to the realities of unquenchable resource consumption needs. However, this position unwittingly advances the argument establishing China's insecurity and increasing ambition. Despite growing economic power by way of productive measures, China shows signs of insecurity and fear of continued US hegemony and an inability to satisfy its resource needs under the continued unipolar US-led world order. China is like a swarm of locusts voraciously consuming resources, moving from one location to the next to satisfy the swarm. China seeks to enhance its global power position on the basis of a power-as-resources strategy, circumventing international institutions in the polar regions and elsewhere to serve as potential cornerstones to securing resources to satisfy this thirst.[91]

China is demonstrating strategic ambitions for challenging US hegemony. To meet its power-as-resources goal, Beijing's ambitious, entitled, self-righteous government and military pursue global influence via international infrastructure investments in an attempt to stay relevant on the global stage. China's approach to global influence through infrastructure investments via debt-trap diplomacy creates new spaces of power. Chinese actions have met the necessary preconditions for realization of the Thucydides Trap. While this so-called trap is an abstract academic conceptualization, we should consider its applicability to the polar regions. Complicating this equation is the addition of Russian ambition, which rivals, and in some areas surpasses, that of China.

Russian Conditions

While the Chinese only recently developed polar flying squadrons, purchased nuclear icebreakers, and created policies outlining their polar region interests, Russia began its own polar pivot almost two decades ago. Remember that in 2001, Russia filed the first of three unsuccessful (to date) territorial shelf claims to the United Nations (UN) seeking to extend its exclusive economic rights from the coast to the North Pole.[92] Recall also that in 2007, as if to demonstrate both its Arctic capability and intent, the Russian Federation symbolically planted its flag on the geographic North Pole Arctic seabed.[93] Such Russian symbolism extends to Antarctica as well. In 2004, Russia built an Orthodox Church in Antarctica on one of its research stations. As a year-round operation, the church services Russian researchers and is a visible demonstration of Moscow's sustainable presence and influence on the continent.[94] These self-important efforts have dovetailed with expanded military infrastructure projects in the Arctic, hostile actions in Georgia and Ukraine, and disingenuous claims that US military forces deployed to the Baltics are a threat to Russian sovereignty.[95] In raising concerns about US actions, Russia feeds the narrative that the United States is a global bully. Moscow "explicitly advocates for the end of the American-led liberal international order and a turn to polycentric world of spheres of influence and more pragmatic governing arrangements."[96] President Putin's continued anti-Western rhetoric advances the argument that Russia seeks alternative institutional structures whereby the United States no longer serves as the default leader in geopolitical affairs and where Moscow enjoys status as a regional hegemon over Eurasia and the Arctic.

Russian sense of entitlement and self-importance mirrors that of the Chinese; but given geographic proximity, coastal access, and economic importance, Russia's ambitions are focused in the Arctic rather than seeking global eminence. Moscow's aggressive posture toward the Northern Sea Route and threats to use military force against ships refusing Russian requirements indicate its intent to control what it believes it legally owns, or what it is entitled to control.[97] Such actions are a direct challenge to freedom of navigation and Washington's desire to command the commons toward this end, but Moscow pursues its agenda with supposed economic intent.

Approximately 20 percent of the Russian economy is dependent on the Arctic. The resources provide enduring Arctic interest for Russia to continue its contested claims to the High North. With the Russian economy tied the "primordial homeland," the Arctic is a vital national interest. Considering Russia's economic dependence on natural resources, its Arctic interest is survival, as it seeks alternative means to support its economy and declining population. This, coupled with Russia's plans to link its control of the Northern Sea Route with China's Polar Silk Road, indicates a major initiative to influence and control evolving Arctic economic activities.[98] Expanding Russian Arctic military infrastructure will make this a natural outcome, as Russia's unfettered ability to operate in the region will give it power to dictate Arctic rules.

Following the reopening of Cold War–era Arctic military bases and an expanded Arctic footprint, Russia's intent to militarize the Arctic and secure its security interests is broadly advertised. Such a rapid and extensive military infrastructure investment in a targeted region indicates insecurity fueled by a desire to control and exercise sovereignty throughout the High North. Russia's fear of losing—or intent on maintaining—Arctic influence is undeniable.[99] Adding to their physical infrastructure, the Russians have reorganized northern military units and expanded their Arctic asset portfolio in attempts to assert military dominance in the region. The Northern Fleet is the "largest, most powerful, and most modern" of the Russian naval forces, with daily activity throughout the Arctic, though it is not a large fleet in comparison to US naval fleets.[100] In Antarctica, Russia leverages its status as an Antarctic Treaty signatory to influence Antarctic operations in pursuit of its own objectives, despite disagreements with New Zealand and others.[101]

Moscow demonstrated its assertiveness with the December 2019 announcement about operational hypersonic missile deployments in the Arctic.[102] Beyond this, Russia's icebreaker fleet is the largest in the world and growing; it has extensive air defense and electronic warfare capabilities, and its concern about US ballistic missile submarine deployments is well known.[103] As Russia expands the "Ice Curtain," fear and insecurity fuel a military deterrent project in the Arctic. In other words: Russia seeks an aggressive-*looking* Arctic military posture to deter others and to maintain resource access. Russia's economic instability and dependence on the Arctic's natural resources make influence over the Arctic imperative for future national growth and sustainment. However, military expansion alone does not indicate hostile intent.

There is credence to the idea that Arctic conflict is the last thing Russia wants, because war would degrade Russia's economic stability. Still, a militarily ambitious Russia in the Arctic—even if seeking only to deter others—has had the opposite effect. Rather than preventing increased militarization from NATO, the United States and its allies have expanded their Arctic postures and orientation. The security dilemma is now a polar dilemma. Russian Arctic aggression rises to Thucydidean proportion with indicators of intent to aggress toward a situation in which the United States is in a regionally subordinate role.

A potential or attempted shift in the balance of power—as Allison observed in his chosen cases—between today's rivals grows more likely with each passing year of investments in Arctic capabilities. Applying Allison's framework to the polar regions illustrates a rising Chinese power intent on securing influence in both the Arctic and

Antarctica by way of polar flying squadrons; a Polar Silk Road policy; expanding investment in Greenland and Iceland; and a self-proclaimed label as a "near-Arctic state." Likewise, Russia's widening and contested claims to Arctic territory, combined with its buildup of military infrastructure in an effort to secure its posture and interest in the region, make for an equally compelling concern indicative of an increasingly self-important state motivated in part by fear and insecurity. In this context, competing interests and actions toward the polar regions to date are beginning to meet Thucydides's two preconditions for realization of this so-called trap.

AVOIDING A US POLAR TRAP

Critics of Allison's Thucydides Trap argue that his vision of hegemony's rise and fall is too static, that it lacks nuance and consideration for the unique aspects of each time period and the relative dynamics shaping competition and conflict decisions.[104] Despite the critiques, Allison's frame is a useful heuristic for considering the potentialities of great power war stemming from polar region confrontation and conflict. Just as German efforts toward "political hegemony and maritime ascendancy" threatened England in the early pre–World War I era, simultaneous—and sometimes complementary—Chinese and Russian efforts to reject the current international system threaten US hegemony.[105]

Debates over the extent and intent of Chinese and Russian ambition continue. Whether either poses an existential threat to US hegemony is also debatable; but what is not debatable is that the level of Chinese and Russian polar presence, power, posture, and policy that dwarfs Washington's. There is a growing literature arguing that the US-backed world order is in decline, and that Russia and China are the principal challengers to the ecology of this order as they seek to write the obituary to US hegemony. For those rejecting notions of conflict with Russia or China, we know that it "makes no sense to think that hegemonic systems, or international orders more generally, will ever be free from violence and coercion."[106] Or more directly put: "The creation and maintenance of order involves violence and the suppression of certain interests in favor of others."[107]

The evolving situation in the polar regions is indicative of this position. China and Russia are revisionist actors. Absent attention and action by the United States toward the polar regions, Russian and Chinese geostrategic advantages will increase, and the capabilities gap will widen, to an unrecoverable point.

The polar regions are ripe for future power tensions. The year 2019 saw two major shifts in US Arctic military posturing, largely due to increased Russian activity in the High North. The 2019 announcement that the US Air Force will station F-35 squadrons at Eielson Air Force Base (Fairbanks), its northernmost Alaskan base, is a contribution to a necessary force posture capable of deterrence and response.[108] Across the Atlantic, the 2019 reestablishment of the US Navy's Second Fleet as the maneuver arm in the Atlantic and the Arctic provides a ready naval force for international power projection to ensure freedom of the seas and to act as a regional deterrent.[109] While this is not a dedicated Arctic command per se, the Second Fleet's reopening (following its 2010 closure to reallocate budgets to other priorities) is in direct response to increased Russian activity in the Arctic. Also in Europe, US rotational force deployments in the Baltics must continue, despite inflationary Russian rhetoric labeling these a "threat."[110] However, deploying 700 marines to Norway on short-duration rotations remains insufficient for Arctic deterrence, preparation for cold weather conflict, or understanding the limits of equipment and personnel in polar conditions.

US actions are akin to finger-wagging and fall short of consistent military presence, power projection, and strategic orientation. The Second Fleet's area of operations includes the Arctic, but is not dedicated to the High North as its sole operational domain. The Arctic is bisected between US European Command and US Northern Command, further bureaucratizing operational priorities and spans of control. Worse, the lack of US influence in Antarctica is even more pronounced due to current Antarctic Treaty System prohibitions on military activities. Still, China seems to be deviating from the system's restrictions, or at least stretching the allowable limits of military logistics support, and toward questionable ends. This is partly why the Trump administration released its polar memo, the first-of-its-kind White House memo on national security interests in the Arctic and Antarctica, including the hint of developing and deploying weaponized icebreakers for polar region military activities as a counter to similar Russian and Chinese development efforts.

China and Russia can exploit the Arctic and Antarctica because the United States has not prioritized them and thus lacks infrastructure, military capabilities, and policy intent necessary to counter malign actions in each region. As the United States continues meddling in the Middle East, the Russians and Chinese can secure a territorial and economic advantage in the polar regions while holding US interests at bay and under threat of attack on the homeland in Alaska.[111] In this case, we have not one rising power but two, and two rising powers that—despite tension elsewhere—have demonstrated common interest and willingness to collaborate in polar region activities. Russia and China threaten to weaken US global leadership and the United States currently lacks the capability and intent to counter revisionist behavior in the polar regions.

The United States cannot afford to adopt the apologists' passive approach toward the polar regions and falsely assume Russian and Chinese actions as benign. Such a strategic miscalculation will set the stage for future conflict. The naysayers who dismiss potential polar conflict as twenty-first-century paranoia should reconsider Graham Allison thoughts on "man's capacity for folly": "However unimaginable conflict seems, however catastrophic the potential consequences for all actors, however deep the cultural empathy among leaders, even blood relatives, and however economically interdependent states may be—none of these factors is sufficient to prevent war, in 1914 or today."[112]

In 1935, Billy Mitchell argued that Alaska was "the most strategic place in the world."[113] Years later Admiral Cruzen cautioned the United States about confining strategic thinking and military training to the tropic and temperate zones. The US defense establishment has seen this polar problem coming for decades. Now that it has arrived, it should compel action and the consideration for new approaches to meeting this evolving power imbalance. The likelihood of conflict is increasing. The United States must consider the real threat of a modern day Thucydides Trap in the polar regions. Most preconditions for realization of this trap have (or will soon) come to fruition. The United States must learn from history and act now to avoid the so-called polar trap rather than react later. Failure to act now and pursue policy actions to inform posturing, presence, and polar power projection will lead to the first geographic, geopolitical, and military power imbalance the United States has experienced in the post–World War II era. The possibility of the polar trap now raises the specter where not one but two competing powers threaten the ruling power, possibly upending the current global order. Polar conflict is not impossible or implausible; it is both possible and plausible.

Allison's research tells us that, as Cooley and Nexon assert, international orders can "undergo major shifts without a cataclysmic war."[114] However, Allison also tells us that, more often than not when a great power is threatened, avoiding conflict is the exception, not the rule. This is the mindset, the alarmist stance, the United States must adopt if it seeks to avoid the polar trap. Such an imbalance will shift the geostrategic dynamic, presenting a new kind of cold war, one that the United States is more likely to lose. Considering the polar regions as an arena for future conflict, what options exist for addressing US polar myopia?

NOTES

1. "Polar Operations" lecture delivered by Rear Admiral R. H. Cruzen (US Navy) at the Naval War College, Newport, R.I., October 6, 1948.
2. Much of this chapter appeared previously in Burke and Matisek, "The Polar Trap," *Journal of Indo-Pacific Affairs*, 4, No. 7, 2021, pp. 36–66.
3. Burke and Cretella, "Towards a Strategic Value Proposition."
4. Konyshev and Sergunin, "Is Russia a Revisionist Military Power in the Arctic?"; Gjørv, Lanteigne, and Sam-Aggrey, *Routledge Handbook of Arctic Security*.
5. Burke, "Trump's Interest in Greenland Is a Wakeup Call."
6. US Department of Defense, *Arctic Strategy* (Washington, DC, June 2019), p. 3.
7. Burke, "Great-Power Competition." While others have no doubt used the term "Arctic alarmist" in their writing, each is in reference to climate change; none that I know of have used the phrase in reference to the evolving defense and security situation in the Arctic as I did in the Modern War Institute article. Since my article was published, others have used this term in a similar fashion.
8. Devyatkin, "The Pompeo Doctrine in Effect."
9. Graham and Jaffe, "There Is No Scramble for the Arctic."
10. English and Gardner, "Phantom Peril in the Arctic." The Arctic Council has long referred to the Arctic as a "zone of peace" in its public messaging.
11. Käpylä and Mikkola, *On Arctic Exceptionalism*, p. 5.
12. Lundestad and Tunsjø, "The United States and China in the Arctic."
13. Pincus and Berbick, "Gray Zones in a Blue Arctic."
14. Murray, "Do Not Oversell the Russian Threat in the Arctic."
15. Pezard, "How Not to Compete in the Arctic."
16. Pincus, "NATO North?"
17. Gosnell, "Caution in the High North."
18. Auerswald, "Now Is Not the Time for a FONOP in the Arctic."
19. English, "Why an Arctic Arms Race Would Be a Mistake."
20. See, for example, Heather Exner-Pirot, "How to Write an Arctic Story in 5 Easy Steps," *Arctic Today*, December 4, 2018, https://www.arctictoday.com/write-arctic-story-5-easy-steps.
21. US Department of Defense, *Arctic Strategy* (Washington, DC, June 2019), p. 2.
22. "Russia 'Probably' Conducting Banned Nuclear Tests, US Official Says," *BBC News*, May 30, 2019, http://www.bbc.com/news/world-us-canada-48454680.
23. Kraska, *Arctic Security in an Age of Climate Change;* Tamnes and Offerdal, *Geopolitics and Security in the Arctic;* Gjørv, Lanteigne, and Sam-Aggrey, *Routledge Handbook of Arctic Security;* Heininen and Exner-Pirot, *Climate Change and Arctic Security*.
24. Exner-Pirot, "Between Militarization and Disarmament."
25. Nakano, "China Launches the Polar Silk Road"; Axe, "Russia Is Sending S-400 Air Defense Systems to the Arctic."
26. Dillow, "Russia and China Vie to Beat the U.S."
27. Buchanan and Straiting, "Why the Arctic is Not the 'Next' South China Sea."
28. US Department of the Air Force, *Arctic Strategy*, July 2020, p. 7, https://www.af.mil/Portals/1/documents/2020SAF/July/ArcticStrategy.pdf.
29. Nilsen, "Russia's Top General Indirectly Confirms Arctic Deployment."
30. "NORAD and USNORTHCOM Commander SASC Strategic Forces Subcommittee Hearing," April 3, 2019, http://www.northcom.mil/Newsroom/Speeches/Article/1845843/norad-and-usnorthcom-commander-sasc-strategic-forces-subcommittee-hearing.
31. Hui, "China's Arctic Policy."

32. "Major Icebreakers of the World," May 1, 2017, http://www.dco.uscg.mil/Portals/9/DCO%20Documents/Office%20of%20Waterways%20and%20Ocean%20Policy/20170501%20major%20icebreaker%20chart.pdf?ver=2017-06-08-091723-907.
33. Aliyev, "Russia's Military Capabilities in the Arctic."
34. Regehr, "Replacing the North Warning System."
35. Leonkov, "Hypersonic Throw of the 'Dagger.'"
36. Nilsen, "Russia's Top General Indirectly Confirms Arctic Deployment."
37. "Russia Says 'Avangard' Hypersonic-Missile System Now Deployed," *Radio Free Europe Radio Liberty*, December 27, 2019, https://www.rferl.org/a/russia-says-avangard-hypersonic-missile-system-now-deployed/30347625.html; "New Russian Weapon Can Travel 27 Times the Speed of Sound," *CBS News*, December 27, 2019, https://www.cbsnews.com/news/avangard-hypersonic-glide-vehicle-new-russian-weapon-can-travel-27-times-the-speed-of-sound/; "Russia Deploys Avangard Hypersonic Missile System," *BBC News*, December 27, 2019, https://www.bbc.com/news/world-europe-50927648.
38. Conley and Bermudez, "Ice Curtain."
39. US House Armed Services Committee, "National Security Challenges and U.S. Military Activity in North and South America," Washington, DC, March 11, 2020, https://armedservices.house.gov/hearings?ID=8313A04A-DB88-4037-9811-925864674E14.
40. Garamone, "Northcom Commander Calls for 21st Century Tools."
41. "NORAD and USNORTHCOM Strategy: Executive Summary," Joint Training Education and Academic Workshop (JTEAW), Colorado Springs, CO, July 2019, pp. 3–4.
42. Bouffard and Carlson, "A Surface Presence for the US Navy in the Arctic?" p. 28.
43. US House Armed Services Committee, "National Security Challenges."
44. US Senate Armed Services Committee, Subcommittee on Readiness and Management Support, "Hearing to Received Testimony on U.S. Policy and Posture in Support of Arctic Readiness," Washington, DC, March 3, 2020, https://www.armed-services.senate.gov/imo/media/doc/20-09_03-03-2020.pdf.
45. Portions of this section appeared in my previously published work Burke, "Great-Power Competition"; and Burke, "Trump's 'Super Duper Missile.'"
46. Joyner, *Antarctica and the Law of the Sea;* Hemmings, Rothwell, and Scott, *Antarctic Security in the Twenty-First Century.*
47. "The Protocol on Environmental Protection to the Antarctic Treaty," 1998, art. 2, https://documents.ats.aq/cep/handbook/Protocol_e.pdf.
48. *The Antarctic Treaty,* October 15, 1959. The treaty went into effect in 1961 for members Argentina, Australia, Belgium, Chile, France, Japan, New Zealand, Norway, the Soviet Union (Russian Federation), South Africa, the United Kingdom, and the United States. There are now fifty-four signatories. For the most up-to-date information on the treaty, see https://www.ats.aq/index_e.html.
49. Joyner, "Nonmilitarization of the Antarctic"; Carter, Brady, and Pavlov, "Russia's 'Smart Power' Foreign Policy and Antarctica"; Brady, *China as a Polar Great Power.*
50. Pompeo, "Looking North"; O'Rourke et al., "Changes in the Arctic"; Tiezzi, "China to Establish Antarctic Air Squadron."
51. Brady, *China as a Polar Great Power.*
52. The Antarctic Treaty does not expire in 2048. The Madrid Protocol (which is part of the broader Antarctic Treaty System) entered into force in 1998 and commits

Antarctica to status as "a natural reserve, devoted to peace and science" (art. 2). It enters a window for renegotiation in 2048, or "after the expiration of 50 years from the date of entry into force of this protocol" (art. 25). Additional citation: "Antarctic Mission Ends as Icebreakers Reach Home After Traveling 130,000 km in 198 Days," *China Daily*, April 23, 2020, http://www.ecns.cn/news/sci-tech/2020-04-23/detail-ifzvtuth8158877.shtml.

53. Pawlyk, "More US Military Power Needed."
54. Green, "China's Maritime Silk Road"; Volpe, "The Tortuous Path."
55. Pawlyk, "More US Military Power Needed."
56. The most southern Chinese region, Hainan, is approximately 5,800 miles from the nearest part of Antarctica. American Samoa is the nearest US territory to Antarctica, less than 4,000 miles away.
57. Kline, "Joint Task Force."
58. Webb and Krasner, "Hegemonic Stability Theory."
59. Wittkopf, *World Politics*.
60. Gorenburg, "An Emerging Strategic Partnership."
61. Allison, "The Thucydides Trap."
62. Allison, *Destined for War*, p. 41.
63. Miyake, "Thucydides's Fallacy, Not a Trap."
64. Thucydides, "The History of the Peloponnesian War."
65. Allison, "The Thucydides Trap."
66. "Thucydides's Trap," 2020, http://www.belfercenter.org/thucydides-trap/overview-thucydides-trap.
67. Cooley and Nexon, *Exit from Hegemony*, p. 55.
68. Ibid., p. 3.
69. Ibid.
70. Cooley and Nexon, *Exit From Hegemony*, pp. 87–118.
71. NATO member states with signed memorandums of understanding indicating intent to collaborate with China on its Belt and Road Initiative: Albania, Bulgaria, Croatia, Czech Republic, Estonia, Hungary, Italy, Latvia, Lithuania, Luxembourg, Montenegro, North Macedonia, Poland, Portugal, Romania, Slovakia, Slovenia, Turkey. "Countries of the Belt and Road Initiative," https://green-bri.org/countries-of-the-belt-and-road-initiative-bri.
72. Cooley and Nexon, *Exit from Hegemony*, p. 40.
73. Ridgewell, "US Labels China 'Greatest Potential Adversary.'"
74. Cooley and Nexon, *Exit from Hegemony*, p. 9.
75. Ibid., p. 15.
76. Allison, Blackwill, and Wyne, *Lee Kuan Yew*.
77. Perlez, "Leader Asserts China's Growing Presence."
78. Mazarr, Heath, and Cevallos, *China and the International Order*, p. 124.
79. Ibid.
80. Vine, *Base Nation*. According to Vine, the United States has some 800 bases and installations around the world. Of these 800 or so, it has but one military base within the Arctic Circle (Thule in Greenland). It has several sub-Arctic army and air force bases in Alaska but no coastal Alaskan defense presence within the Arctic Circle. The United States has research stations in Antarctica but no permanent military infrastructure, though it does fly air force cargo aircraft to Antarctica as part of its seasonal logistics support mission to the US Antarctic Program.
81. Hui, "China's Arctic Policy."
82. Brady, "China's Undeclared Foreign Policy at the Poles."
83. Personal communication with air force general, April 10, 2020.

84. Peltier, "China's Logistics Capabilities for Expeditionary Operations," p. 34.
85. Seidel, "China's Bold New Fishing Plan."
86. Ibid.
87. "In Pic: China's 5th Research Station in Antarctic on Inexpressible Island," February 8, 2018, http://www.xinhuanet.com/english/2018-02/08/c_136958901.htm.
88. Personal communication with air force general, April 10, 2020.
89. Allison, "The Thucydides Trap."
90. Beckley, "The Power of Nations."
91. Ibid.
92. Russia revised and refiled a similar petition to the United Nations in 2015. The United Nations has not ruled on this second petition as of this writing.
93. Parfitt, "Russia Plants Flag on North Pole Seabed."
94. "How Russians Built an Orthodox Church in the Antarctic," January 27, 2020, https://www.rbth.com/travel/331601-russian-orthodox-church-antarctic.
95. MacAskill, "Russia Says US Troops Arriving in Poland Pose Threat."
96. Cooley and Nixon, *Exit from Hegemony*, p. 25.
97. O'Rourke et al., "Changes in the Arctic," p. 25.
98. Pompeo, "Looking North."
99. Aliyev, "Russia's Military Capabilities in the Arctic."
100. Ibid.
101. Headley, "Russia Resurgent."
102. Nilsen, "Russia's Top General Indirectly Confirms Arctic Deployment."
103. Isachenkov, "Russia Voices Concern."
104. Jonathan Kirshner, "Handle Him with Care: The Importance of Getting Thucydides Right," *Security Studies* 28, no. 1 (2019): 1–24, DOI: 10.1080/09636412.2018.1508634.
105. Allison, "The Thucydides Trap."
106. Cooley and Nixon, *Exit from Hegemony*, p. 24.
107. Mukherjee, "Two Cheers for the Liberal World Order," p. 2.
108. Miller, "Eielson Reactivates Fighter Squadron."
109. "U.S. 2nd Fleet at a Glance," https://www.c2f.navy.mil/Portals/24/Documents/U.S.%202ND%20FLEET%20AT%20A%20GLANCE_28%20JAN.pdf?ver=2019-04-22-144707-180.
110. MacAskill, "Russia Says US Troops Arriving in Poland Pose Threat."
111. Burke and Matisek, "The Illogical Logic."
112. Allison, "The Thucydides Trap."
113. Murkowski, "Unveiling Arctic Legislation."
114. Cooley and Nexon, *Exit from Hegemony*, p. 56.

7

Toward a US Grand Strategy

THE POLAR REGIONS ARE COMPETITIVE AND CONTESTED, SO it follows that, assuming trends continue, polar region conflict is coming. What it will look like and how it will unfold is anyone's guess, but we can assume its inevitability based on the emerging global tensions of today's international security environment. The status quo model has come and gone. China and Russia are no longer satisfied with their positions in the international order and actively seek change via increasingly assertive international action and rhetoric. Though their respective global ambitions differ—Moscow seeks multipolarity and polycentrism whereas Beijing seeks Chinese unipolarity at best and US-Chinese bipolarity at worst—Russia and China have adopted revisionist narratives informing their approach to international relations, and the polar regions have assumed new relevance in the reemergence of twenty-first-century great power competition.

Accepting the premise that the polar regions are relevant contested commons in the crosshairs of revisionist state ambition and with the potential to serve as destabilizing regions leading to strategic spillover elsewhere, the polar trap is a plausible outcome of this evolving dynamic. With that, the United States has a decision to make: seek to maintain global hegemony, even in the polar regions, by restricting Russia and China, or seek an alternative arrangement aimed at avoiding conflict through accommodation while maintaining US interests.

To some, the latter proposition signals retrenchment, or worse: retreat. This is not the solution. Retrenchment leaves the United States vulnerable to a changing international order and one that will quickly, absent checks and balances on China in particular, descend into further anarchy. More aptly stated: "The best way to ensure the longevity of a rules based international system favorable to U.S. interests is not to retreat behind two oceans, lower American standards, or raise the tolerance level for risk."[1] However, those advocating for worldwide US power projection tend to focus on the three widely held regions assumed to be most significant to maintenance of international stability: Asia, Europe, and the Middle East.[2] But this is a regional argument emphasizing mostly sovereign state territories. It says little about the significance of the contested commons to the international order. Rather than retrench and leave the commons to the makings of an anarchic system, the United States needs a "strategic concept that informs its approach to those areas of the world that no state commands, which it does not aspire to control, but in which chaos would threaten US interests."[3]

Given the evolving nature of the international system as it pertains to emerging security challenges of the day, the promise of global stability enabled via institutional liberalism is a false premise. Those espousing the virtues of liberalism are anchored to the old way of doing things. The old way is tired. We need a new approach, a new strategic concept that recognizes the realities of the day and operates within them, rather than an approach that ignores the realities of the day in favor of an emotional plea anchored in ideology. In recognition of the geopolitical realities of the day, this strategic concept should be informed by neorealist thought streams rather than liberal idealism.

The assumptions we make to inform strategic dialogue and solutions to these challenges must be based on observations rather than emotion, on pragmatism rather than optimism. We need to see the world for what it is now and will become, not for what we want or hope it to be in the future. To this end, the world is anarchic such that the assumption of interminable international institutional legitimacy is blindly rooted in the illogical logic of global good.[4] Regardless of their public narrative, state actors today seek self-interest first and above all else. The strategic concept we adopt must reflect these assumptions and recommend the guideposts for future actions on the basis of the same. Within this thread, I propose a neorealist-inspired alternative approach that I call transactional balancing for tending to the polar regions as among the most pressing twenty-first-century security challenges for the United States.

THE REALIST CASE FOR DEALING WITH CHINA AND RUSSIA IN THE POLAR REGIONS

Some say let Russia and China have the poles, claiming that the polar regions are not in the geopolitical or strategic interests of the United States. For this camp, avoidance of the polar trap as previously discussed amounts to simply cooperating with regional actors, avoiding competition, abiding by international norms, and sidestepping confrontation to rely on legal regimes to resolve disputes. These Arctic apologists (or polar optimists if we include Antarctica) view the polar regions as cold, remote, and peaceful domains devoid of military competition. They hope for passivity as an enduring polar condition and hinge their arguments on US maintenance of international leadership and diplomacy while avoiding deliberate investment in polar military capabilities for the militarization it may produce. This position either deliberately rejects or passively overlooks the lessons of history, which is a fool's folly.

As Allison and history tell us, when a rising power threatens a ruling one, the likely result is war. While nuclear weapons and economic interdependence may serve as sufficient deterrents for rational states to avoid nuclear conflict, the prospect of military conflict below the nuclear threshold—or even the idea of "limited" nuclear war—remains. If the United States fancies itself a global power in the twenty-first century and intends to endure as such, ignoring the rise of not one but two competitors in the polar regions only enables the ascension of the threatening powers and the inevitable displacement of itself as the dominant one. International laws, norms, and treaties have not stopped Chinese and Russian actions in the South China Sea and Ukraine, respectively. What is to stop them from doing the same in the Arctic and Antarctica?

If, on the other hand, the United States acknowledges the evolving nature of the international system and the increasing cost and risk of maintaining global primacy such that it no longer seeks worldwide hegemony, then the next best option is to engage in balancing behavior and to promote a bipolar order with China as another global power where material preponderance and primacy are not required for global conditions favorable to the United States. This is a departure from longstanding US tradition but is a reflection of the times. We have to consider the reality of today's nuclear world and the now prominent and increasingly ambitious peer powers. Global rule through coercive means is unsustainable in the twenty-first century.

In 1945 the United States had a nuclear monopoly; the preponderance of global firepower; and one-third of the world's gross domestic product (GDP). The United States was the quintessential global hegemon in that it had "the ability to establish rules of action and enforce them, and the willingness to act on this ability," as it demonstrated with the use of nuclear weapons that same year.[5] The United States had unmatched economic and military power following World War II and for much of the Cold War such that primacy was not only possible, but also inevitable. We cannot say that same today.

In this way, there are alternative approaches to achieving a bipolar balance, which, according to neorealists, is the most stable type of international system.[6] Ensuring that the United States remains a global leader while avoiding the polar trap requires that it remain among the active states in the polar regions. Passively condemning Russian and Chinese action in the polar regions with stiff rhetoric from afar or promoting institutional solutions to advancing mutual polar interests absent complementary military power—as has been suggested by the majority of the scholarly base to date—is a utopian approach rooted in liberalism.

With the polar trap as a plausible if not probable outcome absent increased US attention and orientation to the polar regions, attempts at liberalism through diplomacy and cooperation are optimistically naive. Such utopianism disregards reality and does little to secure or advance US national interests. It only ensures that the United States is left behind in great polar power competition. When it comes to polar region policy and strategy, liberalism is a submissive, or worse, dismissive, approach. The United States needs to recognize twenty-first-century polar region realities, specifically in the Arctic. Russia, even in its chairmanship position from 2021 to 2023 in the Arctic Council, proffers mostly ceremonial involvement as an Arctic border state intent on maintaining self-preservation at all costs. Moscow does not abide by the pacific notion of Arctic exceptionalism and only continues military expansion, deploying more capabilities into the High North and holding swaths of the Arctic Circle at bay due to its military advantage. Whether Moscow intends to threaten the Arctic and those operating within is up for debate, but their Arctic capabilities and military posture is nonetheless formidable, as the Arctic is critical to Russia's economic survival.

The United States cannot continue its irrational reliance on the notion of Russian defensiveness and passivity in the Arctic. Moreover, the United States must see China's advancing Arctic and Antarctic policies, posture, presence, and power as the objective indicator it is: China wants to be a polar power and a world power by extension. The United States must consider the Arctic and Antarctica for what they have become: anarchic arenas of strategic competition pitting rival powers against each other. The United States needs to approach the polar regions from the neorealist lens and guide actions toward this end, actions that seek to maintain US power, security, and influence while leveraging the inherent anarchy of the international system. Continued reliance on international institutions, argued as a necessary complement to US polar interests, is insufficient in today's polar region landscape absent increased US military orientation and presence. In this way, future strategies and resulting actions should consider the polar regions for what they will be in ten to fifteen years rather than what they used to be. If the United States does not want the polar regions to descend into conflict, it must maintain influence. Realist-inspired balancing behavior and not idealistic liberalism should be the US polar prescription for the twenty-first century.

BALANCING FOR TWENTY-FIRST-CENTURY POLAR REALITIES

Current US grand strategy, namely liberal hegemony, holds that state intervention in other states' affairs—inclusive of military, economic, and diplomatic intervention—is necessary to promote a liberal world order. Liberal hegemony as practiced by the United States previous to the Trump administration viewed intervention as the means to global stability, translating into a need for US involvement in various world affairs. This approach invokes Madeline Albright's label of the United States as the "indispensable nation" with the responsibility and unmatched insight to influence local politics and promote world order favorable to the West— informed by the logic of free markets and international institutions.[7]

In essence, liberal hegemony is a platform of global democracy promotion rooted in the liberalist school's vision of the United States as the world's exemplar and one that—through institutions and cooperation— can compel equally productive and mutually beneficial behavior among other states toward global benefit. This platform sees the United States as the global hegemon, but through its ability to influence global norms, institutions, procedures, and rules toward the common good. Whereas liberalism at its core assumes that international order and conflict avoidance can be achieved through diplomacy, cooperation, and compliance with international institutions, norms, and standards, the realist platform emphasizes three pillars: anarchy, sovereignty, and power. While liberalists see the world and its many actors as seekers of peace and cooperation toward the common good, for neorealists the international environment is anarchic and decentralized in that it lacks a global governing authority. Given the lack of a universal authority, realist thought streams emphasize the pursuit of power and security to advance self-interests first, of which all states hold the same basic desires but where there are disparate capabilities among the states to achieve these needs.

Specifically, neorealists contend that the capability disparity injects fear into the system and compels states to seek ways to enhance their power relative to others. Unlike liberalists, who assume conflict avoidance is achieved through communication, the neorealist paradigm assumes competing state interests such that conflict is inevitable. Assuming the inevitability of conflict, neorealists further hold that trust among states is a false premise such that we should not assume the sanctity of institutions as reliable self-binding mechanisms of establishing order but rather non-binding "marriages of convenience."[8] Because states do not trust each other, they seek military and economic means to ensure their own survival. As more and more states seek expanded military postures, this creates an ever-increasing security dilemma and points toward eventual conflict as a result.

Considering the inevitability of conflict, neorealist policy prescriptions therefore maintain that states will pursue power thereby resulting in a unipolar, bipolar, or multipolar international balance of power.[9] Within this balancing construct, states engage in internal or external balancing where internal balancing emphasizes economic and military spending to strengthen state security and external balancing emphasizes alliance engagement and participation toward the same ends. The amount and type of balancing behaviors states engage in produces the international polarity system. Realism, broadly, was the bedrock principle of the Trump administration's foreign policy agenda and influential in producing the current geopolitical dynamic motivating the writing of this book.

In contrast to liberal hegemony's insistence on global interventionism to promote favorable world order, democracy, and the defense of human rights, realism heralds several strands of analysis with a common assumption of international anarchy and the resulting premise that states seek survival and self-interest first; to achieve each requires power. The power that states seek to achieve is relative to their perception of other states' power. This perception informs the balancing behaviors (internal/external) that states engage in toward their relative ends. The resulting effect of the combined balancing behaviors on the global stage then becomes the basis for the balance of power between and among states. For realists, balancing produces unipolar, bipolar, or multipolar dynamics.

There is opportunity to adopt a new balancing approach in the contested commons that are the polar regions today, one that detaches from entrenched ideology and seeks to promote mutually beneficial reciprocal relations between even the most unlikely parties. This new balancing concept must adequately describe the evolving nature of polar region interactions and interstate dynamics, explain why they are occurring, and sufficiently predict the likely outcomes on the basis of the same. Adopting the concept of transactional balancing, discussed as a potential outcome in Chapter 5, as the guiding approach for US polar region affairs, the United States can likely avoid the polar trap.

Transactional Balancing in the Polar Regions

Grand strategy is inflexible and mechanistic. It is a one-size-fits-all solution. The polar regions are fluid such that what might fit one day by way of strategic approach will not fit the next. The literal and figurative landscapes are too dynamic in the polar regions to insist upon an ideologically driven grand strategy. To this point, consider Eliot Cohen's insistence that the "very idea of grand strategy, then, runs on the rocks when it confronts the power of accident, contingency, and randomness that pervade human affairs."[10] The accident, contingency, and randomness are just as much constants as they are opportunities in today's world, such that we should seek an approach that leverages each as expected rather than one that seeks to mitigate chance and risk through fixed prescriptions for behavior.

Those who continue to cling to the notion of unchallenged US hegemony fail to account for the real and objective evidence of Russian anti-Western influence campaigns and China's ascendant economic influence, both of which challenge US leadership. While Russia is a descendant power that falls short of China's global influence, Moscow's regional power in the Arctic surpasses that of other states and demands attention. China's ascendance to global power status via economic presence and increasing interstate relationships weakens many of the existing partnerships and alliance structures serving as the fabric of the US-led unipolar movement. Unipolarity is eroding and power balancing evolving, and no more so than in the polar regions. This compels some level of US economic and military involvement.

The United States must maintain, at least, regional hegemony in the Western Hemisphere (including the Arctic) and a leading position in global affairs (including the Antarctic). Though no modern state will seek to emulate China's government, Beijing's rise is sufficiently influential to noticeably alter global affairs as a consequence of US strategic retrenchment. To maintain global leadership and influence does not require unipolarity on the order of that prescribed by liberal hegemony, however. Unipolar maintenance requires US military primacy in regions of geostrategic importance and complementary commitments to sustaining the legitimacy of the very institutions at risk of dissolution. Liberalism works when the United States runs the show. But today the world has reverted back to Cold War dynamics, with China arguably more powerful on a relative scale than the Soviet Union at its height during the twentieth century.

The global appetite for the post–World War II US-led institutions is not as voracious as it was in the twentieth century. Wedge-driving behaviors, deglobalization trends, and the move toward economic reshoring and regionalization strain alliances like North Atlantic Treaty Organization (NATO) and further erode partnerships.[11] As more European states consider "decoupling" from US alliances, NATO's future existence is more threatened now than ever.[12] The arguments for NATO's resilience that once carried the day are quickly becoming more tenuous. Opportunity abounds for Moscow and Beijing to establish themselves as regional and global powers, respectively. Russia and China seek to challenge the United States where it is not present and to further erode US leadership—and the polar regions and its institutions are primed for exploitation. Russia and China seek opportunity for self-advancement. The United States can choose to continue its ideologically driven resistance toward Russia and China and heighten global tensions, or it can choose to abandon ideology for opportunistic transactions—the very opportunities that will be an effective hedge against escalation and polar conflict.

Transactional Balancing Described

Transactional balancing subscribes to a bipolar vision and emphasizes restrained use of force only for targeted regions of geostrategic interest to the United States (and thus rejects liberal hegemony's insistence on global primacy). Primacy via preponderance is past its time. In a world of renewed great power competition and constantly changing global dynamics that can fluctuate on the basis of a Tweet by a world leader, we cannot subscribe to the confines of static "grand strategies" that bind our decisions to infirm ideologies. The United States must remove ideologically informed and thus restrictive grand strategy from the equation and instead pursue and generate influence through relationships with peer powers via an opportunistic mechanisms rooted in pragmatism rather than emotion.

According to Joseph Nye, US preponderance "does not constitute empire or hegemony. The US can influence, but not control, other parts of the world."[13] To influence requires power, and per Nye there are three ways to wield power toward influence: through coercion, payment, or attraction.[14] Transactional balancing offers an approach that can wield power in each of these ways, but on the basis of need and interest rather than ideology and values.

Transactional balancing resides within the neorealist assumption that international anarchy and uncertainty compel states to seek security before power and survival above all else. It is an offshoot subscribing to offshore balancing's broader framework of targeted regional involvement—rather than liberal interventionism—but one that emphasizes the global commons (and the polar regions specifically) rather than the Middle East.[15] Transactional balancing further describes a hybrid of new balancing behavior to best address the unique nature of interstate interactions in the global commons. Like offshore balancing, I root transactional balancing within John Mearshiemer's frame of offensive realism focused on seeking regional hegemony through economic and military power maximization.[16] Transactional balancing seeks a bipolar balance of power, assumes multipolarity, and accepts balancing as a natural and expected outcome of anarchy, accident, contingency, and randomness as each relates to and interacts with state self-interest. The difference here is that unlike offshore balancing and other substrands of realist thought within the broader balance-of-power theory that portend global solutions on the basis of informative frames, transactional balancing is a strategy of the commons.

Lacking territorially established regions of sovereignty and state law to govern behaviors in the commons, states are left to *consider* international laws as nothing more than suggested frames of self-binding behavioral governance mechanisms. Despite the fervent arguments of some, international law is not, in fact, law; this is a misnomer. It is time to stop assuming that the commons are the same as sovereign state territories and that law applies equally in the commons as it does in the sovereigns. Because there is no territorial sovereignty in Antarctica, the high seas (including the Arctic Ocean), outer space, or the atmosphere (the traditionally held common domains), we should not blindly assume the persistent and unchallenged sanctity of international institutions and legal codes as effective bindings of the myriad state actors operating within the commons, and within the polar circles specifically. Rather we should assume states will enter into the international and polar commons seeking their own self-interest first and will act in accordance with these interests, even at the risk of confrontation and resulting conflict. Thus, the descriptive mechanism of future state behavior in the international commons is best conceived as transactional balancing, or a quid pro quo system of state-to-state transactional interactions on the basis of perceived mutual national security interests.

Transactional balancing involves the diplomatic, military, and economic instruments of power employed in ad hoc arrangements with quid pro quo dynamics as the primary drivers of the interaction. In this model, states will interact and transact in the commons via communicated agreements, but absent the overarching label, structure, and self-binding parameters of formal institutions and instead based on self-interested logic. Transactional balancing is realist pragmatism and realpolitik rooted in the tenets of balance of power and compensation theories.

For the United States, a prescription for transactional balancing therefore has two inherent assumptions and two principal objectives. First, it assumes that states are self-interested. Second, it assumes that within the scope of self-interest, states are rational actors that will seek to avoid conflict as a primary motivator of their behavior, though they will of course posture militarily in preparation. These assumptions inform two principal objectives: promoting US national security, and promoting a favorable global power balance absent a lone hegemon. Both of these objectives are achieved via identification of and engagement in mutually constitutive arrangements with state actors in the commons and based on the assumption of the illegitimacy of international law and formal institutions.

Since the global commons are effectively lawless, transactional balancing occurs on the periphery of formal institutions. It assumes the presence of formal institutions or alliance networks in form, but not in function. Therefore, transactional balancing allows states to engage and interact with other states on the basis of mutual diplomatic, military, and economic incentive structures and the resulting balancing against other states. In this way transactional balancing can provide avenues of opportunity for traditionally adversarial states to transact with one another on a bilateral basis of common interests rather than be obstructed by arbitrary formal institutional barriers.

As a strategy of the commons, transactional balancing is bounded within and by state national security interests and is not intended as a blanket foreign policy prescription extending beyond this scope. In this way, we can consider transactional balancing relative to other forms of balancing behaviors states engage in to advance their own self-interest and security. The difference here is that as an accepted strategy of the commons for self-interest first but intended toward mutual benefit, transactional balancing can be the informative frame that avoids the tragedy of the commons, where self-interest alone prevails. The transactional nature of the concept implies multiparty benefit rather than each state pursuing its own interests to the detriment of the whole. This is a key distinction to understanding the resulting balancing behavior likely to occur under this model.

Engaging in transactional-balancing behavior occurs at the nexus of internal and external balancing. It integrates internal balancing behaviors of states seeking growth and security via increased economic and military spending with external balancing of states seeking security via involvement in military relationships aimed at checking other states' powers. Rather than choosing to internally or externally balance as a blanket ideology for achieving state security, transactional-balancing behavior satisfies both internal and external balancing's intent and sees each as occurring in concert with one another, but on the basis of a transactional arrangement.

Transacting states in the commons will seek expanded economic postures via, with, and through bilateral or multilateral interactions so as to have more to offer others within anticipated future transactional relationships. States will likewise seek expanded military footprints in the commons, spurred by increased economic means, so as to improve their security within anticipated future transactions, again on the assumption that even in a transactional arrangement, the potential for destabilization remains. The need for military posture also recognizes that interactions in the commons will occur independent of or without deference to existing, and in some cases restrictive, alliance structures. With that, external balancing via formal alliances is seen as unnecessary to meet state needs.

The problem with external balancing by way of partnerships and alliances is that it assumes static interests. In today's international security environment this is a flawed assumption and necessitates a more flexible balancing construct to enable states to pursue their interests at the time, be it the year, the month, the day, or even the hour. Because of this, transactional balancing presents an alternative to external balancing whereby states can elect to engage in bilateral transactionalism toward security interests on an as-needed basis rather than via indefinite promises that may serve as future obstacles, or worse, unwanted debts.

For example, over 90 percent of current NATO member states are unable to pay the 2 percent GDP mandate for the collective security benefit NATO provides.[17] For the majority of these states, transactional balancing offers a method by which they can instead assess their security needs relative to their means and engage in targeted transactional arrangements with whomever they choose, deliberately tailored to such needs. We can think of this as an à la carte security pursuit whereby the state gets exactly what it seeks, perhaps at a higher per-unit cost, but does not suffer from unnecessary cost outlays as it would in NATO's buffet-style venture where it may pay for things it does not want or need. This allows states to pursue balancing behaviors—via mutually beneficial transactions—when they want or need to rather than indefinitely through questionably necessary institutional commitments.

Transactional balancing enables states to approach their security interests and balance with and against other states on the basis of convergent or divergent interests. These interests may involve perceived threats and spur the desire for mutually supporting military arrangements to balance against the threat. This will also compel blocs of small and weak states to seek economic and security arrangements with more powerful states operating in the commons. In effect, we will likely see the same resulting function of numerous similar arrangements to current institutions, but they will lack the actual form of the same, thereby freeing states to engage when and how they want or are able to rather than comply with institutional mandates.

Through this approach, transactional balancing will serve as an alternative behavioral construct to the formal alliance structure in that it will produce the same net result of advancing mutual security interests among the transacting parties, but without the self-binding commitment of a signed alliance agreement. These mutually beneficial arrangements will inevitably serve as balancing constructs as they accumulate over time. Transactional relations in the commons will continue in the form of an "at will" agreement that can be terminated, broken, or otherwise rendered irrelevant at any time, for any reason, by any party to the transaction. This is, in many ways, the way the international system presently functions though few states are willing to admit it. The reality is state interests change with time and circumstance. When circumstances change, commitments change. States are fickle and cannot be bought; they can only be rented with sufficient interests to satisfy.

By way of example, let us suspend reality for a moment and ask: Can Norway possibly benefit from security transactions with Russia in the Arctic? Probably. But Norway's allegiance to the NATO alliance stands in the way. In transactional relationships, the formality of promised institutional commitments is absent from the equation, thereby removing restrictive parameters and thus allowing and even encouraging states to engage with other states toward specific ends via deliberate and targeted means. This is a more efficient and thus attractive form of international interaction through payments and attraction rather than coercion, which is the more likely outcome, at least in the international commons.

TRANSACTIONAL BALANCING EXPLAINED

Transactional balancing assumes international institutions will either dissolve or become impotent in effecting international governance and motivating (or deterring) state behavior in the future. International covenants inject numerous complications and contradictions when considered against the myriad economic, political, and security interests of the various states party to the agreement; all of which change with evolving circumstance. Assuming decades-old treaties or international forums can compel indefinite stability rejects reality while elevating the present above the past with respect to the lessons of history. Self-interest will prevail. The polar regions specifically are contested commons that—in time—will see increasingly self-interested state behavior and the resulting departures from long-standing international norms and treaties.

The United States, as an example, has led these voluntary self-binding arrangements so as not to be seen as the international bully but rather as an international big brother, a supporter of small and weak states so those with less will look more to the United States as an opportunity instead of as a threat.[18] However, in the era of strongman politics with the likes of Erdogan, Putin, and Xi Jinping, Donald Trump saw opportunity as well to preside over a "dog eat dog" world where the "sheer power of the United States will ensure that it most often comes out on top."[19] This approach established the framework for transactional balancing as something other than an absurd suggestion rooted in chaos and laid the foundation for its potential reality.

While such chaos is far less likely to occur in and between sovereign state relations, this notion of a desired international "free for all" vision lends itself toward the predicted transactional-balancing dynamic in the polar commons at the very least. Trump and his administration approached international relations as a deal-making endeavor for the duration of his term. Trump himself is a self-described negotiator and dealmaker. Trump's "America First" agenda saw the transactional aspect of a relationship as its value proposition, or in today's lexicon: What's in it for me?

Under a second Trump administration, the likelihood of a transactional-balancing dynamic would have been almost certain. Under the Biden administration, however, the future is less clear. Donald Trump did not value international agreements constraining US policy and interests.[20] A

Trump reelection would have advanced America's "What's in it for me?" mentality in foreign affairs. With Biden now in the Oval Office, he has pledged to restore the US commitment to partnerships and alliances, but the inertia toward transactionalism has increased such that it will be hard to slow.

The United States is gradually exiting from hegemony via withdrawing troops from overseas locations; withdrawing from international agreements; and increased reshoring of economic development and interests.[21] Regarding international agreements, Trump withdrew the United States—or declared intent to withdraw—from eight international organizations or treaties during his term. By way of comparison, Obama did not withdraw from any such commitment in his eight years; Bush withdrew from two; and Clinton from three in their respective times in office.[22] Whereas Trump withdrew from more international commitments than past presidents, he appeared to share similar goals as his predecessors in securing greater defense commitments from allies and advancing US manufacturing influence.

The Trump administration took action on NATO's burden-sharing arrangement and followed through on threats to reduce support for countries failing to meet the 2 percent GDP mandate.[23] Beyond NATO, Trump suggested that other countries housing US troops may soon be asked to pay the costs of US troop presence in return for the security benefit they receive.[24] What will these and other transactional demands do for the future of US global leadership? While Trump did not seek the disintegration of the so-called American bloc, his administration—with its "Principled Realism" and "America First" monikers—generally rejected the idea of "liberal internationalist globalism that seeks to fashion a world order in America's own image and spread free-market democracy around the globe using its overwhelming military primacy."[25]

Trump openly questioned the value of military deployments and overseas presence relative to national security gains. Moreover, he challenged the utility of US alliance commitments and the lacking return on investment, saying among other things, "We've made other countries rich, while the wealth, strength, and confidence of our country has dissipated over the horizon."[26] In other words, he viewed US commitments in transactional terms or, in essence, via the "What's in it for me?" test.

This transactional nature indicates an increasing risk to the mere existence of US involvement in formal alliances. It further hints to the instability of the future international order: should the US reject its own agreements and institutions, the likely result is that others will follow suit. This will either fracture the institutions themselves or inject such dissolution that we should not cling to the false hope, premise, or notion of assumed institutional stability simply because they have not been sufficiently challenged to date.

Trump's foreign policy approach rejected "ideals such as human rights or democracy in favor of transactional relationships."[27] Rather than assume the world as a global community of states interested in advancing toward the common good, the Trump administration saw the international arena as a zero-sum stage of competing interests in which states interact and transact toward their personal gains first. Trump, then, naturally approached interactions with states "on the basis of cost-benefit calculations as to how each relationship works in America's perceived economic or political interests."[28] In this way, we saw the budding framework for and continued path toward realizing the transactional-balancing outcome in the commons. Even after Trump's 2020 election defeat, his transactional approach continues to influence, and there is nowhere on the planet more primed for this type of dynamic than the polar regions. With that, what will transactional balancing look like?

TRANSACTIONAL BALANCING PREDICTED

Transactional balancing is both a prescription for and an outcome of the new world order with diplomatic, military, and economic drivers for conditions-based state security. Whereas I present transactional balancing as an implicit argument predicting future behaviors and interactions in the global commons broadly—that is, the high seas, the atmosphere, the Antarctic, and outer space—my focus here remains on the polar regions.[29] In this way, we can think of transactional balancing in the polar regions as polar balancing.

Polar balancing is region-specific transactional balancing characterized by the relational dynamic where state-to-state exchanges in the polar commons are based on the perceived national security benefit each stands to gain from the interaction and independent of institutional encumbrances. As institutions erode and states further adopt transactional balancing as the new norm in the commons, the polar regions will become arenas of both tension and opportunity, leading to a new modus operandi that could reshape our conception of international relations and power dynamics.

The polar regions are petri dishes for potential transactional relations outside the sphere of formal institutional arrangements. There are myriad state actors operating in these common domains absent legitimate governing structures with international enforcement authority. States have divergent and convergent interests and thus different and similar incentives and disincentives for action and inaction. The polar economic resource propositions by way of mineral extraction and fisheries as well as alternative shipping and overflight routes are significant incentives for polar region presence and influence. The unique nature, as well of relatively—compared with most other regions—unpopulated, uninhabited, and unexplored areas, is equally intriguing for ambitious states such that there is a broad and substantive incentive structure compelling interest, commitment, and presence in the polar regions for myriad agendas. Because the Arctic and Antarctica are different, we can and should expect a different form of balancing behavior than we see and expect elsewhere. The polar regions are in some ways today's equivalent of the Wild West—lawless, remote, and intriguing. Transactional balancing, or polar balancing, will be the new form of balancing that satisfies the central aim of internal, external, and even soft balancing as currently recognized balancing approaches in a single behavioral model.

Transactional balancing in the global commons—and polar balancing in the polar commons—will succeed via steady accumulations of bilateral micro-transactions producing outcomes advancing state security interests. With transactional balancing's objectives broadly focused on promoting US national security and a favorable global power balance absent a lone hegemon, polar balancing's objectives—as a region-specific strand of transactional balancing—are to maintain US regional hegemony in the polar regions via a military polar pivot and avoidance of uncontested regional threats first, and to preserve the international norm of freedom of navigation in polar waters second.[30] Both of these objectives can be achieved through the transactional security arrangements discussed to this point.

Under polar balancing, the US focus will be on complementary regions of critical importance in great power competition, and ones that are most geographically concerning to the United States since it no longer enjoys a status as an insular great power. This model will see mutually constitutive agreements emerge to create a new normative structure for polar region interactions in contested commons. Common interests will be the condition for common transactions. The micro-transactions and mutual benefit accumulation over time will manifest as the basis of this new operating model informing interstate behaviors. Transactions will not take the form of mutual material gain always, but will generally produce mutual benefit. There will inevitably be scenarios where one transacting party, by way of greater military and economic means, is the superior actor in the equation and thus better positioned to generate its desired outcome. In this way, the subordinate actor may elect to avoid the transaction altogether if it senses a threat. This will in turn compel the subordinate actor to seek transactions with other states to balance against the perceived threat. As a product of this balancing behavior, the originally superior state may then perceive an evolving balancing construct against itself in the region, thus compelling a more reserved approach and, by extension, reduced tension.

For instance, under the transactional model, existing tensions that tend to be exaggerated by policy hawks and politicians may, in some ways, be reduced via transactional benefits occurring outside the scope of otherwise restrictive alliances. The prospect of a US and Russian security arrangement is an albatross in today's international security environment. This is the product of NATO's existence as a collective security deterrent to balance against Russia in the European theater, and the position of the United States as the leading power within the alliance. The natural result of NATO's existence, then, is the formal designation of Russia as a US and NATO adversary and the resulting internal and external balancing behaviors we have seen since its inception that, in some ways, have done more to antagonize and alienate Moscow, thus creating a more precarious environment. This has led Moscow toward more aggressive internal balancing behavior and the equally enhanced threat to European state security. NATO no longer provides the same utility it once did, such that some European actors crave something different.

There was an appetite in the 1990s for US-led institutions like NATO when the United States was the undisputed hegemon. That hunger has been satisfied and is shifting toward a different flavor of world order. If we remove NATO from the equation, for instance, and assume an environment whereby transactional balancing occurs absent the existence of formally binding institutions, Russia may be more likely to partner with the United States and to balance against an ascendant Chinese power in the Arctic as a perceived threat to Moscow's economic interests and self-preservation. In the Antarctic, however, Russia may seek to transact with expanding Chinese presence and resulting resource access potential on the assumption of economic gain. These behaviors, while seemingly contradictory, can occur under a transactional-balancing construct given the assumed ad hoc and informal nature of the state of affairs driven chiefly by need rather than principle.

Russia is a descendant power. Its population is in decline; its economy is as well. Russia needs economic strength to ensure its own national security. With continued Sino-Russo tensions in other regions and the potential for strategic spillover into the polar regions, Moscow may come to see Beijing as a threat to its economic and security interests in the

Arctic such that it balances against it there with current NATO members. On the contrary, Russia may see China equally as an opportunity in the Antarctic such that it transacts with Beijing below 66° south latitude.

This suggestion no doubt sounds ridiculous to some, but if we consider the nature of transactional balancing as proposed—in that it is free of institutional encumbrances—states are more likely to engage in mutually beneficial transactional arrangements that would otherwise be taboo relative to current alliance structures and resulting assurances. In other words, transactional balancing promotes an international commons environment characterized by complementary arrangements among and between states that, absent this sort of balancing behavior, would traditionally be considered adversaries. The net effect of these transactional activities is conflict avoidance or at least an environment that sees Russia, China, and the United States as transacting partners rather than military adversaries. State transactional arrangements—across the military and economic spheres—may serve as a more effective form of twenty-first-century balancing construct than continued involvement in alliances toward questionable ends.

Transactional Balancing as an Outcome

To consider transactional balancing as a probable outcome in the commons, we need to know what it is and what it is not. The balancing component of the concept occurs as the transactional interactions and their outcomes accumulate over time. Because transactional balancing is epistemologically derived from the realist tradition and conception of global interactions in that states seek their own interests first and no one truly wins, balancing is a natural outcome of these many interactions over time. In the absence of international institutions and constraints, states will choose whether to engage, interact, and transact in the commons. For the polar regions in particular, state participation calculus will be largely based on a state's perception of relative gain through wading into the waters, so to speak, and seeking to interact and transact with other states through bilateral or even multilateral accords.

The reality of the current international environment is such that only a handful of states have enough military and economic clout to truly destabilize this balancing construct through hard power projection. This is how and why the United States, even in its apparent departure from global hegemony under this model, will maintain its status as a global power. This is a page straight from the Trump Doctrine in that it assumes most militarily powerful states will pursue transactional relations with each other first and otherwise "disregard or sacrifice" small and weak states lacking sufficient power for the United States to transact with and benefit from.[31] In this way, "great powers pragmatically cooperate and transact with other great powers while smaller powers lack agency and voice over broad rule-making."[32] This form of balancing results in a bipolar or even multipolar order where the United States and China at least, and possibly Russia too, enjoy coordinated agendas that while ideologically disparate will otherwise result in regional balancing at least in the polar regions sufficient to avoid conflict.

This model also assumes spheres of regional influence and mutually expectant and understood state interactions and transactions for access and resources while simultaneously stable enough to avoid military conflict and absent a lone arbitrator of rules. The additional reality is that despite increasing rhetoric of great power competition, evolving polar battlespaces, and potential conflict, polar powers Russia, China, and the United States do not aspire to polar region conflict. In the age of nuclear weapons and trends toward deglobalization, war is the least-desirable outcome. Bearing the costs of open conflict in the polar regions not only is a strain on the global economy, but also risks sowing greater strife into the security environment that will take decades to recover from. Neither Russia, China, nor the United States seek this, such that none are willing to swing the big stick and risk escalating tensions and possible military conflict in the polar regions or elsewhere, at least not yet. But miscalculations and resulting escalation could happen in the Arctic and Antarctica.

Transactional Balancing in Antarctica

If, for example, China were to—literally and figuratively—plant its flag on Antarctica, deploy military assets, and subsequently claim sovereign territory for exclusive drilling, fishery access, and other resource extraction efforts, the only states currently capable of compelling a change in Beijing's course are Russia and the United States. Herein lies the opportunity for a transactional-balancing approach to guide the way. In this example, we can and should assume that Russia will not do anything in the way of response or retaliation, as Moscow would not consider such action a threat to its security. On the contrary, Moscow may see opportunity in China's departure from a constraining international treaty in this case. Moscow will pursue this as an opportunity to transact with China as a partner in such efforts, with potentially widespread mutual benefits to both states resulting from such a partnership. Likewise, the

United States would see three options as presented in Chapter 5: do nothing, transact, or engage.

The latter of these options is unlikely. The United States would not seek to be the aggressor in such a situation. It is more likely that the United States would level condemnation on Beijing and raise the issue in a future Antarctic Treaty Consultative Meeting as a means of calling attention to bellicose Chinese activities and departures from international norms and agreements. The reality is, though, that this would have little, if any, effect, especially as China continues to galvanize its economic and diplomatic relationships with many countries that the United States would otherwise appeal to in the consultative meetings via the Belt and Road Initiative—which operates on the same ideologically-detached opportunistic bilateral transaction premise as transactional balancing.

Though the United States will do more than nothing and may initially condemn such an action as a bold challenge to the sanctity of the Antarctic Treaty, the United States would not apply compulsory power seeking to compel a change in Beijing's direction. Such a response would inevitably risk escalation and resulting military conflict—which is good for neither power. China knows that neither international finger-wagging nor compulsory power are effective or realistic US responses, respectively, to such a hypothetical scenario. Doing nothing, on the other hand, would also be a detriment to US international standing, as it would convey a pacifist and apathetic platform uncharacteristic of long-standing US global leadership. Transacting with China, however, presents an opportunity to demonstrate assertiveness and leadership that falls short of aggression while maintaining the prospect of mutual gain.

In this sort of hypothetical transactional balance, the United States may seek to bolster its existing relationships with other Antarctic players and even China itself as a means of balancing and conflict avoidance. In seeking multilateral incentive structures via interaction rather than ignorance to apparent Chinese aggression, the United States takes action and balances against China, but in a way that does not cast China as an adversary and rather as a potential transactional opportunity. This further signals to China and any other state seeking similar advancements that the United States and others will not simply turn a blind eye to such actions and will instead seek to interact and transact as well. In the event China refuses to transact and partner with others by way of an access agreement (as the most likely transaction mechanism in this case), this will only encourage more widespread transactional-balancing behaviors among other states seeking to counter a rogue state in this example. If China refuses the proposed transactional arrangement, the United States will seek alternative transactions with other Antarctic states to balance against Chinese activities. Beijing's ties with Australia, as an example, may be put to the test relative to a competing US military or economic proposition aimed at balancing against malign Chinese activities. Eventually, the accumulation of these micro-transactions and partnerships will shift out of China's favor, thus compelling a change in self-serving behaviors and likely incentivizing more transactional relations and cooperative interactions with other states. We can apply similar logic with examples for the Arctic as well.

TRANSACTIONAL BALANCING IN THE ARCTIC

Despite all the rhetoric of icebreaker gaps, a Chinese-Russian "axis," Russia's supposed Arctic grab, and even a new cold war in the Arctic, most of this amounts to uninformed sensationalism. Yes the Arctic is heating up, both literally and figuratively, such that new opportunities compel states to pay more attention to the northern latitudes. And yes there could be an Arctic meltdown in time, both literally and figuratively, resulting in international conflict, especially as we see more military activity within the Arctic Circle. We do not need a reminder of how easy it is for one miscalculation, one misstep, one misperception to catalyze military action that escalates into militarized response, which escalates further into open conflict. Existing and restrictive institutions, alliances, and state alignments are in many cases the culprit of these interstate tensions. In the absence of formal alliances like NATO pitting some states against others by way of a pen stroke, states could be free to assess their own interests without the restrictive consideration for others and thereby seek arrangements with those states most attractive to their own national security needs at any given time. This is a more attractive form of balancing, especially considering that even with NATO, as an example, tensions still present in the Arctic among supposed allies.

We typically do not consider freedom of navigation as a transactional activity. The very word *freedom* implies the exact opposite in that states are free to navigate the international high seas. However, with competing claims in the Arctic, the concept of freedom of navigation is somewhat challenged in particular areas. As a prime example, the Northwest Passage runs along the northern Canadian coastline and throughout its series of coastal islands. The passage is a continued point of tension among the United States and Canada dating back to the 1950s.

As discussed, the United States and other states consider the Northwest Passage an international strait to be navigated freely for those interested and able to do so. Canada, however, sees the passage as its own and within the Canadian exclusive economic zone. These tensions came to a head following the US Coast Guard's Northwest Passage navigation with the *Polar Sea* icebreaker in 1985. In a visible rebuke of Canadian claims to the Northwest Passage as sovereign territory, the *Polar Sea* navigated the passage from Greenland to Alaska without securing official Canadian government permission.[33] Publicly disputed, this incident raised new attention to what had been a long-standing "agree to disagree" dynamic between Washington and Ottawa on the subject of the Northwest Passage.

Years later, in 1988 and after failed Northwest Passage negotiations, then–Canadian prime minister Brian Mulroney famously said to US president Ronald Reagan about the Northwest Passage: "Ron, that's ours. We own it lock, stock, and icebergs."[34] This incident produced the 1988 agreement on Arctic cooperation between the United States and Canada stipulating that the United States would seek Ottawa's consent prior to navigating Canadian-claimed waters in the future.[35] In the 1980s, this agreement was seen as a success story, a feel-good moment of cooperation after decades of unsettled disputes. World affairs in the 1980s were not what they are today. The United States could afford to let Canada have this one back then, for the United States had other policy levers and points of leverage to advance its interests absent unfettered access to the Northwest Passage. As Arctic conditions evolve and the economic prospect of Arctic transit increases, there is increasing interest in Northwest Passage access such that the United States now wonders what it gets in return for this Arctic agreement.

Whereas Northwest Passage crossings have since occurred with little fanfare as a result of the agreement, US-Canadian tensions over the same matter continue. In May 2019, US secretary of state Mike Pompeo poured fuel into this fire in his Arctic Council speech stating that "Russia is not the only nation making illegitimate claims: the US has a long contested feud with Canada over sovereign claims through the Northwest Passage."[36] Pompeo's statement here reflected the Trump administration's continued transactional obsession informing its approach to international affairs and its deeply rooted skepticism "about regimes perceived as encumbering or restricting American freedom of action."[37] If the United States leaves the Northwest Passage to Canada and cedes its insistence of its status as an international strait, what does the United States get in return?

This was the thinking of the Trump administration and the frame by which it approached most of its interstate relations. It is the same frame that continued to influence US foreign policy in the first months of the Biden administration. Continued disagreements over the Northwest Passage provide a transactional opportunity for other states seeking to drive a wedge between the United States and Canada relations and toward their own interests. With its own claim analog on the opposite side of the Arctic by way of the Northern Sea Route, Russia sees the US-Canadian Northwest Passage rift as fertile ground for transactional opportunity with Canada, asserting that the United States disregards Canada and instead simply pays lip service to it as both a partner and an ally. With this, we should ask: What can Russia and Canada offer each other that may be compelling enough to form the basis of a transactional relationship in the Arctic and elsewhere?

Though there is a long history of tension, there is an equally long history of generally avoiding the Northwest Passage dispute in public narrative. The problem here is that attention is the enemy of apathy and ad hoc arrangements. Eventually, someone raises the issue and compels a conversation, and that conversation will more likely than not result in change. As we have seen, these conversations compelling change tend to produce outcomes in the form of treaties, agreements, and otherwise formal institutions resulting in even greater attention, scrutiny, and restriction than what was previously a stable ad hoc arrangement lacking the formality of a signed, restrictive covenant. Rules, stipulations, articles, and conditions present in these formal arrangements further narrow the scope of action, increase scrutiny in compliance, and thereby reduce and bind state behaviors. The intended purpose of the resulting institution—to formalize the previously ad hoc nature of ongoing transactions—frustrates states, further encouraging departures and deviations from the same institutions meant to bind behavior, and thus risking their very existence as a result. Would it not be better to simply avoid this churn and stick to the inherently transactional nature of state-to-state interactions in the global commons if we anticipate returning to the same ad hoc arrangements we once sought to formalize?

Transactional Balancing to Avoid Conflict

This is the future: alliances and partnerships will not be as robust as they were in the past. Blind commitments and obedience to dated alliance provisions shackle states in a dynamic and changing world teeming with opportunity. Formal institutions are in peril with continued deviations and departures. China, primarily through its ambitious Belt and Road Initiative, presents a compelling economic proposition for small and weak states that may exceed the perceived security blanket benefit provided by the structure of formal treaties and alliances such as NATO. In this way Beijing is providing small and weak states a departure incentive from alliance commitments; an attractive alternative transactional opportunity. Russia, too, will balance against anything that it perceives as a threat to its interests and self-preservation. Beijing wedge-driving in the South China Sea between Moscow and Hanoi is just one example of a tense Russian-Chinese partnership. Moscow lacks a calibrated moral compass and will go to and with whichever state can benefit it the most, regardless of ideology; its has signaled its intent toward this approach as recently as in its 2035 Arctic policy document, focused on seeking "stable and mutually beneficial partnerships."[38] If Russia perceives China as a threat to its interests, it is more likely to align, partner, and transact with the United States and others than it is to ally with China.[39]

The same can be said for other interstate dynamics that will play out in the polar regions. Even the United States today signals its dissent toward idealistic foreign policy in favor of more pragmatic and transactional relations. To this point, there is opportunity in the pragmatism of transactional balancing. Putin will align with anti-West state leaders the same as he will with Western ones, provided the price is right. With this, Russia's perception of Chinese ambition and action will determine its alignment with the Far East power. The most likely transaction arenas in the twenty-first-century great power competition include the strategic straits and resulting freedom (or restriction) of navigation of the commons stemming from competing claims, as well as access to fisheries, ports, seabeds, and the cosmos—all of which present in the polar regions as strategically valuable.

Increasing strategic values compelling more state presence and participation in polar region affairs coupled with increasingly fragile international institutions point to a future where transactional balancing is the likely outcome toward avoiding war. As a US approach, transactional balancing within the polar regions, or polar balancing, promotes a polar region balance of power favoring US security interests, but stops short of seeking global hegemony. A characteristic of the transactional nature of this method is followed by military power projection sufficient to signal a commitment to polar region presence and balance while ensuring favorable conditions for interstate activities to occur. In this way, polar balancing derives its approach from offshore balancing's emphasis on "robust nuclear deterrence [and] air power," which is highly applicable to the polar regions.[40] While Layne's original concept of offshore balancing also promoted "overwhelming naval power," achieving this—at least on the surface—in the polar regions is easier said than done, and even more questionably necessary. However, naval power projection—and military presence broadly—is required for transactional or polar balancing to occur as described.

Reorienting and enhancing nuclear deterrence and air power capabilities in the Arctic is a necessary precondition for enabling expanded naval power projection. As the Arctic continues toward ice-free summers and states seek further interests and fewer institutional constraints, naval surface power projection will become the norm in the Arctic. This is especially necessary for the United States in its commitment to homeland defense via Arctic military posturing, given that the United States is no longer the same insular great power it once was.

In 1997, Layne astutely noted: "Insular great powers are substantially less likely to be affected by instability than are states that face geographically proximate rivals."[41] At that time, the United States was an insular great power in every sense of the word. It enjoyed the relative security of weak or pacifist neighbors to its north and south as well as the expansive security of two "protective moats" to its east and west.[42] However, in 1997 the Arctic was not an evolving domain for great power competition, as its climate and year-round ice made sustained operations in the region next to impossible. Over twenty years later, geography, technological advancements, and the environmental suitability of the Arctic have changed. The climate is still challenging, the seasonal darkness still limiting, but the year-round ice is diminishing and transit routes once impassable are now open at certain times of the year.

The Arctic is now a legitimate "avenue of approach to the homeland" for an ambitious great power, and one area of the world where the United States has comparatively little military capabilities relative to the evolving threat.[43] As the revolution in military affairs changed the military dynamic and brought strategic competitors within reach from a greater distance via enhanced technology and capabilities, this notion of US insularity dissolved. Hence the United States is no longer an insular great power protected by oceans and agreeable neighboring states. US strategy and military capabilities must pivot to this northern arena of evolving geopolitical tension, while also recognizing Russian and Chinese apparent or assumed militarization activities in Antarctica as the region continues its own warming and melting trends.[44]

Changing Arctic geography and the dissemination of the revolution in military affairs mean that the United States no longer enjoys the same sense of geographic detachment or protection that it once did. Late-twentieth and early-twenty-first-century globalization trends made the world smaller, flatter, and more connected and accessible.[45] Recent twenty-first-century deglobalization trends, on the other hand, have injected increased economic and diplomatic tensions, resulting in continued internal balancing behaviors where states have independently increased their military capacities as a result of the trends toward reshoring, regionalization, and even hinted-at isolationism.[46] The polar regions matter more today than ever before, compelling a US military polar pivot sufficient to contend with the new geostrategic landscape.

US policymakers should consider transactional balancing in the polar regions as an approach to avoid the aforementioned polar trap while simultaneously seeking to balance against China while keeping an eye on Russia. To some, expanded US military presence in the polar regions risks advancing toward a new security dilemma whereby the polar regions become ensconced in the same militarized chest-puffing plaguing other areas of the world. This is a legitimate concern. The counterargument holds that if the United States fails to see the significance of the polar regions to evolving great power competition, each will succumb to the potentially malign nature of Chinese global ambition as a launching pad for unchecked power projection.

China's strategic goal is to ascend to a position of global hegemony, and its "growth as a truly global economic, political, and military power is inextricably linked to the Arctic and Antarctic."[47] For its military specifically, "polar access is vital" for China's global reach via ballistic missiles and its BeiDou satellite navigation system.[48] The United States—as a leading polar power—needs to recognize the importance of the polar regions to China's hegemonic ambition. In this same context, the United States also needs to recognize the balancing opportunity present in current and future US-Chinese polar relations. China and the United States maintain the same strategic interests in the polar regions: security, resources, and science.[49] According to Anne Marie Brady, "there is considerable potential for cooperation between China and the United States in the polar regions, but there is also significant potential for conflict where their interests diverge or clash."[50]

Since China sees the current US alliance network and Washington's strategic pivot to Asia Pacific as a threat to its national security, there is opportunity here via a transactional-balancing approach to improve US-Chinese relations through reoriented postures leveraging mutual interests. Absent a major miscalculation resulting in military escalation, the United States is not going to go to war with China in the Arctic or

Antarctica in an attempt to cling to the increasingly unsustainable premise of liberal hegemony. That said, like China and Russia, security interests for the United States are inextricably linked to and with the polar regions, such that the United States must remain influential in each.

The Need for a Pragmatic Polar Strategy

The elders of the US foreign policy regime are anchored to ideological platforms like millennials are to their cell phones. They cannot imagine a world without adherence to their chosen theory or prescription for international relations. What we are facing today is a battle of ideology versus pragmatism. Those anchored to ideology and still informing policy and strategy decisions refuse to consider alternative approaches that depart from their preferred prescriptions. A pragmatic US approach to the polar regions is necessary in the twenty-first century, one informed by international relations discourse but also willing to depart from the norm to consider alternative realties for what the polar regions will be in the next ten to fifteen years and not what we hope they will be. With that, current US foreign policy toward the polar regions misses the mark, electing to consider the Arctic and Antarctica as regions of peripheral curiosity rather than central concern in favor of continued focus toward problems of a previous generation.

China and Russia have made and continue to make hegemonic strides toward the polar regions. The United States has not executed any competing or rival pivot. Superficial defense strategies need to be inclusive of both polar regions, rather than a singular focus on the Arctic alone.[51] The United States should learn from the Australian government, which in 2016 released an Antarctic strategy and twenty-year action plan.[52] Moreover, Australian defense officials have noted that "Antarctica is especially useful for command, control, communications, computers, surveillance and reconnaissance system capabilities, as well as missile timing and missile positioning."[53] This all points to an ally accepting the burden of defense in Antarctica, but through US support. The Department of Defense must have a polar strategy document, one that coherently links the importance of each region to US influence and the future of space power.

The polar regions are the backdrop of the twenty-first-century strategic competition, and the United States is losing. To keep pace with China and Russia, the United States must invest in polar infrastructure, logistics, and military capabilities, first to enable productive transactional arrangements and second to avoid conflict. However, military investment in the polar regions is not cheap or fast and it will take years to appropriate funds and realize the benefit of such investments. In the interim, the United States must consider alternative approaches to maintaining regional influence in each polar region and a favorable balance of power in an increasingly multipolar world order. As the future of alliances is unclear, the transactional nature of geopolitics will prevail, thus compelling broadened though informal security arrangements focusing on access, navigation, and resource sharing in the international commons. In modern international politics and strategic competition, no state can achieve global hegemony. Attempting to do so is a futile enterprise mired in waste and irresponsibility. Accepting this reality is a necessity in strategic competition such that states must seek opportunistic and reciprocal arrangements via transactions.

At their core, all international interactions can be reduced to transactions. Transactional balancing satisfies the interests of the United States in seeking to remain an influential leader in polar region affairs while also providing an avenue of approach to avoid future conflict despite global instability and lawlessness. If instead of engaging in transactional balancing the United States elects not to wade into the polar commons as a transacting party, it will be left behind and seal its fate as a third-place nation in the era of polar power competition. This will produce strategic spillover effects elsewhere that may render China as the new global leader, and the United States in the back seat.

Notes

1. Campbell et al., "Extending American Power," p. 2.
2. Ibid.
3. Cohen, *The Big Stick*, p. 193.
4. Mearsheimer, "The False Promise of International Institutions."
5. Brown, *Understanding International Relations*, p. 43.
6. Kenneth. Waltz, "The Origins of War in Neorealist Theory," in R. Rotberg & T. Rabb, *The Origin and Prevention of Major Wars* (Cambridge University Press, 1988)
7. Scowcroft, "The Dispensable Nation?"
8. John J. Mearsheimer, *The tragedy of great power politics*. WW Norton & Company, 2001, p. 33.
9. Glaser, *Rational Theory of International Politics.*
10. Cohen, *The Big Stick,.*, p. 205.
11. Hammes, *Deglobalization and International Security.*
12. Cooley and Nexon, *Exit from Hegemony*, p. 174.
13. Nye, "Get Smart," p. 163.
14. Nye, *Foreign Affairs,* p. 160.
15. Layne, "From Preponderance to Offshore Balancing."
16. Mearsheimer, *The Trajedy of great power politics*
17. Browne, "NATO Report."

18. Cooley and Nexon, *Exit from Hegemony.*
19. Ibid., p. 15.
20. Cooley and Nexon, *Exit from Hegemony.*
21. Cooley and Nexon, *Exit from Hegemony,* p. 169; Hammes, *Deglobalization and International Security.*
22. Cooley and Nexon, *Exit from Hegemony,* p. 169.
23. Woodward, "Trump Says He Is Reducing US Troops."
24. Cooley and Nexon, *Exit from Hegemony,* p. 174.
25. Lind, "John Mearsheimer on International Relations"; Stokes, "Trump, American Hegemony," p. 135.
26. "Trump Inauguration: Transcript of Donald Trump Speech," *Time,* January 20, 2017, http://time.com/4640707/donald-trump-inauguration-speech-transcript.
27. Stokes, "Trump, American Hegemony," p. 136.
28. Ibid., p. 137.
29. United Nations, "UN System Task Team."
30. Burke and Matisek, "The American Polar Pivot."
31. Wolff, *Fire and Fury,* p. 227.
32. Cooley and Nexon, *Exit from Hegemony,* p. 195.
33. Briggs, "The Polar Sea Voyage."
34. Lajeunesse, *Lock, Stock, and Icebergs.*
35. "Agreement Between the Government of the United States of America and the Government of Canada on Arctic Cooperation," https://books.google.com/books?id=I7yt5vzN-dsC&pg=PA2&lpg=PA2&dq=%E2%80%9CAgreement+Between+the+Government+of+the+United+States+of+America+and+the+Government+of+Canada+on+Arctic+Cooperation,%E2%80%9D&source=bl&ots=YOBLOiOHXf&sig=ACfU3U28zcRZezhEUU7y8dXg-VJSiCzStA&hl=en&sa=X&ved=2ahUKEwjv5_Tpnt7zAhXGmuAKHfoOC9gQ6AF6BAgDEAM#v=onepage&q=%E2%80%9CAgreement%20Between%20the%20Government%20of%20the%20United%20States%20of%20America%20and%20the%20Government%20of%20Canada%20on%20Arctic%20Cooperation%2C%E2%80%9D&f=false.
36. Cecco, "Mike Pompeo Rejects Canada's Claims."
37. Stokes, "Trump, American Hegemony," p. 137.
38. Putin, "Foundations of the Russian Federation State Policy."
39. Klimenko, "Russia's New Arctic Policy Document."
40. Layne, "From Preponderance to Offshore Balancing," p. 113.
41. Ibid., p. 116.
42. O'Shaughnessy, "Hearing to Receive Testimony."
43. Ibid.
44. Specktor, "Antarctica Just Saw Its All-Time Hottest Day Ever"; Amos, "315 Billion-Tonne Iceberg."
45. Friedman, *The world Is Flat.*
46. Hammes, *Deglobalization and International Security.*
47. Brady, *China as a Polar Great Power,* p. 245.
48. Ibid.
49. Ibid., p. 259.
50. Ibid., p. 230.
51. *Report to Congress: Department of Defense Arctic Strategy* (Washington, DC: Office of the Under Secretary of Defense for Policy, Department of Defense, 2019).
52. Turnbull, *Australian Antarctic Strategy.*
53. Gothe-Snape, "Defence Wants to Roll Out Military Tech."

8

Balancing on the Pivot: The Future of Polar Security

SCHOLARS WRITING ABOUT STRATEGY FIND IMPECCABLE CLARity in post-facto arguments. Practitioners, however, formulate strategy and generate lines of effort without the luxury of clarity. They are stepping into the unknown and struggle to infer the contours of the strategic horizon. And in that milieu, those best capable of navigating the tumult of strategic contexts are those audacious enough to think from outside safe confines. This book operates outside the traditional limits and notions of these convenient (safe) confines and makes a competing argument than what is otherwise advanced within the polar region security conversation. As I conclude this look at the polar regions in the context of renewed great power competition, my arguments remain consistent with these departures and examine atypical remedies for attending to the inevitable polar problems of tomorrow.

From our discussion, we see the significance of the polar regions to international security such that any argument dismissing the poles as irrelevant lacks historical grounding. Moreover, the unique nature of the polar regions as contested commons with competing claims, tenuous covenants, and access to the cosmos makes the Arctic and Antarctica even more compelling to state interests, especially with the increasing threat of resource scarcity and the need to go beyond one's borders to secure more.

Understanding polar actor status, in terms of polar peripherals, perceivers, players, and powers, is an important frame to view which states are best positioned by way of capability and intent, as measured by polar policy, posture, presence, and power, to inform and influence future polar region affairs. In determining the polar powers, we see clear policy and strategic commitment to the polar regions by Russia and China, but less so by the United States such that it provides an opportunity to exploit a strategic gap for revisionist powers intent on shifting the global narrative and power balance in their favor. Polar power policies and postures indicate a progression toward a future polar trap in the absence of comparable US attention to the regions. However, the United States can maintain a favorable power balance in and out of the polar regions through recognizing geopolitical realities and adopting a realist's prescription for meeting its polar region security objectives.

Through transactional balancing, Washington can seize opportunity to pursue its security and defense agenda in concert, rather than in conflict, with Russia and China as a means of competing productively and avoiding the potential polar trap. Adopting transactional balancing, the United States will enter into the evolving polar fray with its eyes wide open rather than blindly clinging to the dated ideology of US exceptionalism seeking liberal hegemony. This leaves us at the final departure point for the concluding discussion: What should the future US polar strategy look like in terms of policy, posture, presence, and power projection and to best enable successful balancing?

TOWARD A POLAR STRATEGY

The United States needs to do something about the polar regions. Washington must consider pursuing a comprehensive polar policy and complementary strategy now, while it can, rather than later when it must. Current US strategic priorities are superficial, resulting in a geographic pivot in the wrong direction. To reorient strategic attention toward objectively greater challenges, the United States should execute a polar pivot and prioritize the Arctic and Antarctica as foundations of its future defense and security posture.

The polar pivot is a prescription for polar region stability and US influence, but one that falls short of plunging the polar regions into great power conflict. As with transactional balancing, the polar pivot roots its recommendations in realism and contends that the prognosis for returning to liberal hegemony is strategically myopic.

Prioritizing defense and security commitments in the maze of international security concerns is an intellectual puzzle requiring incisive strategic acuity. It is apparent today that US strategic priorities lack such acuity. Determinants of "strategic value" are often superficial and lack analytical depth.[1] According to Eliot Cohen, "In theory, political and military leaders at the top of the US decision making pyramid should establish national security priorities and devote adequate time to the most important of them."[2] Anthropogenic climate changes have objectively altered polar landscapes in the twenty-first century, making these regions some of the most strategically important areas for both influence and control.[3] Since 1980, Arctic sea ice has steadily declined at a rate of 12.8 percent per decade.[4] This steady decline leads to expanding navigable waters and underscores the opportunity for ambitious actors. Polar cooperation and competition are occurring. Absent a US approach toward productive competition mechanisms in the polar regions, confrontation and conflict will follow.[5]

THE POLAR PIVOT

With current strategic rebalancing focused on countering great power adversaries like China and Russia, the United States has—mistakenly—emphasized the specific geographic regions near these actors as the renewed focus of military presence. In doing so, the United States continues to overlook Russian and Chinese actions elsewhere, missing strategic opportunities to steer the Antarctic and Arctic regions into favorable power balances. This is a strategic error decades in the making. A polar pivot to these regions is needed, including militarization of assets and capabilities intended to compete with Russia and China and contest where necessary.

The 2017 National Security Strategy claims that "China and Russia want to shape a world antithetical to U.S. values and interests" in an attempt to "challenge American power, influence, and interests ... to erode American security and prosperity."[6] Before retiring, Secretary of Defense James Mattis explicitly identified China and Russia as "revisionist powers" trying "to create a world consistent with their authoritarian models."[7] Flowing from such logic, the 2018 National Defense Strategy views China and Russia as strategic competitors requiring a renewed US military focus on lethality, strengthened partnerships and alliances, and reforming of the Department of Defense for the right balance of performance and affordability.[8] Despite intense focus on China and Russia, the National Defense Strategy is superficially bent on their respective regions. Current US strategic visions miss adversarial actions in the polar regions. Such a strategic omission is salient, as neither region is explicitly identified as a focus area in the National Security Strategy or National Defense Strategy.[9]

Whereas the United States has established infrastructure throughout Europe and Asia from which it can exert influence, the polar regions remain conspicuously bare. There is too much US emphasis on competing in Asia and Eastern Europe for the polar regions to matter. US deterrence efforts in the Asia Pacific region have been ineffective; China continues expanding its artificial island construction, with the total reclaimed area exceeding 3,200 acres.[10] US rhetoric has amounted to veiled threats and toothless policy statements that lack budgeted intent. These statements are irrelevant and ineffective as there have been numerous occasions in which Congress has budgeted for polar capabilities but funds were reallocated for different priorities.[11]

The Arctic situation is a potential multipeer adversarial environment with geographic proximity that should warrant US attention similar to its South China Sea focus. To the south, Antarctica is also a multipeer environment, with multiple countries claiming to have discovered the continent—or least expressing imagined claims to its resources—with ambition to project power from the continent in time.[12] This should concern the United States and allies, compelling real action. Yet the United States remains comparably uncommitted to the polar regions.

EXECUTING THE PIVOT

Russia continues to push the boundaries of acceptable behavior, especially against the Arctic Circle neighbors of Canada, Greenland (Denmark), and Norway. North Atlantic Treaty Organization (NATO) members, and Norway especially, are concerned that Russian military activities are creating an "anti-access/area denial 'bubble' that would cover a significant portion of their territory and prevent NATO from coming to [their] defense."[13] Around the Antarctic Circle, China poses the greatest threat—or competing opportunity—to South Africa, Australia, New Zealand, Chile, and Argentina. Similarly, Australia has demonstrated substantial apprehension regarding China's numerous activities and new scientific bases in Antarctica that blur lines of legality in the region.[14] With potential strategic competition at the border of the US homeland in the Arctic, it is understandable that the United States has a formal Arctic strategy. However, these challenges are not reserved to the Arctic alone but rather to the polar regions as a whole. The United States needs to acknowledge a true polar emphasis through the adoption of a wholly polar strategy rather than one that solely focuses on the geographic proximity of the Arctic.

While "fully ice-free summers probably remain a decade or more away," this gives the United States time to prepare for the future strategic environment in the Arctic and to more fully predict Antarctica's future.[15] A polar strategy should contain general prescriptions for developing dedicated polar hard power capabilities, creating a dedicated polar military command, training specialized polar-capable troops and creating polar-oriented units, modernizing existing military weapons systems to operate in polar climates, guidance for conducting military operations in and around the polar regions, and prescriptions for expanded polar presence. But beyond the tangible to-do list, a polar strategy should outline enduring US polar interests and develop polar military engagement criteria for when those interests are threatened. It should stipulate the necessary military capabilities required for successful polar engagement and the complementary infrastructural support. Finally, the polar strategy should detail the polar security environment and the known and assumed interests of relevant polar actors as potential transactional partners as well as potential conflict brokers.

THE STRATEGIC FRAMEWORK

The Arctic and Antarctica are different in some ways, but similar in others. The polar strategy needs to attend to these issues and present an executable framework for realizing US national security interests and desired continuing states—not end-states—in the regions, because the former are continuous; the latter are a "kind of strategic pixie dust" that sounds good on paper but does not exist in reality.[16] To this point, the future polar strategy must think in terms of maintenance and balance rather than in terms of containment and hegemony. Given the operational limitations coupled with the sheer expanse of each polar region, it is difficult to imagine anyone achieving regional hegemony in either the Arctic or Antarctica.

With these factors in mind, the polar strategy should outline the necessary policy positions to inform polar defense postures as well as the polar military presence required to sustain US polar power and influence. Each of these requirements can be anchored to the notion of the polar regions as contested commons. Thinking about the Arctic and Antarctica in this way and relative to the need to develop policy informing posture that promotes presence and achieves power, four themes emerge: projection, protection, prevention, and preservation.

PROJECT POWER

Nobody ever won a medal for avoiding a crisis. If the United States intends to remain a polar power, it must project military power into each region as a demonstrated commitment to this status rather than avoiding the potential conflict trap. More directly, the United States needs to aggress toward this challenge rather than passively react to it. By projecting power into the polar regions, the United States will create opportunities to shape and influence polar affairs consistent with its own interests first rather than react to an already shaped and restrictive environment in its absence.

The polar regions are challenges now; if the United States ignores them they will become crises. There will be increased military posturing and presence in the polar regions, especially as the world continues to question whether the Antarctic Treaty and Arctic Council are fit for their respective purposes. With that, the United States needs to set the conditions by which it wants to live, or accept living within the conditions others set. Those advocating for polar restraint are lobbying the same anti-antagonist rhetoric that motivated Russia and China toward the regions in the first place, where they are now in the position of advantage to set the conditions. Asserting presence by way of power projection is a necessary effort toward changing this course, but can be done in a way that avoids conflict while still maintaining polar power. But as with most things when it comes to the poles, it is easier said than done.

Projecting power in the polar regions is a challenge. From the United States, Antarctica takes days for planes and weeks for ships to reach. Acknowledging the Antarctic Treaty restriction on military maneuvers and casting it aside for the sake of argument (and future predictions that it will be nullified or abandoned), projecting power to Antarctica is a logistical effort in overcoming time and distance. For this we can briefly look to the challenges the British faced during the Falklands War as a close analog for what it might look like to sustain military power projection south of the Antarctic Circle.

THE FALKLANDS ANTARCTIC ANALOG. The United Kingdom (UK) first claimed sovereignty over the Falkland Islands in 1833. From this southern British territory, the UK expanded its claims in 1908 to include "South Georgia, the South Orkneys, the South Shetlands, and the (South) Sandwich Islands, and Graham's Land, situated in the South Atlantic Ocean and on the Antarctic continent to the south of the 50th parallel of south latitude, and lying between the 20th and the 80th degrees of west longitude."[17] As a claimed British territory, the UK has since maintained presence on the islands, leading to tensions between the British and the Argentinian government on the basis of competing territorial claims. The tensions escalated in April 1982 following an

Argentinian invasion of and attempt to take the Falklands, prompting the British to dispatch military forces to defend their territory.

Though short-lived, the implications of this campaign were significant. The Falklands War told us that not only could a modern military (at the time) project power over 8,000 miles from its home; the war also told us that a modern military would project power that far, especially in the case of protecting territorial claims. For the British, Ascension Island, a small island in the middle of the Atlantic Ocean, proved invaluable in the logistics of military power projection to the Falklands.[18] The analog of the Falklands War demonstrates that there is no limit to the will and intent to project military power when sovereignty is at stake, provided the logistical infrastructural support is in place. It also serves as a reminder that the current unresolved sovereignty issues on Antarctica are ripe for tension and potential conflict, thus necessitating a more thorough look at potential basing analogs enabling future power projection to and from Antarctica.

Those arguing that the Antarctic Treaty will remain a sufficient compliance mechanism rely on the assumption that humans are inherently good-natured. But this is the flaw of liberalism relative to polar region philosophy. Assuming polar institutions will indefinitely motivate compliance, regardless of changing environments, is naive. It assumes collective agreement, strength, and shared sacrifice for the greater good. In today's international security landscape, powerful states—fueled by nationalism—are unlikely to surrender their power and self-constrain their interests, be they military or economic, to consensus-based international institutions. Operating on the notion of future treaty dissolution, absent Antarctic governance, and increased US interest on the continent for resources and influence, how should the United States project power in Antarctica? And what about the Arctic?

US MILITARY POWER. While the United States needs more military surface presence in the polar regions, it does not need to drop Navy SEALs from 33,000 feet in the Arctic to militarily compete with Russia, or to build additional LC-130 Skibirds to compete with China's Antarctic air squadron.[19] And despite the growing narrative of the "icebreaker gap," the United States does not need to develop dozens of icebreakers to keep up with Russia and maintain its polar power status. The majority of the polar waters and ports worth sailing between and to are ice-free most of the year, such that investing in polar icebreakers is an unnecessary commitment that will inevitably see a majority of the icebreaker fleet in dry dock as a visible waste of money. To more colorfully argue the point, the mechanisms of the US defense acquisition that would secure new icebreakers make even the largest glaciers seem swift and nimble by comparison.

It will take a decade or more to proceed from an idea to a tangible series of operational icebreakers with any hope of using toward influential power projection means. For instance, the 2020 White House memo calling for a "ready, capable, and available fleet of polar security icebreakers" does not expect them to be deployable until late 2029.[20] It would, in theory, be more practical and cost-efficient to modify a selection of current US Navy amphibious ships to operate in polar waters with ice-hardened hulls.[21] Rather than seek new and more polar capabilities that will take decades to deploy, the US military can project power through its existing force structure, but can be more effective in doing so through expanded presence in the regions.

THE ARCTIC CRESCENT. The 2018 National Defense Authorization Act committed $14 million for the US Air Force to "acquire real property and carry out the military construction projects" in Iceland's Keflavik Air Station.[22] Iceland was until 2006 home to US Naval Air Station Keflavik (NASKEF) and was an active hub for monitoring Soviet activity during the Cold War.[23] Since its 2006 closure, there have been calls to reopen the base to US personnel rather than use it as a transit hub for training and rotational force operations. Renewing the US Arctic commitment via a reestablished permanent military basing in Iceland is a necessary step toward operationalizing the US military's flurry of Arctic strategies in recent years.

A revitalized NASKEF-like installation, be it an air base or a naval station, satisfies navy and air force Arctic lines of effort from their respective strategies. It would provide a static location from which the navy can maintain enhanced presence as well as strengthen cooperative partnerships and even build a more capable Arctic force.[24] A renewed presence in Iceland would, conceivably, enable the air force and army to meet some of its Arctic lines of effort as well, including vigilance, preparation, competition, and defense in the Arctic.[25] The Iceland base would also serve as an ideal location for monitoring the Greenland–Iceland–United Kingdom Gap while doubly serving as a central location for a competing US "Arctic Crescent" to match Russia's "Ice Curtain." A permanent Icelandic base would enable the United States to resume training in extreme cold weather conditions in a location other than Norway and potentially even station Arctic regiments; similar to the US Marine Corps' littoral-regiment trial concept.[26]

Establishing Arctic regiments within Iceland is a necessary step in demonstrating commitment and ability to operate in the Arctic. The infrastructure to sustain such a suggestion is a bigger ask than the $14 million commitment affords. But it is worth considering as a strategic investment for future Arctic presence. Yet the proposed benefits of the suggestion cannot be realized independent of similar commitments elsewhere. More important still, if the United States were to adopt a more robust Arctic presence by way of permanent basing and increased military presence, this would necessitate a dedicated command currently absent from the Unified Command Plan.

THE (NOT-SO) UNIFIED COMMAND PLAN. The Unified Command Plan establishes the current US geographic combatant commands, segmenting the globe into six command areas of responsibility:[27]

- US Northern Command (NORTHCOM)
- US Southern Command (SOUTHCOM)
- US European Command (EUCOM)
- US Indo-Pacific Command (INDO-PACOM)
- US Africa Command (AFRICOM)
- US Central Command (CENTCOM)

Each of these regions has nicely defined boundaries delineating responsibility. The complication of the world being round is that where these lines intersect in the north and south produces further segmentation of the Arctic and Antarctica among the geographic commands.

The polar regions are the only areas violating the Unified Command Plan principle of geographic segmentation. In the Arctic (see Figure 8.1), NORTHCOM's area of responsibility extends off the northern Alaskan and Canadian coasts, out to and around the geographic North Pole, along the western edge of Greenland, abutting Thule Air Force Base, and into the Atlantic Ocean. NORTHCOM is the US Arctic advocate. NORTHCOM's Arctic interest comes and goes with the passing of the guidance from one commander to the next.[28] Despite the fact that Greenland is on the North American continental shelf, adjacent to the NORTHCOM area of responsibility, and that Thule Air Force Base houses a NORTHCOM/North American Aerospace Defense (NORAD) unit in the Twenty-First Space Wing, the island sits within the EUCOM area of responsibility as a territory of Denmark, in Europe. In essence, the geographic combatant commands, at least in the case of NORTHCOM and EUCOM relative to Greenland, might better be called the geopolitical combatant commands.

Figure 8.1 Combatant Command Boundaries in the Arctic

Source: US Department of Defense, "Unified Command Plan 2011," https://archive.defense.gov/ucc.

Contrary but analogous to the Greenland logic, the EUCOM area of responsibility boundary does not extend in the southern Atlantic and to the west of the Falkland Islands, even though the Falklands are a British territory. So why, then, does the EUCOM boundary extend to Greenland when it is otherwise part of the North American continent and thus should be part of NORTHCOM's area of responsibility? Because the geographic combatant command boundaries are cluttered in the High North. But simply redrawing the NORTHCOM lines to include Greenland, as logical as this is, does not solve the entire polar problem, as the situation is as complicated or more with Antarctica.

Balancing on the Pivot 211

Unified Command Plan segmentation is messier in the Southern Hemisphere. The plan places the entire continental landmass of Antarctica within the INDO-PACOM area of responsibility, yet the command boundaries of both SOUTHCOM and AFRICOM naturally reach south to cover nearly half of the Antarctic coastline (see Figure 8.2). The Antarctic Peninsula in particular, of which the US Palmer Station on Anvers Island is near the extreme northern tip, extends over a thousand miles into the SOUTHCOM area of responsibility, but only the maritime domain is part of SOUTHCOM while the peninsula remains part of INDO-PACOM. The effect of this Antarctic segmentation is that

Figure 8.2 Combatant Command Boundaries in Antarctica

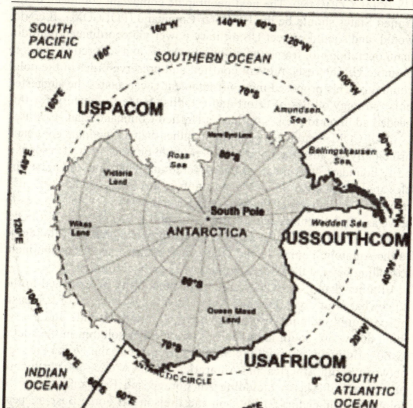

Source: US Department of Defense, "Unified Command Plan 2011," https://archive.defense.gov/ucc.

INDO-PACOM is responsible for thousands of miles of SOUTHCOM and AFRIRCOM Antarctic shoreline. Fortunately, the current prohibition of Antarctic military operations means the need for command deconfliction is nonexistent, as INDO-PACOM oversees US military Antarctic support missions. Regardless, the Unified Command Plan segmentation of the polar regions is a curious line-drawing exercise injecting questions relative to the need for a dedicated polar command, especially if the United States advances toward a more robust polar military presence. A dedicated polar command not only delineates polar region areas of responsibility but also produces the dedicated command expertise and commitment to polar region presence and power projection the US currently lacks relative to Russia and China.

US POLAR COMMAND. The next geographic combatant command of the United States should be the US Polar Command (POLCOM). It could, would, and should project US military power via coordinated multidomain operations to, from, and within the Arctic and Antarctic Circles to promote US interests, prevent conflict, and preserve order in the polar commons. This proposed mission statement encapsulates the suggested polar strategy's lines of effort and establishes the framework for this needed addition to the US military's Unified Command Plan structure.

POLCOM should be a geographic rather than a functional command principally because the polar circles provide obvious area of responsibility boundaries for polar military operations. That said, the polar circles are located at 66°33' north and south, respectively. To the north, this boundary excludes Eielson Air Force Base in Alaska, which figures to serve as a prominent basing location to support Arctic operations if POLCOM is established. To the south, a similar problem presents with regard to the Antarctic Peninsula and other small protrusions of the continent extending beyond the circle's boundary. There is a solution.

Rather than POLCOM's area of responsibility be confined to the somewhat arbitrary Arctic and Antarctic Circles, the area of responsibility should include everything above 60° north latitude and everything below 60° south latitude. This is a cleaner solution in the south, as 60° south cuts through the Southern Ocean and the Drake Passage between South America and Antarctica. In the Arctic, 60° north captures most of Alaska including Anchorage and Fairbanks (home to Joint Base Elmendorf-Richardson and Eielson Air Force Base, respectively); all of the Canadian Northwest Territories, Greenland, and Iceland; most of Scandinavia, including 95 percent of Norway and nearly 100 percent of Finland; and 100 percent of the Russian Northern Fleet

Joint Strategic Command's posture. The nature of a command with two independent areas of responsibility requires a northern and southern headquarters. There are several existing locations that would make ideal POLCOM headquarters.

POLCOM-NORTH. With established infrastructure capable of supporting a future command mission, Eielson Air Force Base, Alaska, is the best candidate for POLCOM-North headquarters. Thule Air Force Base, Greenland, presents another compelling northern headquarters location with port access, but lacks the space, infrastructure, and accessibility to support a command headquarters.[29] A reestablished US base at Keflavik, Iceland, is another location worthy of consideration. However, given the current absence relative to the existence of others, Keflavik is not a viable option. Therefore, establishing an Alaskan northern headquarters POLCOM would enable the command to absorb NORTHCOM's northern homeland defense mission while allowing NORTHCOM to focus exclusively on the defense and civil support within the conterminous United States, or the lower forty-eight states.[30] As well, POLCOM could draw forces from units in Joint Base Elmendorf-Richardson and Eielson Air Force Bases without compromising Alaskan-based units providing support for INDO-PACOM's combat mission in the Asia Pacific theater. The United States may not yet require the full contingent of Alaska-based military units to commit to the Arctic domain, but having the northern headquarters established in Alaska would lay the foundation for the future pivot when necessary.

POLCOM-SOUTH. Antarctica is a different dynamic than the Arctic. A POLCOM-South recommendation assumes Antarctica will become a militarized domain with several countries projecting power to and from the continent either through an agreed revision to the Antarctic Treaty (less likely) or a deliberate departure by some (more likely). The notional POLCOM-South headquarters should be located either in Christchurch, New Zealand, or in the British Falkland Islands. The US Air Force operates its Antarctic support efforts via Christchurch International Airport, but this is not a permanent basing location or sustainable long-term partnership, especially considering the burgeoning Chinese influence in New Zealand and increasing wariness of the Kiwis toward the United States.[31] At a distance of 2,380 miles, Christchurch is the gateway to McMurdo Research Station on Ross Island, the largest US Antarctic station.[32] It is approximately 3,200 miles to the Amundsen-Scott Station at the South Pole and 4,400 miles to Palmer Station on the Antarctic Peninsula.[33]

Between Chinese wedge-driving and New Zealand's small-state status, there is less potential for transactional benefits for continued United States–New Zealand partnership for Antarctic access.

The United Kingdom, in comparison, through the Falkland Islands, provides an attractive alternative Antarctic access point by way of the Royal Air Force's Mount Pleasant airbase and its adjacent Mare Harbor. Mount Pleasant and Mare Harbor sit in the east-central region of East Falkland Island and only 900 miles to the US Palmer Station on the Antarctic Peninsula. Mount Pleasant is 2,646 miles to the US Amundsen-Scott Station at the South Pole and 3,283 miles to McMurdo Station.[34] Though this distance is greater, the value proposition for the United States, given that the UK is a nuclear state and US ally with a military presence in the extreme South Atlantic, through a potential transactional balancing arrangement is greater than that with New Zealand. Moreover, a potential US military presence bolsters UK defense posture on the Falklands and may act as an increased deterrent against ongoing Argentinian reclamation rhetoric.[35] This is a winning transactional arrangement for the United States and United Kingdom. The infrastructure on the British base may be incapable of sustaining a US command now, but if the United States and United Kingdom agree to such an arrangement, anything can happen.[36] A US military presence in the Falklands, however, would compel a restructuring of current US polar units designed to support Arctic and Antarctic missions.

US POLAR UNITS. To realize the benefits of the polar pivot, the enhanced polar force presence, the reorganized command structures, and the resulting strategy, the United States needs to commit forces to this mission. Sustaining forces in the polar regions is a limited goal requiring substantial logistics support—two contradicting aims. Future polar operations may involve the simultaneous challenge of fighting the adversary and the environment, similar to the effects of the weather on combat effectiveness in the Korean War. Put another way: "everything in the Arctic is trying to kill you," such that preparing for polar military operations is a necessity that should be executed by the services to provide polar-capable forces for a polar-dedicated command.[37]

Whereas the services are responsible for organizing, training, and equipping their personnel for employment within and by the combatant commands, there are standing units now that the United States should consider making a permanent fixture within the proposed POLCOM structure. The US Marine Corps should build upon its rotational force concepts in Australia and Norway and establish static (vice rotational) polar regiments for sustained cold weather presence and power projection. Norway, Iceland, and Alaska are ideal basing locations for these new marine contingents to operate "in the snow of far off northern lands."[38] Similarly, the army should establish Arctic brigades for sustained Arctic ground presence. Again, Norway, Alaska, and Iceland make for obvious basing considerations to be deconflicted with the location of the proposed marine polar regiments. The US Navy's reestablished Second Fleet's area of responsibility includes the North Atlantic up to the North Pole.[39] But like the US Navy's Third, Sixth, and Seventh Fleets, whose areas of responsibility extend to both the Arctic and Antarctica, the Second Fleet's area encompasses more than just the Arctic.[40] These are not exclusively polar units, but the navy should develop platforms specific to polar missions that are exclusively trained for and deployed to the polar regions within this construct of bifurcated fleet areas of operations. Finally, the US Air Force has the 109th Airlift Wing, an Air National Guard unit based out of Schenectady, New York, which has the US Air Force polar airlift mission and operates the only ski-equipped LC-130s (Skibirds) in the world. With this unique capability, the 109th supports three different combatant commands depending on its location—and this is part of the problem. While operating in Greenland, the 109th falls under EUCOM's area of responsibility, under NORTHCOM in Alaska and in the Arctic, and under INDO-PACOM (through the Joint Task Force–Support Forces Antarctica) when supporting operations to and from Antarctica. Instead, the United States should commit the 109th to support operations in the Arctic and Antarctica, as it does now, through a singular POLCOM mission alignment. Whereas the unit may be better served as an active-duty unit for operational support reasons, it can remain as a US National Guard force under this construct and still maintain its state support role while simultaneously providing forces to the POLCOM commander when requested in the Arctic or Antarctica.

To this end, the Joint Task Force–Support Forces Antarctica, with operational oversight and execution of US Antarctic support missions to the National Science Foundation's US Antarctic Program, should reside under POLCOM. Currently, the headquarters of the Joint Task Force–Support Forces Antarctica, as a INDO-PACOM and Pacific Air Forces (PACAF) asset, is located in Joint Base Pearl Harbor, Hawaii. For the airmen and other personnel of the support forces, this is an unpopular suggestion given the choice between Hawaii and the Falkland Islands.[41] However, removing the support forces from PACAF and INDO-PACOM—and their area of operations by extension—is a necessary effort in command organization and force commitment toward both streamlined and transactional ends. The Joint Task Force–Support Forces Antarctica in Hawaii does little for the United States by way of transactional balancing. Relocating it to a shared US-UK base in the Falklands, while still enabling Antarctic power projection, would provide a mutually beneficial arrangement and demonstration of transactional commitments by two nuclear-power states toward Antarctic security that would have marked effects on the motivations and resulting actions of competing near-peer powers Russia and China in Antarctica. In committing dedicated polar units to a dedicated polar command to execute a dedicated polar mission, the United States can and will demonstrate its commitment to the future defense and security dynamic in the polar regions.

Protect Interests

All state-to-state arrangements fundamentally rest on the basis of perceived threat from military force. To enable military polar presence that promotes transactional balancing, US arrangements with polar states need to expand to ensure continued force posture and future influence in the contested commons. We have already seen examples of alliance efforts countering China in the Arctic, with the Pentagon convincing Denmark to fund infrastructure (e.g., airports) in Greenland to prevent Chinese investment and basing there.[42] The United States needs to double-down on these efforts and seek greater presence in Greenland beyond the opening of a consulate in Nuuk in 2019.[43] To protect its Arctic interests, the United States needs to own Greenland.

THE GREENLAND PROPOSITION. Greenland is primed to be among the most strategically valuable pieces of real estate on Earth in the coming years. Recall Truman's attempt to purchase Greenland in 1947. Those who mocked Donald Trump for stating his interest in purchasing the island territory from Denmark in 2019 conveniently forgot this history lesson. Between Arctic gateway access and resulting regional influence, immense undeveloped land, natural resources, military training and basing, and even commercial uses resulting from increasingly thinning ice and accessible lands, Greenland's military, strategic, diplomatic, and economic values will be unparalleled in the future. Lacking resources and the ability to leverage its location through infrastructure investment, Denmark has been largely unable to realize the strategic value of the largest island in the world and can command a hefty price for its purchase. The price may be worth it for the United States, however, such that the conversation should compel Washington to enter into serious transactional discussions with Copenhagen over Greenland's future, not unlike its approach with Ottawa in a similar area.

ALERT FORCES. Given Canada's proximity and NATO alliance with the United States, the polar pivot could be actualized through a transactional arrangement involving US support of base expansion at Canadian Forces Station Alert, Ellesmere Island, Nunavut, Canada. Alert is a weather and intelligence station and the world's most northern military base.[44] Developing it into a robust military installation with expanded barracks, an improved and extended airstrip, and a deep-water port would provide an additional hub for Arctic influence, both militarily and economically, and from which to pursue expanded transactional arrangements. Moreover, it would serve Canada's strategic interests as well, given the vast amounts of resources trapped within Canada's Arctic exclusive economic zone.[45] This sort of transactional arrangement would also tighten US-Canadian relations over the use of the Northwest Passage and serve as a balancing mechanism advancing US interests against revisionist power projection along Canada's Arctic coastline.

Other potential interest-based transactional arrangements center on control of economic trade routes, imposition of passage tolls, and restricted access to (and control of) vital and profitable energy resources in the polar regions. Newly expanded trade routes and strategic interest in the Arctic region will fundamentally change global trade and advantage those willing to transact in the polar commons. If the notional Transpolar Sea Route (see Figure 8.3) ever becomes a reality—as some predict—states will be able to navigate through the center of the Arctic Circle such that the Arctic will become a competing Northern Hemisphere route in time.[46]

The Arctic interest proposition then becomes a race for territorial control and expansion, garnering influence over global trade. In this vein, we can even envision a scenario where Russia, in asserting uncontested military control of its claimed Arctic exclusive economic zones on the backs of competing territorial shelf claims, would extract tolls and impose permit requirements for operation in and transiting of its claimed territorial waters, much as it is already doing in the Northern Sea Route. While more difficult to impose such control in Antarctica, China has already demonstrated its desire to exploit fisheries to the maximum extent possible, causing disruptions to Antarctic food chains.[47] If both Russia and China were to further militarize the Arctic in a visible rebuke to international norms, the United States and allies

Figure 8.3 Arctic Shipping Routes

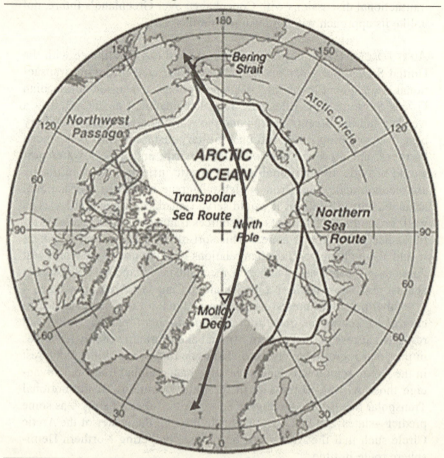

Source: Adapted from Central Intelligence Agency, *World Factbook,* "Arctic Ocean," November 24, 2020, https://www.cia.gov/library/publications/the-world-factbook/geos/xq.html (Transpolar Route line added).

would need to consider revoking the Svalbard Treaty, which prevents Norway from militarizing its sovereign archipelago.[48] This would enable Norway and NATO allies to position military forces and infrastructure on Svalbard (as opposed to only being able to land at Jan Mayen) as a means of deterring future hostilities from China and Russia.[49] It would also require the expulsion of Chinese and Russian intelligence personnel working on Svalbard, which is considered a critical node for communicating with their respective spy satellites. US efforts should also be pursued with Sweden and Finland as nonaligned countries that are participating in US-NATO Arctic military exercises as "enhanced opportunities partners."[50]

A failure to defend US interests in the Arctic and Antarctica will have lasting impacts on the environment, free trade, and global security. The Western status quo will spark disagreements over resources and territorial claims in the polar regions. It is not a question of if but rather when and how. The American people must have the willingness and intent to diplomatically, militarily, and economically transact in the polar regions. Without such resolve, China and Russia will rapidly establish an advantage at each pole, and such an advantage will compel a US response to recalibrate the balance of power, potentially aggravating rival states and leading to conflict.

PREVENT CONFLICT

In the post–World War II era, the United States voiced concerns that the Soviets would unilaterally claim Antarctic territory and that deterring this required an agreement to ensure Antarctica did not succumb to international strife. The resulting covenant after nearly a decade of international discussion was the 1959 Antarctic Treaty, requiring that "Antarctica shall be used for peaceful purposes only."[51] Today there are approximately seventy permanent research stations in Antarctica representing twenty-nine countries. Although the entirety of the Antarctic Treaty System bans military activity, except for logistics support of scientific research, there are growing indicators of Antarctic militarization around the continent. There are substantial increases in China and Russia having installed "dual-use" military technology in Antarctica.[52] China and Russia employ extractive economies, and the resource-rich Antarctic continent is a primary target of national interest for both.[53]

China is already well positioned for Antarctic influence as the leading trading partner of both Australia and New Zealand, two of the most prominent Antarctic access points on Earth. The United States cannot ignore these "Five Eyes" allies and must bolster its relationship with both. Australia has followed the United States into every major military conflict since World War I. Though Australian defense officials may be reluctant to politicize Antarctica within the international security context, a visible US commitment to ensuring Antarctic security and stability in the face of questionable Chinese and Russian activity is something Australia will support.[54] New Zealand's interests—or willingness to support in various world affairs—are less aligned with the United States than Australia's, but New Zealand's proximity to Antarctica is a compelling motivator for Wellington to back Washington and maintain peace on the continent. It is, perhaps, the threat of Antarctic conflict that will mend relations in updating the 1951 security treaty between Australia, New Zealand, and the United States, or provide an alternative transactional construct for pursuit of mutual interests between the reluctant allies. To the north, US relations with Arctic ally states are equally opportunistic for alternative transactional arrangements to balance with or against Russian and Chinese interests toward conflict avoidance.

Regardless of platform, these and other international agreements remain critical to meeting desired states through transactional balancing. Ensuring polar region stability and conflict prevention in the face of strategic competition requires the United States to identify various state interests and seek transactional opportunities aimed at preventing malign polar hegemony. Where interests diverge, this extends an even greater need for transactionalism and ideologically distant informal negotiations toward mutually constructive ends. Where negotiations cannot produce such transactions, states will be better served—on the basis of their security interests—to depart from the interaction and seek alternative means to achieving their intent. Of course, this construct relies on the premise of rational state behavior for conflict prevention as an assumed collective interest toward the preservation of order.

Preserve Order

For the majority of the twentieth century and the beginning of the twenty-first, the United States has forged relationships with polar states that are now even more critical to maintain. For realists, an assumed anarchic international system compels strong states to direct and influence weak-state activities. The United States perceived threats to the homeland via a Soviet attack over the High North in the Cold War, but did not perceive a threat to international order broadly in the Arctic or in Antarctica. Today, both polar regions are contested commons and the subject of competing territorial claims, and of fragile covenants guiding increasingly impatient and worried state behaviors, and are critical for advancing national interests via the cosmos, or space. Because of these overlapping and overarching dynamics, the Arctic and Antarctica are now squarely in the crosshairs of powerful states' interests. Though the polar regions are on the map's periphery, they are moving closer to the center of the geopolitical and geostrategic frame of great power competition. Each region is now among the priority geographic foci of great power competition such that the United States and other commonly interested states need to take action now to promote and preserve order.

Since the Battle of the Aleutian Islands (1942–1943) and with the exception of regular intercepts of Russian aircraft inside the Alaskan Air Defense Identification Zone, the United States has had no need to exercise military combat power in the sub-Arctic or Arctic.[55] Likewise, since the late 1940s, there has been no compelling need to project military combat power in Antarctica. Significant cost, extreme conditions, extraordinary distance, and relatively uninhabited areas have long provided sufficient reasons for the United States to avoid sustained military presence in and around the polar regions. As a result, the US military has conducted limited training and exercises in the polar regions relative to myriad military engagements of the past seventy-five years, choosing instead to implement other methods of influence via its involvement in the very international institutions that China and Russia now seek greater influence in themselves.

Arctic sea ice retreat has established new routes of access for self-interested states to control and economically threaten. Anticipated Antarctic ice melt into the twenty-first century may render the world's largest frozen desert another rock in the ocean ready for social inhabitance beyond research purposes. Contemporary issues in the polar regions transcend the bounds of human, economic, and environmental security. The United States can no longer afford to remain idle in the polar power conversation. Neutrality begets apathy, and apathy begets weakness when strategic competitors are otherwise aggressively pursuing presence and influence in the polar regions. The United States cannot continue overreliance on smaller states to maintain liberal order at the poles. To this end, the United States must renew its leadership position in the polar regions in the twenty-first century similar to the leadership role it ironically assumed in the establishment of the many international polar institutions we know today—but today's and tomorrow's polar leadership role will look different than in the past.

THE FUTURE OF POLAR SECURITY

The United States is losing its hegemony. Whether Washington should seek to rebuild its international brand and reestablish itself as the global hegemon is the subject of debate among scholars and policymakers today. While the academic debate rages, the United States continues its global retreat as China seeks greater power and influence. Russia is interested in self-preservation such that it will continue building Arctic defenses not as a means of preparing for war but rather as a deterrence mechanism intended to keep military conflict from spilling into the Arctic, where for Russia, "conflict is bad for business."[56]

While Russia seeks self-preservation, it also seeks beneficial strategic partnerships but refuses self-binding alliances or state agreements. Russia is a self-interested state with a questionably calibrated moral compass that will balance with or against any state on a cost-benefit calculation. Moscow will continue meddling in global politics toward its desired ends; it will persist with its support of some regimes while decrying others; and Moscow will, ultimately, maintain itself as a polar power for both its own economic well-being and its influence in global affairs. But the real challenge for the future of polar security is not Moscow; it is Beijing and its global ambition that is manifesting in the Arctic and Antarctica.

Tenuous Polar Partnerships and Access

China will continue its ambitious plan to realize its Polar Silk Road via expanding economic agreements with northern European states like Norway, Iceland, Denmark (Greenland), and Sweden. Berthing agreements, resource extraction, commercial shipping, and infrastructure investment projects are all on the table as Beijing moves toward an expanded European influence posture, as enabled by its access to the Arctic as an alternate route. China and Russia will seek mutually beneficial arrangements in the Arctic and Antarctica, provided they can maintain productive relations despite tensions in the South China Sea and elsewhere. As China continues harboring productive economic and diplomatic relations with the European Union, this injects greater rifts into NATO's increasingly fragile collective security arrangement.

To the south, China socialized in its culture that it is destined to rule Antarctica, which is why Beijing insists on befriending Australia and New Zealand, albeit through subversive political means, and much to Washington's dismay.[57] These efforts cast further doubt on the ability of the United States to sustain arrangements like the Five Eyes partnership or the security treaty between Australia, New Zealand, and the United States. Given the current state of international politics and the developing distrust others have in US reliance, New Zealand is far more likely to pursue relations with China than it is with the United States. As a small state in the evolving great power politics game, New Zealand will be forced to suffer what small states usually suffer, which is benefiting from neutrality within the broader competition of great power investment on its home turf, with the ultimate goal, in this case, of Antarctic exploitation by China.

Australia, too, is a reluctant US ally weary from following the United States through decades of interventionism. Regarding Antarctic access, Australia aims to suppress the notion of aggression and militarization in Antarctica. Australians seek to avoid politicizing Antarctica because of concerns over optics, given that such rhetoric would likely pit Beijing and Washington as adversaries. This puts Australia in a difficult position relative to its robust economic ties with China and its established history with the United States. But this "do nothing, say nothing" strategy is misguided and passive, leaving Australia open for business to the highest bidder and thus putting China at a geographic and strategic advantage over the United States in the Australian Antarctic access discussion.

Both Australia's and New Zealand's relations with the United States are tenuous and ripe for Chinese wedge-driving. This risks the United States losing the diplomatic and security high ground to China in the Southern Hemisphere and to the principal Antarctic access states, hinting at further erosion of US polar influence. Beijing's approach puts it on a trajectory toward the position of diplomatic, economic, or even military advantage in each of these relationships in the not-too-distant future, assuming Washington does nothing to alter this course. This ultimately amounts to an accessibility issue.

POLAR ACCESS POINTS

Polar region accessibility is the fundamental challenge to operating in the regions. Time, distance, and environmental factors challenge the most capable states to maintain consistent polar access for scientific, economic, or even military purposes. Polar region influence is directly proportional to a state's ability to access each region and conduct its activities. Given this, the future polar strategic competition will converge as much in the regions themselves as it will on Arctic and Antarctic gateways. Since both polar regions are difficult to operate from and within for sustained periods, it follows that it is easier for states to manage access rather from afar than seek to control from within. Assuming states will be more compelled to establish presence and influence in the Arctic and Antarctic access points, the United States needs to consider instructive analogs where this dynamic occurs to inform its approach to polar region access.

ANTARCTIC ACCESS. In Australia, the preponderance of the population lives on the periphery of the continent and ventures into the center for resource extraction activities. Antarctica is similar in that there is much state interest in reaching into the continent's center for extractive intent and economic gain, but where the preponderance of the human activity occurs along the peripheral and more habitable shorelines. Australian cities like Perth, Melbourne, Sydney, and Adelaide serve as similar access points for the Australian outback as countries like New Zealand, Australia, South Africa, and Argentina are for Antarctic accessibility. These gateway countries should be the principal focus of future US transactional balancing if the United States remains intent on maintaining Antarctic presence and influence, especially with the driving assumption that the Antarctic Treaty will—in time—dissolve. The United States needs to proactively manage Antarctica and emphasize balancing behavior to avoid conflict. Washington needs to abandon the false premise that the Antarctic Treaty is a sustainable governance construct for a continent with unresolved sovereignty and an increasingly attractive resource extraction proposition. Antarctica is now and will remain a compelling expansion opportunity for the next twenty to thirty years, and those who guide their approach in accordance with this assumption will be best positioned to exploit the southern continent to their own advantage, just as states are currently doing in the Arctic today.

ARCTIC ACCESS. The access dynamic is similar in the Arctic, with the critical access points occurring—beyond the United States and Russia—in Canada, Greenland (Denmark), Iceland, and Norway, each of which China is pursuing bilateral agreements with on the basis of the same logic as the proposed US approach. China's transactional approach toward Greenland and Norway, in particular, is precisely the model the United States needs to adopt as a counterbalance to Beijing's expansionist propositions. The United States should not continue its ignorant assumption that international institutions like NATO and the Arctic Council will remain intact with sufficient influence to govern, guide, or even deter Arctic behavior based solely on a consensus model of self-compliance. Transactional bilateralism has arrived and will prevail, and with it will emerge normative balancing behaviors based on transactional relations.

Transactional balancing will be the preferred form of international agreement for and between more powerful states and the leading predatory power practice used against weaker states. China has already started down this path and has developed productive transactional relationships with dozens of states, including most of those states critical to polar region accessibility. The United States can choose to continue espousing the virtues of multilateralism and pin its hopes of global influence to the increasingly false premise of institutional stability, or it can elect to forgo ideology in favor of pragmatism and realpolitik and step into the transactional-balancing environment that will define geopolitics and twenty-first-century strategic competition.

Whatever the case, rather than idly observing Beijing's rise to global prominence through prioritizing polar region presence via transactional arrangements with gateway state partnerships, many of which are longtime US allies, Washington must take a proactive approach and reemphasize polar region presence through strengthening its own relationships with critical Arctic and Antarctic access states. Those states that succeed will be the ones that adopt a pragmatic rather than ideological approach.

REALPOLITIK AND POLAR SECURITY

Returning to the assumption that councils and treaties are insufficient to ensure state compliance as we progress into more aggressive twenty-first-century geostrategic resource competition, the future of the polar regions will play out in one of two ways. Without treaty-oriented status quo stability as discussed in Chapter 5, and absent another productive balancing construct, polar conflict will occur due to a zero-sum competition among China and the United States where one of the two powers emerges as the polar hegemon, making and enforcing the rules according to their own governance model and thus injecting more tension into the system. The alternative is to pursue a transaction-based balancing dynamic characterized by negotiations in which neither China nor the United States has the influence or dominance to set the terms of international standards, commerce, or culture. In this space, we will see smaller states with a place at the table the same as powerful states seeking to negotiate outcomes consistent with national interests. The transactional model is even more plausible with nearly thirty years of globalization trends.

Today, people are more informed and thus less likely to buy into the "the bad guys over there" model that pervaded twentieth-century rhetoric. Populations and states have spent more time interacting with and learning about each other today such that the notion of a future characterized by productive transactional balancing operating independent of formal institutions and avoiding conflict is entirely possible. To this end, there is a future where the United States, Russia, and China cast aside ideological differences and enter into quid pro quo arrangements benefiting each state's interest first while avoiding tension. There is an opportunity to consider ways in which the future can be different, but it requires the suspension of flawed assumptions of the future looking like the past. This is where Western leaders who are twentieth-century hegemonic ideologues will inject their own revisionist narratives disguised as a progressive agenda. Those espousing the assumed virtues of institutional liberalism are not in tune with evolving realities. Ideology is fading, realpolitik is emerging, and transactional balancing is the globalist's realpolitik solution for management of the commons.

This is, admittedly, an optimistic model requiring—and thus assuming—a greater degree of global maturity and a shared vision than is currently present in the international system. In this model, there will likely be some form of proportional representation on states interacting in the global commons, including in the Arctic Ocean and on Antarctica. There would be a resulting incentive for states to take on more climate refugees, as an example, due to the proportional underpinnings of the agreement regime that supports the common good—a "you take some, I'll take some" dynamic leading to mutually beneficial outcomes rooted in first achieving self-interest. Within this logic thread, a club solution to polar region governance is an option.

A club solution entails an organizational construct whereby participating state actors agree in principle to behavior stipulations and promise contributions to the system that are enforceable through penalties for noncompliance. Club arrangements like the G-7 or G-20 differ from treaties chiefly in that they impose penalties on members who fail to meet the agreed commitments. Because of the penalty proposition, club solutions have come under scrutiny as unrealistic constructs for promoting international behavior and compliance. NATO is in many ways representative of a club system in theory, but in practice its refusal to enforce penalties on member states for failing to meet spending commitments keeps it removed from club status.

The Antarctic Treaty and Arctic Council are not club solutions to polar management, as they do not require contributions or enforce penalties; rather, each simply functions as a consensus-driven forum for states to agree on behavior principles. As well, each entity serves only to include state voices that are involved in the dialogue and fails to deter self-interested behavior anyway. A transactional club system could work as an alternative model of polar management.

States participating in the Arctic and Antarctic clubs will seek access based on need. There will be no membership contract or recurring price for admission. The polar club system will operate on a "pay as you go" model free of institutional encumbrances and managed through transactional relations with states presiding over the critical polar access points. Within the regions themselves, bilateral transactions will occur at will, but those states with territorial claims will be in the positional advantage in the arrangement. In this future model, states with Arctic territory will likely enforce territorial claims on the basis of continental shelf extensions. These will come to be accepted, even if disputed by some, as the international norm and standard, such that Arctic states will make and enforce the rules in the High North independent of the Arctic Council and its future. This is where the transactional nature of the balancing construct will likely play out, at least with regard to China as an example.

Here, China will continue to seek Arctic access for trade purposes, but on what basis will Beijing seek this access if it continues to block access to the South China Sea? Arctic states and others within balancing relationships feeling the effects of South China Sea constraints will be less likely to transact with China in the Arctic, unless there is a transactional arrangement allowing quid pro quo access to the Arctic for China in return for South China Sea access for Arctic states. In this way, the Arctic can serve as a transactional point of leverage for restoring limited access to the South China Sea. In Antarctica, the situation is—at risk of an obvious pun—the polar opposite.

Here, several states have claims, but the claims are unrecognized by those states with the most power in the current international system. Several without territorial claims, and even those with, are building more bases on Antarctica as a prelude to future lodging expectations and independent of the Antarctic Treaty. Eventually this will compel strategic competition relative to the global underpinnings of an increasingly resource-driven, self-interested equation chiefly motivated by China and the United States.

As the two primary influencers of the future international system, China and the United States will have military parity within the next two decades and an equally aggressive interest in Antarctic influence. Antarctic governance will need to be reconciled, be it the acceptance of transactional balancing via a club system or even a more formalized arrangement akin to today's increasingly fragile treaties. This will happen—on the basis of accelerating access and changing conditions—sooner than 2048, when the Antarctic Treaty's Madrid Protocol enters its renegotiation period, which may, as some have warned, lead to the removal of restrictions on military maneuvers and the resulting dissolution of the Antarctic Treaty System as we know it. States adopting and posturing for this eventuality will be best positioned for future Antarctic opportunity.

Parting Shot

It is easy to say that the polar regions are too far and too harsh to matter for international security. It is always easier to say why something cannot or will not happen than it is to contend with the realities that it might. To this point, Antarctica is rarely shown fully on modern maps. This is anecdotal to its position on the periphery of most people's minds. Great power competition in Antarctica extends beyond the imagination and conceivable realities of most. Antarctica enjoys neither ownership nor governance such that it is, effectively, an ongoing geopolitical research experiment. But Antarctica is enormous and full of attractive resources. So it logically follows that in progressively strained resource environments, states will continue seeking influence and presence in areas with resources, as they have for centuries. To the extent oil is needed, it can—and will—come from the polar regions. Resource competition for oil and other commodities will compel state expansion, and those states pursuing polar expansion will be the ones shaping the future of these regions culturally and strategically. When Europeans colonized North America, they did so at a time when social justice ideology was the driving force. South American colonization occurred prior with a feudal elitist system ascendant. What point of history are we in now and how will current ideologies influence the inevitable settlement of the last big chunk of ungoverned space on Earth?

The post–World War II model of globalism and cooperation has dominated effectively for seventy-five years. However, as Thomas Kuhn suggested as early as 1960 and as recently as 2012, we are exiting this period of romanticized ideology on the basis of market economics and entering a period of competing systems that will come to dominate the global environment.[58] Idealists will of course seek the globalist model of cooperation, but pragmatists will assume a transactional model of self-interested behaviors. The dominant model will be the one built on the back of the current international situation, and the current situation increasingly looks to be one of self-interested bilateral transactionalism rather than multilateralism. It will be, most certainly, a historic alignment point, whichever model prevails.

With this in mind, climate change is driving access to the poles and will be the dominant element of global interaction by the midpoint of the twenty-first century. This will induce pressures for migration and create refugee crises on a scale never seen before. Those states leading the charge in addressing and responding to migration crises and management of the global commons will set the global agenda, including in the polar regions. This portends transactional balancing as the preferred pragmatic approach to realpolitik in the polar regions and elsewhere, regardless of who sits behind the Resolute Desk in the White House. Even with the election of Joe Biden as the forty-sixth president of the United States, the seeds of Trumpism and transactional dynamics have been sown into the fabric of the international system for years.

Biden claimed that the US commitment to the NATO alliance "is sacred, not transactional."[59] But perhaps a transactional approach has merit. Trump's decision to reduce US troop levels in Germany on the basis of "delinquent" defense spending was purely transactional.[60] The Obama administration promoted the same commitment but stopped short of Trump's threats to withdraw US support.[61] Biden countered and claimed that values are stronger than cash. But China and 142 states committed to Beijing's Belt and Road Initiative disagree, in some cases setting aside competing values and ideologies in favor of interest-based transactional arrangements.[62] China's economic arrangements with more than half of the NATO member states indicate two things: cash is still king, and NATO's value system is compromised.[63] The United States should favor a pragmatic approach to foreign relations, one that seeks competing transactional arrangements with countries on China's bucket list to prevent Beijing's unfettered economic and military expansion. Doubling down on the US International Development Finance Corporation's efforts is a good start.[64]

As of this writing, the United States is $27 trillion in debt. Defense spending cuts are possible and the United States must be more deliberate with its interventions and overseas commitments. The United States needs to recognize the fiscal realities and Washington's weakened position from which to set the rules in an increasingly contested world where forward-deployed forces are less influential and at greater risk. The United States should engage in transactional-balancing behavior—rather than seeking hegemony—by maintaining a deterrent military, reserving forward engagement for existential threats to US vital interests, and pursuing mutually constitutive state economic and security arrangements premised on institutional fallibility and avoidance of self-binding ideology.

Seeking liberal hegemony may or may not lead the United States to war, but if Washington attempts to contain China, then conflict is inevitable. Things are different today. The pragmatist's approach removes ideology from the equation and adopts the necessity of US polar power through capability and intent as demonstrated via polar policy, posture, and presence. Investments are early indications of decisionmaking priorities and the United States has not invested in the polar regions to the extent other powers have. Where does this leave Washington as states jockey and position to compete over claims and influence the polar commons in the assumed absence of covenants and heightened necessity of access to the cosmos? Here again we see the creeping issues of territoriality, resource competition, and space domain access creating the conditions for confrontation and conflict that could lead the United States into a polar trap. To avoid the trap the United States needs to dismiss the apologist narrative pervading the conversation and adopt a sense of urgency in its orientation to the polar regions.

The Arctic and Antarctica are as strategically valuable as other regions compelling US presence and focus today. Rather than continue the Asia Pacific pivot, the United States should consider executing a polar pivot that seeks to project power, protect interests, prevent conflict, and preserve order in the polar regions. Developing a comprehensive polar strategy executed by a US Polar Command with dedicated polar capabilities and trained polar units is a good start toward signaling an expanded US commitment to the Arctic and Antarctica. This commitment will promote favorable conditions for the United States to adopt a transactional-balancing approach in the polar regions that complements its aims.

Without such an approach, continued subtle actions below the threshold of war will create an environment of strategic brinksmanship in the polar regions, extending the regional dynamics from cooperation, to competition, to confrontation, to conflict. Miscalculation and escalation are increasingly likely as states proceed through this continuum. We need to accept the reality that the current polar laws and norms are not fit for purpose in the twenty-first century. International institutions do not exist in perpetuity. When these seemingly infallible covenants eventually reach their tipping points, the United States will have a choice to make: it can watch as these international institutions crumble, and then it must be willing to operate in a region where it may not get to call the shots; or it can take action now and prevent the situation from happening, and at least be able to influence the outcome and still call some of the shots. There is opportunity in the pragmatism of transactional balancing. The future US defense posture calls for logic and measure rather than disconnected ideology. In the twenty-first-century international security environment, it is the pragmatist's approach that will prevail.

Notes

1. Burke and Cretella, "Towards a Strategic Value Proposition."
2. Cohen, *The Big Stick*, p. 199.
3. Kraska, *Arctic Security in an Age of Climate Change*.
4. Arctic Research Consortium of the United States, *2018: Interim Post-Season Report* (Fairbanks, Alaska, October 11, 2018).

Balancing on the Pivot   231

5. For example, many prominent authors do not consider the polar regions in their analysis of great power competition. See Mearsheimer, "The Gathering Storm"; Bechev, *Rival Power*; Wright, *All Measures Short of War.*

6. Donald J. Trump, *National Security Strategy of the United States of America* (Washington, DC: White House, 2017), pp. 1–2.

7. Ali, "U.S. Military Puts 'Great Power Competition' at Heart of Strategy."

8. Mattis, *Summary of the National Defense Strategy.*

9. The Arctic is passively mentioned once: "A range of international institutions establishes the rules for how states, businesses, and individuals interact with each other, across land and sea, the Arctic, outer space, and the digital realm." Trump, *National Security Strategy*, p. 40.

10. "China Island Tracker," https://amti.csis.org/island-tracker/china/.

11. Bernal, "House Funding Bill."

12. Hook and Mander, "The Fight to Own Antarctica."

13. Pezard, *The New Geopolitics of the Arctic*, p. 3.

14. Young, "What's China Up to in Antarctica?"

15. Gonzalez, "The Arctic and Antarctica."

16. Cohen, *The Big Stick*, p. 203.

17. Francioni and Scovazzi, *International Law for Antarctica*, p. 652.

18. Privratsky, *Logistics in the Falklands War.*

19. Nilsen, "Paratroopers Jump at 10,000 Meters."

20. Trump, "Memorandum on Safeguarding U.S. National Interests."

21. Personal communication with US Navy surface warfare officer who deployed with a US carrier strike group into the North Atlantic between 2018 and 2020.

22. *Fiscal Year 2018 National Defense Authorization Act*, December 12, 2017, p. 594.

23. Winger and Petursson, "Return to Keflavik Station."

24. US Department of the Navy, "A Blue Arctic: A Strategic Blueprint for the Arctic" (Washington, DC: Pentagon, January 5, 2021).

25. US Department of the Air Force, *Arctic Strategy*, July 2020, https://www.af.mil/Portals/1/documents/2020SAF/July/ArcticStrategy.pdf.

26. Athey, "Corps to Launch 3-Year Marine Littoral Regiment Experiment."

27. Feickert, "The Unified Command Plan and Combatant Commands."

28. Conversation with NORTHCOM officials about Arctic postures since 2002.

29. Summary of conversations with active-duty air force officers in various command positions (past/present) with experience operating to, from, and around Thule Air Force Base, Greenland.

30. "What Constitutes the United States? What Are the Official Definitions?" https://www.usgs.gov/faqs/what-constitutes-united-states-what-are-official-definitions?qt-news_science_products=0#qt-news_science_products.

31. Email conversation with New Zealand defense officials.

32. Measured via Google Maps, April 21, 2021.

33. Ibid.

34. Ibid.

35. Ferguson, "Falkland Islands Threat."

36. Conversation with US senior defense official on the feasibility of the Falklands proposal, November 29, 2020.

37. Conversation with US Air Force official on location at the US Air Force Arctic Survival School, Eielson Air Force Base, Alaska, February 2021.

38. "The Marines Hymn," https://www.marineband.marines.mil/about/library-and-archives/the-marines-hymn.

39. US Navy Fleet Forces Public Affairs, "Navy Establishes U.S. 2nd Fleet, Vice Adm. Lewis Assumes Command," August 24, 2018, https://www.navy.mil/Press-Office/News-Stories/Article/2250097/navy-establishes-us-2nd-fleet-vice-adm-lewis-assumes-command.

40. The US Navy's Fourth Fleet covers the SOUTHCOM area of responsibility including the Antarctic peninsular shorelines but does not have any permanently assigned vessels. Its Third Fleet area of responsibility extends throughout the Pacific Ocean north to the Arctic region by way of the Bering Strait and south to Antarctica in the Southern Ocean. The Sixth Fleet area of responsibility extends into the European Arctic waters to the north and south to Antarctica by way of the Atlantic Ocean. The Seventh Fleet does the same by way of the Pacific, extending out from Asia and Australia, meeting the Third Fleet area of responsibility in Hawaii.

41. Conversations with Joint Task Force–Support Forces Antarctica personnel.

42. Hinshaw and Page, "How the Pentagon Countered China's Designs."

43. "Consul, US Consulate, Nuuk, Greenland," https://dk.usembassy.gov/embassy-consulate/nuuk/consul.

44. Brockman, "Life North of 80."

45. James, *Canada and Conflict.*

46. Bennett et al., "The Opening of the Transpolar Sea Route."

47. Cirino, "Overfishing of Krill."

48. Wither, "Svalbard."

49. "Polar Bears: The King of the Arctic," https://en.visitsvalbard.com/visitor-information/polar-bears#:~:text=The%20polar%20bear%20population%20in,which%20exceeds%20the%20human%20population.&text=Of%20these%20a%20little%20less,on%20the%20drifting%20sea%20ice.

50. Nilsen, "Northern Sweden and Finland Play Key Role."

51. *The Antarctic Treaty,* October 15, 1959.

52. Gothe-Snape, "Defence Wants to Roll Out Military Tech."

53. Feiger and Wilson. "The Countries Taking Advantage of Antarctica."

54. Conversation with Australian security and defense policy expert, August 2020.

55. Burke, "Great Power Competition." The Arctic Monitoring and Assessment Programme (AMAP) is an Arctic Council working group that stipulates its region of coverage to include both areas in the Arctic Circle proper as well as those areas in the sub-Arctic, which includes the Aleutian Islands.

56. Buchanan, "The Overhaul of Russian Strategic Planning."

57. Brady, *China as a Polar Great Power.*

58. Kuhn, *The Structure of Scientific Revolutions.*

59. Ibid.

60. Woodward, "Trump Says He Is Reducing US Troops."

61. "Trump Confirms He Threatened to Withdraw from NATO," August 23, 2018, https://www.atlanticcouncil.org/blogs/natosource/trump-confirms-he-threatened-to-withdraw-from-nato.

62. "Green Belt and Road Initiative," March 2020, https://green-bri.org/countries-of-the-belt-and-road-initiative-bri.

63. Portions of the proceeding sections previously appeared in *Defense One.* Citation: Ryan Burke, "The Hidden Dangers in Biden's Foreign Policy," December 7, 2021, https://www.defenseone.com/ideas/2020/12/hidden-dangers-bidens-foreign-policy/170519/. Reused here with permission.

64. See website of the US International Development Finance Corporation, https://www.dfc.gov.

Bibliography

Ali, Idrees. "U.S. Military Puts 'Great Power Competition' at Heart of Strategy: Mattis." *Reuters,* January 19, 2018.
Aliyev, Nurlan. "Russia's Military Capabilities in the Arctic." June 25, 2019. https://icds.ee/en/russias-military-capabilities-in-the-arctic.
Allison, Graham. *Destined for War: Can America and China Escape Thucydides's Trap?* New York: Houghton Mifflin Harcourt, 2017.
———. "The Thucydides Trap: Are the U.S. and China Headed for War?" *The Atlantic,* September 24, 2015. http://www.theatlantic.com/international/archive/2015/09/united-states-china-war-thucydides-trap/406756.
Allison, Graham, Robert Blackwill, and Ali Wyne. *Lee Kuan Yew: The Grand Master's Insights on China, the United States, and the World.* Cambridge: MIT Press, 2013.
Amos, Jonathan. "315 Billion-Tonne Iceberg Breaks Off Antarctica." *BBC News,* September 30, 2019. http://www.bbc.com/news/science-environment-49885450.
Antarctic and Southern Ocean Coalition. *The Antarctic Oil Myth.* April 20, 2014. https://www.asoc.org/component/content/article/9-blog/1184-the-antarctic-oil-myth.
Arctic Council. *Declaration on the Establishment of the Arctic Council.* Joint Communiqué of the Governments of the Arctic Countries on the Establishment of the Arctic Council. 1996. https://arctic-council.org/en/about.
Athey, Philip. "Corps to Launch 3-Year Marine Littoral Regiment Experiment Using Hawaii Marines." *Marine Corps Times,* September 22, 2020. https://www.marinecorpstimes.com/news/your-marine-corps/2020/09/22/corps-to-begin-3-year-marine-littoral-regiment-experiment-using-hawaii-marines.
Åtland, Kristian. "Mikhail Gorbachev, the Murmansk Initiative, and the Desecuritization of Interstate Relations in the Arctic." *Cooperation and Conflict* 43, no. 3 (2008): 290.
Atta, Lee Van. "A Bordo del Monte Olimpo en Alta Mar." *El Mercurio* (Santiago), March 5, 1947.

Auerswald, Dave. "Now Is Not the Time for a FONOP in the Arctic." October 11, 2019. http://www.warontherocks.com/2019/10/now-is-not-the-time-for-a-fonop-in-the-arctic.

Axe, David. "Russia Is Sending S-400 Air Defense Systems to the Arctic (and That's Just for Starters)." *National Interest,* March 26, 2019.

Barrett, Barbara. "Department of the Air Force Arctic Strategy." Washington, DC: US Department of Defense, July 21, 2020.

Bechev, Dimitar. *Rival Power: Russia in Southeast Europe.* New Haven: Yale University Press, 2017.

Beck, Peter J. *International Politics of Antarctica (Routledge Revivals).* London: Routledge, 2014.

Beckley, Michael. "The Power of Nations: Measuring What Matters." *International Security* 43, no. 2 (2018): 7–44.

Bennett, Mia M., Scott R. Stephenson, Kang Yang, Michael T. Bravo, and Bert De Jonghe. "The Opening of the Transpolar Sea Route: Logistical, Geopolitical, Environmental, and Socioeconomic Impacts." *Marine Policy* (2020): 104–178.

Bernal, Rafael. "House Funding Bill Scraps Arctic Icebreaker Program." *The Hill,* December 13, 2018.

Berry, Dawn Alexandrea. "Cryolite, the Canadian Aluminium Industry, and the American Occupation of Greenland During the Second World War." *Polar Journal* 2, no. 2 (2012): 219–235.

Bertuca, Tony. "NORTHCOM Lists Unfunded Needs for Arctic Communications, Counter-Drone." February 21, 2020. https://insidedefense.com/daily-news/northcom-lists-unfunded-needs-arctic-communications-counter-drone.

Beschloss, Michael. "Dividing the Spoils." *Smithsonian Magazine,* December 2002.

Beukel, Erik. "The Greenland Issue." In *Phasing Out the Colonial Status of Greenland, 1945–54: A Historical Study,* edited by Erik Beukel, Frede P. Jensen, and Jens Elo Rytter. Copenhagen: Museum Tusculanum, 2009.

Biden, Joseph R., Jr. "Why America Must Lead Again: Recusing US Foreign Policy After Trump." *Foreign Affairs* 99 (2020): 64.

Bishop, Caitlyn. "A Look into the International Research Stations of Antarctica." https://oceanwide-expeditions.com/blog/a-look-into-the-international-research-stations-of-antarctica.

Blakemore, Erin. "Who Really Discovered Antarctica? Depends Who You Ask." *National Geographic,* January 27, 2020. https://www.nationalgeographic.com/history/article/who-discovered-antarctica-depends-who-ask.

Bouffard, Troy, Elizabeth Buchanan, and Michael Young. "Arctic Security and Dialogue: Assurance Through Defence Diplomacy." July 11, 2020. https://moderndiplomacy.eu/2020/07/11/arctic-security-and-dialogue-assurance-through-defence-diplomacy.

Bouffard, Troy, and Cameron Carlson. "A Surface Presence for the US Navy in the Arctic?" *Canadian Naval Review* 15 no. 2 (2019): 28.

Brady, Anne-Marie. *China as a Polar Great Power.* Cambridge: Cambridge University Press, 2017.

———. "China's Expanding Antarctic Interests." Canberra: Australian Strategic Policy Institute, 2017.

———. "China's Undeclared Foreign Policy at the Poles." *The Interpreter,* May 30, 2017. https://www.lowyinstitute.org/the-interpreter/china-undeclared-foreign-policy-poles.

Braithwaite, Kenneth, II. "A Blue Arctic: Department of the Navy—A Strategic Blueprint for the Arctic." Washington, DC: US Department of Defense, January 5, 2021.

Briggs, Philip J. "The Polar Sea Voyage and the Northwest Passage Dispute." *Armed Forces & Society* 16, no. 3 (1990): 437–452.

Brockman, Alex. "Life North of 80: Meet the People Living at the Top of the World." *CBC News*, September 3, 2018.

Brown, Chris. *Understanding International Relations.* 5th ed. London: Red Globe, 2019.

Browne, Ryan. "NATO Report Says Only 7 Members Are Meeting Defense Spending Targets." March 14, 2019. https://www.cnn.com/2019/03/14/politics/nato-defense-spending-target/index.html.

Buchanan, Elizabeth. "The Overhaul of Russian Strategic Planning for the Arctic Zone to 2035." May 19, 2020. http://www.ndc.nato.int/research/research.php?icode=641#_edn3.

———. "There Is No Arctic Axis." *Foreign Policy,* July 21, 2020. https://foreignpolicy.com/2020/07/21/no-arctic-axis-china-russia-relationship-resources-natural-gas-northern-sea-route.

———. "West Must Cooperate with Russia in the Arctic." *Moscow Times,* November 3, 2015. https://www.themoscowtimes.com/2015/11/03/west-must-cooperate-with-russia-in-the-arctic-a50614.

Buchanan, Elizabeth, and Bec Straiting. "Why the Arctic Is Not the 'Next' South China Sea." November 5, 2020. http://warontherocks.com/2020/11/why-the-arctic-is-not-the-next-south-china-sea.

Burke, Catharine. "The Northwest Passage Dispute." February 26, 2018. https://www.oxfordresearchgroup.org.uk/blog/the-northwest-passage-dispute.

Burke, Ryan. "Great-Power Competition in the 'Snow of Far-Off Northern Lands': Why We Need a New Approach to Arctic Security." April 8, 2020. https://mwi.usma.edu/great-power-competition-snow-far-off-northern-lands-need-new-approach-arctic-security.

———. "The Hidden Dangers in Biden's Foreign Policy," December 7, 2021, https://www.defenseone.com/ideas/2020/12/hidden-dangers-bidens-foreign-policy/170519/

———. "Trump's Interest in Greenland Is a Wakeup Call About Arctic Influence." *The Hill,* August 27, 2019. thehill.com/opinion/national-security/458823-trumps-interest-in-greenland-is-a-wakeup-call-about-arctic.

———. "Trump's 'Super Duper Missile' Is Super Duper Necessary." *The Hill,* May 19, 2020. https://thehill.com/opinion/national-security/498274-trumps-super-duper-missile-is-super-duper-necessary.

Burke, Ryan, and Olivia Cretella. "Towards a Strategic Value Proposition: Redefining 21st Century Defense Priority Assessments." *Over the Horizon Journal,* April 26, 2021. https://othjournal.com/2021/04/26/towards-a-strategic-value-proposition-redefining-21st-century-defense-priority-assessments.

Burke, Ryan, and Jahara Matisek. "The American Polar Pivot: Gaining a Comparative Advantage in Great Power Competition." *Marine Corps University Journal* 10, no. 2 (October 2019): 70–91.

———. "The Illogical Logic of American Entanglement in the Middle East." *Journal of Strategic Security* 13, no 1 (2020): 1–25.

———. "The Polar Trap: China, Russia, and American Power in the Arctic and Antarctica." *Journal of Indo-Pacific Affairs* 4, no 7 (2021): 36–66.

Byers, Michael. "Cold, Dark, and Dangerous: International Cooperation in the Arctic and Space." *Polar Record* 55, no. 1 (2019): 32–47.

Byrd, Richard E. "All-Out Assault on Antarctica." *National Geographic* 110, no. 2 (1956): 141–179.

Campbell, Kurt, Eric Edelman, Michèle Flournoy, Richard Fontaine, Stephen J. Hadley, Robert Kagan, James P. Rubin, Julianne Smith, James Steinberg, and Robert Zoellick. "Extending American Power: Strategies to Expand US Engagement in a Competitive World Order." Washington, DC: Center for a New American Security, 2016.

Carter, Perry, Anne-Marie Brady, and Evgeny Pavlov. "Russia's 'Smart Power' Foreign Policy and Antarctica." *Polar Journal* 6, no. 2 (2016): 259–272.

Cecco, Leyland. "Mike Pompeo Rejects Canada's Claims to Northwest Passage As 'Illegitimate.'" *The Guardian,* May 7, 2019. https://www.theguardian.com/us-news/2019/may/07/mike-pompeo-canada-northwest-passage-illegitimate.

Chatzky, Andrew, and James McBridge. "China's Massive Belt and Road Initiative." January 28, 2020. https://www.cfr.org/backgrounder/chinas-massive-belt-and-road-initiative.

Chernov, Vitaly. "New Port Planned for Russia's Growing Northern Logistics Chain." March 14, 2020. https://www.maritime-executive.com/blog/new-port-planned-for-russia-s-growing-northern-logistics-chain.

Clark, Helen. "Oil and Gas Fueling South China Sea Tensions." *Asia Times,* July 22, 2020. https://asiatimes.com/2020/07/oil-and-gas-fueling-south-china-sea-tensions.

Cohen, Eliot A. *The Big Stick: The Limits of Soft Power and The Necessity of Military Force.* London: Hachette, 2017.

Conley, Heather, and Joseph Bermudez. "Ice Curtain: Why Is There a New Russian Military Facility 300 Miles from Alaska?" March 24, 2020. https://www.csis.org/analysis/ice-curtain-why-there-new-russian-military-facility-300-miles-alaska.

Conley, Heather, and M. Melino. "The Implications of US Policy Stagnation Toward the Arctic Region." Washington, DC: Center for Strategic and International Studies, May 3, 2019.

Conley, Heather A., and Caroline Rohloff. *The New Ice Curtain: Russia's Strategic Reach to the Arctic.* Lanham: Rowman and Littlefield, 2015.

Cooley, Alexander, and Daniel Nexon. *Exit from Hegemony: The Unraveling of the American Global Order.* Oxford: Oxford University Press, 2020.

Council on Foreign Relations. "Conflict in Ukraine." April 2021. https://www.cfr.org/global-conflict-tracker/conflict/conflict-ukraine.

Cirino, Erica. "Overfishing of Krill Is Disrupting Antarctic Food Chains." *Pacific Standard,* March 30, 2018.

Dahl, Robert. "The Concept of Power." *Behavioral Science* 2 no. 3 (1957): 201–215.

Desjardins, Jeff. "This Infographic Shows How Gigantic the Arctic's Undiscovered Oil Reserves Might Be." *Business Insider,* April 7, 2016.

Devyatkin, Pavel. "The Pompeo Doctrine in Effect: Poking the Russian Bear or Countering China in the Arctic?" May 26, 2020. https://responsiblestatecraft.org/2020/05/26/the-pompeo-doctrine-in-effect-poking-the-russian-bear-or-countering-china-in-the-arctic.

Dewing, Charles, and Laura Kelsay. "Records of the United States Antarctic Service." National Archives, Preliminary Inventories 90, Record Group 126, Publication 56-8. Washington, DC, 1955.

Digges, Charles. "Putin Unveils More Plans to Boost Northern Sea Route." March 7, 2020. https://www.maritime-executive.com/editorials/putin-unveils-more-plans-to-boost-northern-sea-route.

Dillow, Clay. "Russia and China Vie to Beat the U.S. in the Trillion-Dollar Race to Control the Arctic." *CNBC,* February 6, 2018.

Dresen, J. F. "The Prospects for a Sino-Russian Strategic Partnership." In *Kennan Institute Meeting Report,* vol. 11. Washington, DC: Kennan Institute, 2011.

Durkee, Jack. "China: The New 'Near-Arctic State.'" February 6, 2020. https://www.wilsoncenter.org/article/china-the-new-near-arctic-state.

Eckstein, Megan. "Theodore Roosevelt Strike Group in Alaska for High-End." May 14, 2019. https://news.usni.org/2019/05/14/theodore-roosevelt-strike-group-in-alaska-for-high-end-joint-exercise-northern-edge-2019.

———. "Truman Carrier Strike Group Operating North of Arctic Circle." October 19, 2018. https://news.usni.org/2018/10/19/truman-carrier-strike-group-operating-north-arctic-circle-first-time-us-navy-since-1991.

———. "U.S., U.K. Surface Warships Patrol Barents Sea." May 4, 2020. https://news.usni.org/2020/05/04/u-s-u-k-surface-warships-patrol-barents-sea-for-first-time-since-the-1980s.

Embassy of the People's Republic of China. "China Opens 1st Research Station in Arctic Area." July 28, 2004. http://www.china-embassy.org/eng/gyzg/t144196.htm.

English, Robert. "Why an Arctic Arms Race Would be a Mistake." *Arctic Today*, June 18, 2020. https://www.arctictoday.com/why-an-arctic-arms-race-would-be-a-mistake.

English, Robert, and Morgan Gardner. "Phantom Peril in the Arctic: Russia Doesn't Threaten the United States in the Far North—but Climate Change Does." *Foreign Affairs*, September 29, 2020. https://www.foreignaffairs.com/articles/united-states/2020-09-29/phantom-peril-arctic.

Exner-Pirot, Heather. "Between Militarization and Disarmament: Challenges for Arctic Security in the Twenty-First Century." In *Climate Change and Arctic Security*, edited by Lassi Heininen and Heather Exner-Pirot. New York: Springer International, 2020.

Farquhar, John T. "Arctic Linchpin: The Polar Concept in American Air Atomic Strategy, 1946–1948." *Air Power History* 61, no. 4 (2014): 34–45.

Feickert, Andrew. "The Unified Command Plan and Combatant Commands: Background and Issues for Congress." Washington, DC: Congressional Research Service, 2013.

Feiger, Leah, and Mara Wilson. "The Countries Taking Advantage of Antarctica During the Pandemic." *The Atlantic*, May 15, 2020.

Ferguson, Emily. "Falkland Islands Threat: Argentina to Lay Claim to Islands with Major Event This Week." November 3, 2020. https://www.express.co.uk/news/world/1355410/falklands-islands-Argentina-news-claim-britian-malvinas-islands-David-Jewett-1820.

Fogarty, Ellie. *Antarctica: Assessing and Protecting Australia's National Interests*. Sydney: Lowy Institute for International Policy, 2011.

Francioni, Francesco, and Tullio Scovazzi. *International Law for Antarctica*. Leiden: Martinus Nijhoff, 1996.

Friedman, Thomas L. *The World Is Flat: The Globalized World in the Twenty-First Century*. New York: Penguin, 2006.

Friedman, Uri. "The New Concept Everyone in Washington Is Talking About." *The Atlantic*, August 6, 2019.

Garamone, Jim. "Northcom Commander Calls for 21st Century Tools to Defeat Current Threats." March 11, 2020. https://www.defense.gov/Explore/News/Article/Article/2109462/northcom-commander-calls-for-21st-century-tools-to-defeat-current-threats.

Gautier, Donald L., et al. "Circum-Arctic Resource Appraisal: Estimates of Undiscovered Oil and Gas North of the Arctic Circle." Fact Sheet 2008-3049. Washington, DC: US Geological Survey, 2008.

Gjørv, Gunhild Hoogensen, Marc Lanteigne, and Horatio Sam-Aggrey, eds. *Routledge Handbook of Arctic Security*. London: Routledge, 2020.

Glaser, Charles L. *Rational Theory of International Politics: The Logic of Competition and Cooperation.* Princeton: Princeton University Press, 2010.

Gonzalez, Marvin. "The Arctic and Antarctica." Washington, DC: Office of the Director of National Intelligence, 2018.

Gothe-Snape, Jackson. "Defence Wants to Roll Out Military Tech in Antarctica Despite Treaty Ban on Military Activity." *ABC News,* August 19, 2019. https://www.abc.net.au/news/2019-08-19/australia-antarctica-military-dual-use-technology/11427226?nw=0.

Gorenburg, Dmitry. "An Emerging Strategic Partnership: Trends in Russia-China Military Cooperation." April 2020. https://www.marshallcenter.org/en/publications/security-insights/emerging-strategic-partnership-trends-russia-china-military-cooperation-0.

Gosnell, Rachael. "Caution in the High North: Geopolitical and Economic Challenges of the Arctic Maritime Environment." June 25, 2018. http://warontherocks.com/2018/06/caution-in-the-high-north-geopolitical-and-economic-challenges-of-the-arctic-maritime-environment.

Gosnell, Rachael, and Andreas Hildenbrand. "Emerging Challenges in Arctic Security and Recommendations for the Future: Perspectives from the European Security Seminar North 19-05." *Security Insights* no. 24 (March 2019).

Graham, Thomas, and Amy Myers Jaffe. "There Is No Scramble for the Arctic." *Foreign Affairs,* July 27, 2020. https://www.foreignaffairs.com/articles/russian-federation/2020-07-27/there-no-scramble-arctic.

Green, Mark. "China's Debt Diplomacy." *Foreign Policy,* April 25, 2019. https://foreignpolicy.com/2019/04/25/chinas-debt-diplomacy.

Green, Michael. "China's Maritime Silk Road: Strategic and Economic Implications for the Indo-Pacific Region." April 2, 2018. http://www.csis.org/analysis/chinas-maritime-silk-road.

Hammes, T. X. *Deglobalization and International Security.* Amherst: Cambria, 2020.

Hatherton, Trevor. "Antarctica Prior to the Antarctic Treaty: A Historical Perspective." In National Research Council, *Antarctic Treaty System: An Assessment.* Washington, DC: National Academies Press, 1986.

Havnes, Heljar, and Johan Martin Seland. "The Increasing Security Focus in China's Arctic Policy." July 16, 2019. https://www.thearcticinstitute.org/increasing-security-focus-china-arctic-policy.

Headley, James. "Russia Resurgent: The Implications for New Zealand." In *Small States and the Changing Global Order,* edited by Anne-Marie Brady. New York: Springer, 2019.

Heininen, Lassi, and Heather Exner-Pirot. *Climate Change and Arctic Security.* New York: Springer International, 2020.

Hemmings, Alan D., Donald R. Rothwell, and Karen N. Scott, eds. *Antarctic Security in the Twenty-First Century: Legal and Policy Perspectives.* London: Routledge, 2012.

Hinshaw, Drew, and Jeremy Page. "How the Pentagon Countered China's Designs on Greenland." *Wall Street Journal,* February 10, 2019.

Hook, Leslie, and Benedict Mander. "The Fight to Own Antarctica." *Financial Times,* May 23, 2018.

Hopko, Hanna. "What Putin Must Hear in Munich." February 14, 2019. https://www.atlanticcouncil.org/blogs/ukrainealert/what-putin-must-hear-in-munich.

Hui, Lu, ed. "China's Arctic Policy." January 26, 2018. http://www.xinhuanet.com/english/2018-01/26/c_136926498.htm.

Humpert, Malte. "Russia Elevates Importance of Northern Fleet." January 13, 2021. https://www.highnorthnews.com/en/russia-elevates-importance-northern-fleet-upgrading-it-military-district-status.

Bibliography 239

Hurt, Martin. "Russia Continues to Test Western Resolve: Spetsnaz Units Operating in Norwegian Territory." October 2019. http://www.icds.ee/russia-continues-to-test-western-resolve-spetsnaz-units-operating-in-norwegian-territory.

Isachenkov, Vladimir. "Russia Voices Concern over New US Submarine-Launched Nuclear Weapon." *Air Force Times,* February 5, 2020. http://www.airforcetimes.com/news/your-military/2020/02/05/russia-voices-concern-over-new-us-nuclear-weapon.

James, Patrick. *Canada and Conflict: A Hard-Hitting Look at Canadian Security Post-9/11, from the Afghanistan War to US Relations and Arctic Sovereignty.* Oxford: Oxford University Press, 2012.

Joint Staff. *Description of the National Military Strategy 2018.* Washington, DC: US Department of Defense, 2018.

Joyner, Christopher C. *Antarctica and the Law of the Sea.* Boston: Martinus Nijhoff, 1992.

———. "Nonmilitarization of the Antarctic: The Interplay of Law and Geopolitics." *Naval War College Review* 42, no. 4 (1989): 83–104.

Käpylä, Juha, and Harri Mikkola. *On Arctic Exceptionalism: Critical Reflections in the Light of the Arctic Sunrise Case and the Crisis in Ukraine.* Helsinki: Finnish Institute of International Affairs, 2015.

Kearns, David A. *Where Hell Freezes Over: A Story of Amazing Bravery and Survival.* New York: Macmillan, 2005.

Kissinger, Henry. *Diplomacy.* New York: Simon and Schuster, 1994.

Kirshner, Jonathan. "Handle Him with Care: The Importance of Getting Thucydides Right." *Security Studies* 28, no. 1 (2019): 1–24, DOI: 10.1080/09636412.2018.1508634.

Klimenko, Ekaterina. "Russia's New Arctic Policy Document Signals Continuity Rather Than Change." April 6, 2020. https://www.sipri.org/commentary/essay/2020/russias-new-arctic-policy-document-signals-continuity-rather-change.

Kline, Mikaley. "Joint Task Force Kicks Off 64th Year of DoD Antarctic Mission Support." September 10, 2019. http://www.pacaf.af.mil/News/Article-Display/Article/1956772/joint-task-force-kicks-off-64th-year-of-dod-antarctic-mission-support.

Konyshev, Valery, and Alexander Sergunin. "Is Russia a Revisionist Military Power in the Arctic?" *Defense & Security Analysis* 30, no. 4 (2014): 323–335.

Kraska, James, ed. *Arctic Security in an Age of Climate Change.* Cambridge: Cambridge University Press, 2011.

Kuhn, Thomas S. *The Structure of Scientific Revolutions.* Chicago: University of Chicago Press, 2012.

Lajeunesse, Adam. *Lock, Stock, and Icebergs: A History of Canada's Arctic Maritime Sovereignty.* Vancouver: University of British Columbia Press, 2016.

Layne, Christopher. "From Preponderance to Offshore Balancing: America's Future Grand Strategy." *International Security* 22, no. 1 (1997): 86–124.

Leapman, Ben. "Denmark Joins Race to Claim North Pole." *Daily Telegraph,* August 12, 2007.

Leonkov, Alexey. "Hypersonic Throw of the 'Dagger': Competitors Are Still in 'Swaddling Clothes.'" May 23, 2018. https://zvezdaweekly.ru/news/t/20185211547-L3aOs.html.

Lind, Michael. "John Mearsheimer on International Relations, Great Power Politics, and the Age of Trump." December 15, 2018. https://nationalinterest.org/feature/john-mearsheimer-international-relations-great-power-politics-and-age-trump-38772?page=0%2C1.

Lino, Marissa. "Understanding China's Arctic Activities." February 25, 2020. https://www.iiss.org/blogs/analysis/2020/02/china-arctic.

Lüdecke, Cornelia, and C. P. Summerhayes. *The Third Reich in Antarctica: The German Antarctic Expedition 1938–39.* Norwich: Erskine, 2012.

Lundestad, Ingrid, and Øystein Tunsjø. "The United States and China in the Arctic." *Polar Record* 51, no. 4 (2015): 392–403.

MacAskill, Ewen. "Russia Says US Troops Arriving in Poland Pose Threat to Its Security." *The Guardian,* January 12, 2017. https://www.theguardian.com/us-news/2017/jan/12/doubts-over-biggest-us-deployment-in-europe-since-cold-war-under-trump.

Mahan, Alfred Thayer. *The Influence of Seapower on History, 1660–1783.* New York: Little, Brown, 1890.

Mani, N. Mangala, et al. "Challenges in Operations and Maintenance of Antarctica Ground Station for Earth Observation Satellites." *International Archives of the Photogrammetry: Remote Sensing and Spatial Information Sciences* 42 (2018): 281–283.

Maquieira, Christian. "Antarctica Prior to the Antarctic Treaty: A Political and Legal Perspective." In National Research Council, *Antarctic Treaty System: An Assessment.* Washington, DC: National Academies Press, 1986.

Mattis, James. *Summary of the 2018 National Defense Strategy of the United States of America.* Washington, DC: US Department of Defense, 2018.

Mazarr, Michael J., Timothy R. Heath, and Astrid Stuth Cevallos. *China and the International Order.* Santa Monica: RAND, 2018.

McCannon, John. *Red Arctic: Polar Exploration and the Myth of the North in the Soviet Union, 1932–1939.* Oxford: Oxford University Press on Demand, 1998.

McCarthy, Ryan. "Regaining Arctic Dominance: The US Army in the Arctic." Washington, DC: US Department of Defense, January 19, 2021.

McDermott, Roger. "Brothers Disunited: Russia's Use of Military Power in Ukraine." In *The Return of the Cold War: Ukraine, the West, and Russia,* edited by J. L. Black and Michael Johns. London: Routledge, 2016.

McFaul, Michael. "Russia's 2000 Presidential Elections: Implications for Russian Democracy and US-Russian Relations." Testimony Before the US Senate Committee on Foreign Relations. Washington, DC, April 12, 2000.

Mearsheimer, John J. "The False Promise of International Institutions." *International Security* 19, no. 3 (1994): 5–49.

———. "The Gathering Storm: China's Challenge to US Power in Asia." *Chinese Journal of International Politics* 3, no. 4 (Winter 2010): 381–396. https://doi.org/10.1093/cjip/poq016.

Meier, W., et al., *2018: Sea Ice Outlook Interim Post-Season Report.* Fairbanks, Alaska: Arctic Research Consortium of the United States, 2018.

Melino, Matthew, and Heather Conley. "The Ice Curtain: Russia's Arctic Military Presence." March 24, 2020. https://www.csis.org/features/ice-curtain-russias-arctic-military-presence.

Miller, Kent. "Eielson Reactivates Fighter Squadron Ahead of F-35's Arrival." *Air Force Times,* October 12, 2019. http://www.airforcetimes.com/news/your-air-force/2019/10/12/eielson-reactivates-fighter-squadron-ahead-of-f-35s-arrival.

Miyake, Kuni. "Thucydides's Fallacy, Not a Trap." *Japan Times,* September 25, 2018. http://www.japantimes.co.jp/opinion/2018/09/25/commentary/world-commentary/thucydidess-fallacy-not-trap/#.XjHcrehKjD5.

Moon, Twila, et al. "The Expanding Footprint of Rapid Arctic Change." *Earth's Future* 7, no. 3 (2019): 212–218.

Moran, Dan. "200 Years of Exploring Antarctica—The World's Coldest, Most Forbidding, and Most Peaceful Continent." *The Conversation,* January 24, 2020.

https://theconversation.com/200-years-of-exploring-antarctica-the-worlds-coldest-most-forbidding-and-most-peaceful-continent-129607.

Mukherjee, Rohan. "Two Cheers for the Liberal World Order: The International Order and Rising Powers in a Trumpian World." February 22, 2019. https://issforum.org/roundtables/policy/1-5bo-two-cheers.

Murray, Robert. "Do Not Oversell the Russian Threat in the Arctic." May 16, 2016. http://warontherocks.com/2016/05/do-not-oversell-the-russian-threat-in-the-arctic.

Nakano, Jane. "China Launches the Polar Silk Road." Washington, DC: Center for Strategic and International Studies, February 2018.

National Research Council. *Antarctic Treaty System: An Assessment.* Proceedings of a workshop held at Beardmore South Field Camp, Antarctica, January 7–13, 1985. Washington, DC: National Academies Press, 1986.

Nelson, Dale W. "Wanna Buy Greenland? The United States Once Did." *Associated Press,* May 2, 1991.

Nelson, James Carl. *The Polar Bear Expedition: The Heroes of America's Forgotten Invasion of Russia, 1918–1919.* New York: Morrow, 2019.

Niiler, Eric. "Hitler Sent a Secret Expedition to Antarctica in a Hunt for Margarine Fat." August 31, 2018. https://www.history.com/news/hitler-nazi-secret-expedition-antarctica-whale-oil.

Nilsen, Thomas. "Northern Sweden and Finland Play Key Role as NATO Kicks Off Trident Juncture." *Barents Observer,* October 23, 2018.

———. "Paratroopers Jump at 10,000 Meters over Russian Arctic Base." April 26, 2020. https://thebarentsobserver.com/en/security/2020/04/paratroopers-jump-10000-meters-over-russian-arctic-base.

———. "Russia's Top General Indirectly Confirms Arctic Deployment of the Unstoppable Kinzhal Missile." December 19, 2019. https://thebarentsobserver.com/en/security/2019/12/russias-top-general-indirectly-confirms-arctic-deployment-unstoppable-missile.

Nye, Joseph S., Jr. "Get Smart: Combining Hard and Soft Power." *Foreign Affairs* (2009): 163.

O'Rourke, Ronald, et al. "Changes in the Arctic: Background Issues for Congress." January 23, 2020. http://fas.org/sgp/crs/misc/R41153.pdf.

O'Shaughnessy, Terrance. "Hearing to Receive Testimony on U.S. Policy and Posture in Support of Arctic Readiness." March 3, 2020. http://www.armed-services.senate.gov/imo/media/doc/20-09_03-03-2020.pdf.

Ostenso, Need Allen. "Arctic Ocean." April 6, 2020. https://www.britannica.com/place/Arctic-Ocean.

Parfitt, Tom. "Russia Plants Flag on North Pole Seabed." *The Guardian* 2, no. 8, August 2, 2007.

Parker, Geoffrey. *The Thirty Years' War.* London: Routledge, 2006.

Patten, Dary. "Soldier Pierces Through Snow to Improve Life in Antarctica." January 10, 2020. https://www.army.mil/article/231506/soldier_pierces_through_snow_to_improve_life_in_antarctica.

Pauwelyn, Joost, Ramses Wessel, and Jan Wouters. "When Structures Become Shackles: Dynamics in International Lawmaking." *European Journal of International Law* 25, no. 3 (2014): 733–763.

Pawlyk, Oriana. "More US Military Power Needed in Antarctic to Deter Malign Activity, General Says." July 30, 2019. https://www.military.com/daily-news/2019/07/30/more-us-military-power-needed-antarctic-deter-malign-activity-general-says.html.

Peltier, Chad. "China's Logistics Capabilities for Expeditionary Operations." *Jane's,* April 2020.
People's Republic of China. "China's Arctic Policy." January 2018. http://www.scio.gov.cn/zfbps/32832/Document/1618243/1618243.htm.
Perlez, Jane. "Leader Asserts China's Growing Presence on Global Stage." *New York Times,* November 30, 2014. http://www.nytimes.com/2014/12/01/world/asia/leader-asserts-chinas-growing-role-on-global-stage.html.
Pezard, Stephanie. "How Not to Compete in the Arctic: The Blurry Lines Between Friend and Foe." February 27, 2019. http://warontherocks.com/2019/02/how-not-to-compete-in-the-arctic-the-blurry-lines-between-friend-and-foe.
———. *The New Geopolitics of the Arctic: Russia's and China's Evolving Role in the Region.* Santa Monica: RAND, November 3, 2018.
Pincus, Rebecca, and Walter Berbick. "Gray Zones in a Blue Arctic: Grappling with China's Growing Influence." October 24, 2018. http://warontherocks.com/2018/10/gray-zones-in-a-blue-arctic-grappling-with-chinas-growing-influence.
Pincus, Rebecca. "NATO North? Building a Role for NATO in the Arctic." November 6, 2019. http://warontherocks.com/2019/11/nato-north-building-a-role-for-nato-in-the-arctic.
Pompeo, Mike. "Looking North: Sharpening America's Arctic Focus." May 6, 2019. http://www.state.gov/looking-north-sharpening-americas-arctic-focus.
Posen, Barry R. "Command of the Commons: The Military Foundation of US Hegemony." *International Security* 28, no. 1 (2003): 5–46.
Privratsky, K. L. *Logistics in the Falklands War: A Case Study in Expeditionary Warfare.* Barnsley: Pen and Sword, 2017.
Pruitt, Sarah. "How a Five-Day War with Georgia Allowed Russia to Reassert Its Military Might." August 8, 2018. https://www.history.com/news/russia-georgia-war-military-nato.
Putin, Vladimir. "Foundations of the Russian Federation State Policy in the Arctic for the Period up to 2035." March 5, 2020. https://dnnlgwick.blob.core.windows.net/portals/0/NWCDepartments/Russia%20Maritime%20Studies%20Institute/ArcticPolicyFoundations2035_English_FINAL_21July2020.pdf?sr=b&si=DNNFileManagerPolicy&sig=DSkBpDNhHsgjOAvPILTRoxIfV%2FO02gR81NJSokwx2EM%3D.
Regehr, Ernie. "Replacing the North Warning System: Strategic Competition or Arctic Confidence Building?" March 1, 2018. http://www.thesimonsfoundation.ca/highlights/replacing-north-warning-system-strategic-competition-or-arctic-confidence-building.
Rhode, Benjamin. "The GIUK Gap's Strategic Significance." *International Institute for Strategic Studies* 25, no. 29 (October 2019).
Rhodes, Ben. "Inside the White House During the Syrian 'Red Line' Crisis." *The Atlantic,* June 3, 2018.
Ridgewell, Henry. "US Labels China 'Greatest Potential Adversary.'" February 15, 2020. https://www.voanews.com/europe/us-labels-china-greatest-potential-adversary.
Rogan-Finnemore, Michelle. "What Bioprospecting Means for Antarctica and the Southern Ocean." In *International Law Issues in the South Pacific,* edited by Barbara Von Tigerstrom. Burlington: Ashgate, 2005.
Rosen, Mark E., and Cara B. Thuringer. *Unconstrained Foreign Direct Investment: An Emerging Challenge to Arctic Security.* CNA, 2017.
Russian Federation. "One Plan: Measures to Implement the Fundamentals of State Policy of the Russian Federation in the Arctic for the Period up to 2035 and the Development Strategy of the Arctic Zone of the Russian Federation and Ensur-

ing National Security for the Period up to 2035." April 15, 2021. http://static.government.ru/media/files/p8DfCI0Pr1XZnAk08G7J3jUXUuDvswHr.pdf.

Russian Federation. "Strategy for the Development of the Activities of the Russian Federation in Antarctica for the Period up to 2020 and for the More Distant Future." March 31, 2011. https://rg.ru/2011/03/31/antarktika-site-dok.html.

Russian Federation. "The Antarctic Treaty in the Changing World." May 5, 2019. https://cdn.theatlantic.com/assets/media/files/the_antarctic_treaty_in_the_changing_world_(1).pdf.

Russian Federation. "The Foundations of Russian Federation Policy in the Arctic Until 2020 and Beyond." September 18, 2008. http://www.arctic.or.kr/files/pdf/m4/rusia_eng.pdf.

Russian Federation. "The Foundations of the State Policy of the Russian Federation in the Arctic for the Period up to 2035." March 5, 2020. http://static.kremlin.ru/media/events/files/ru/f8ZpjhpAaQ0WB1zjywN04OgKiI1mAvaM.pdf.

Salsig, E. B. "Operation Frostbite: A Strategic Success." *Proceedings* 72, no. 523 (1946): 1199–1206.

Scowcroft, Brent. "The Dispensable Nation?" *National Interest* 90 (2007): 4–6.

Seidel, Jamie. "China's Bold New Fishing Plan on Australia's Doorstep Increases Tensions." December 13, 2020. https://www.news.com.au/technology/innovation/military/chinas-bold-new-fishing-plan-on-australias-doorstep-increases-tensions/news-story/a27224ce439fe490a93a7be81efb6148.

Shea, N., and Louie Palu. "A Thawing Arctic Is Heating Up a New Cold War." *National Geographic,* August 15, 2019.

Slaughter, Kahdija. "F-35 Fleet Doubles at Eielson." June 29, 2020. https://www.eielson.af.mil/News/Article-Display/Article/2241941/f-35a-fleet-doubles-at-eielson.

Sorokina, Anna. "How Russians Built an Orthodox Church in the Antarctic." January 27, 2020. https://www.rbth.com/travel/331601-russian-orthodox-church-antarctic.

Specktor, Brandon. "Antarctica Just Saw Its All-Time Hottest Day Ever." February 14, 2020. http://www.livescience.com/antarctica-record-high-temperature.html.

Staalesen, Atle. "Putin Steps Up Talks with Beijing over Arctic Shipping." *Independent Barents Observer* 30 (2019).

Staalesen, Atle. "Russia Sets Out Stringent New Rules for Foreign Ships on the Northern Sea Route." March 8, 2019. https://www.arctictoday.com/russia-sets-out-stringent-new-rules-for-foreign-ships-on-the-northern-sea-route.

Stokes, Doug. "Trump, American Hegemony, and the Future of the Liberal International Order." *International Affairs* 94, no. 1 (2018): 135.

Summerhayes, Colin, and Peter Beeching. "Hitler's Antarctic Base: The Myth and the Reality." *Polar Record* 43, no. 1 (2007): 1–21.

Takahashi, Minori, Shinji Kawana, K. Saito, Yu Koizumi, Shino Hateruma, and Ayae Shimizu. "Autonomy and Military Bases: USAF Thule Base in Greenland as the Study Case." In *Arctic Yearbook 2019:* 7.

Tamnes, Rolf, and Kristine Offerdal, eds. *Geopolitics and Security in the Arctic: Regional Dynamics in a Global World.* London: Routledge, 2014.

Teller, Matthew. "Why Do So Many Nations Want a Piece of Antarctica?" *BBC News,* June 20, 2014.

Thucydides. "The History of the Peloponnesian War." 431 B.C.E. Translated by Richard Crawley.

Thompson-Jones, Mary. "Why America Should Lose Sleep over Greenland (Think China)." April 18, 2018. https://nationalinterest.org/feature/why-america-should-lose-sleep-over-greenland-think-china-25447.

Tiezzi, Shannon. "China to Establish Antarctic Air Squadron in 2016." February 17, 2016. http://thediplomat.com/2016/02/china-to-establish-antarctic-air-squadron-in-2016.

Tranter, Emma. "'You Cannot Claim Any More:' Russia Seeks Bigger Piece of Arctic." April 11, 2021. https://www.cbc.ca/news/canada/north/russia-arctic-ocean-canada-united-nations-continental-shelf-1.5983289.

Trump, Donald J. "Memorandum on Safeguarding U.S. National Interests in the Arctic and Antarctic Regions." Washington, DC: White House, June 9, 2020. https://www.whitehouse.gov/presidential-actions/memorandum-safeguarding-u-s-national-interests-arctic-antarctic-regions.

Turnbull, Malcolm. *Australian Antarctic Strategy and 20 Year Action Plan.* Caberra: Commonwealth of Australia, 2016.

United Nations. "UN System Task Team on the Post-2015 UN Development Agenda: Global Governance and Governance of the Global Commons in the Global Partnership for Development Beyond 2015." January 2013. https://www.un.org/en/development/desa/policy/untaskteam_undf/thinkpieces/24_think piece_global_governance.pdf.

van Creveld, Martin. *Supplying War: Logistics from Wallenstein to Patton.* 2nd ed. Cambridge: Cambridge University Press, 2004.

Vicuna, Francisco Orrego. "Antarctic Conflict and International Cooperation." In National Research Council, *Antarctic Treaty System: An Assessment*. Proceedings of a workshop held at Beardmore South Field Camp, Antarctica, January 7–13, 1985. Washington, DC: National Academies Press, 1986.

Vine, David. *Base Nation: How U.S. Military Bases Abroad Harm America and the World.* Dallas: Metropolitan, 2015.

Volpe, Marco. "The Tortuous Path of China's Win-Win Strategy in Greenland." March 24, 2020. http://www.thearcticinstitute.org/tortuous-path-china-win-win-strategy-greenland.

Walker, Christopher, Shanthi Kalathil, and Jessica Ludwig. "Forget Hearts and Minds." *Foreign Policy* 14 (2018).

Wallwork, Ellery D., and Kathryn A. Wilcoxson. *Operation Deep Freeze: 50 Years of US Air Force Airlift in Antarctica, 1956–2006.* Scott Air Force Base: Office of History, Air Mobility Command, 2006.

Waltz, Kenneth N. "The Emerging Structure of International Politics." *International Security* 18, no. 2 (1993): 44–79.

———. "The Origins of War in Neorealist Theory," in R. Rotberg and T. Rabb, *The Origin and Prevention of Major Wars* (Cambridge: Cambridge University Press: 1988).

Watts, Arthur. "The Antarctic Treaty as a Conflict Resolution Mechanism." In National Research Council, *Antarctic Treaty System: An Assessment*. Proceedings of a workshop held at Beardmore South Field Camp, Antarctica, January 7–13, 1985. Washington, DC: National Academies Press, 1986.

Webb, Michael, and Steven Krasner. "Hegemonic Stability Theory: An Empirical Assessment." *Review of International Studies* 15, no. 2 (April 1989): 183–198.

Weingartner, Katherine A., and Robert W. Orttung. "U.S. Arctic Policymaking Under Trump and Obama." *Polar Record* 55, no. 6 (2019): 402–410.

Whelan, Nathaniel. "The Oceans of the World by Size." September 7, 2020. https://www.worldatlas.com/articles/the-oceans-of-the-world-by-size.html.

Winger, Gregory, and Gustav Petursson. "Return to Keflavik Station: Iceland's Cold War Legacy Reappraised." *Foreign Affairs* 24 (2016).

Wither, James K. "Svalbard: NATO's Arctic 'Achilles' Heel.'" *RUSI Journal* 163, no. 5 (2018): 28–37.

Wittkopf, Eugene R. *World Politics: Trend and Transformation*. New York: St. Martin's, 1997.
Wolfers, Arnold. *Discord and Collaboration: Essays on International Politics*. Baltimore: Johns Hopkins Press, 1962.
Wolff, Michael. *Fire and Fury: Inside the Trump White House*. New York: Holt, 2018.
Woodward, Alex. "Trump Says He Is Reducing US Troops in 'Delinquent' Germany, Wrongly Saying It Owes NATO Billions of Dollars." *The Independent*, June 16, 2020. https://www.independent.co.uk/news/world/americas/us-politics/trump-germany-us-troops-military-nato-a9567791.html.
Woody, Christopher. "The US Air Force Is Fixing Up a Remote Base That Could Help Keep an Eye on Russia." January 14, 2020. https://www.businessinsider.com/us-air-force-fixing-up-norwegian-base-arctic-near-russia-2020-1.
Wright, Thomas. *All Measures Short of War: The Contest for the Twenty-First Century and the Future of American Power*. New Haven: Yale University Press, 2017.
Young, Claire. "What's China up to in Antarctica?" *The Strategist*, September 20, 2018.

Index

Afghanistan, US war in, 11–12, 38
Air Defense Identification Zone, 40
Air Force, US, 124, 147, 215
alarmist position on geostrategy, 142, 145–148, 165, 166(n7)
Alaska: cold weather military exercises, 39–40; Russian maritime reconnaissance aircraft, 136; strategic importance, 24–25, 165; US Polar Command, 212; US polar military units, 215; US undermanning polar regions, 168(n80)
Albright, Madeleine, 175
Alert forces (Canada), 217–218
Aleutian Islands Campaign, 25–26
Allison, Graham, 154–155, 165, 173
anarchic system, the world as, 172
Antarctic Air Squadron (China), 158
Antarctic Treaty: China's Antarctic goals and policies, 103; China's special managed area, 105; club solutions, 226–227; compliance and noncompliance, 64; consultative meeting, 134; history and tenets of, 32–34, 43(n37); history and territorial conflict, 56–59; importance and role of, 9–10; Madrid Protocol, 103, 151, 167–168(n52), 227; Norway's polar power status, 78; polar perceivers, 87(table); polar peripherals, 88(table); polar powers and polar players, 86(table); polar typology, 83; restriction on military maneuvers, 123–124, 205–206, 219–220; Soviet Union as signatory, 95; territorial claims, 54–55; treaty-oriented stability model, 126–128; US polar policy, 112
Antarctic Treaty consultative meeting, 33, 105, 134, 139(n57), 190
Antarctic Treaty System, 32–33, 36, 43(n36), 67, 107
Antarctica: access points, 223–224; China's policies and ambitions, 103–108, 222–223; China's research presence, 73(n55), 104, 106, 158–159; concerns over China's expansion, 204; control of the space domain, 66–68; defining the polar regions, 4–10; Falklands analog, 205–206; global commons network, 48; great power competition over, 14; human settlement, 22(n14); polar states and polar powers, 78; polar typology, 83; potential conflict, 133, 138(n44); resource exploitation,

223–224; Russia's economic and research expansion, 89; Russia's policies, 95–96; temperature rise, 16–17; territorial claims, 54–56; transactional balancing, 131, 189–191; Trump policies ignoring, 119; US lack of policy for, 122; US military presence during WWII, 26–28, 31–32, 43(n11); US POLCOM-South, 213–214; US 2020 presidential polar memo, 122–124

Antarctica 2049 (film), 103

apologist position on geostrategy, 142–145, 165

Arctic Coast Guard Forum, 60

Arctic Council: China's policies challenging the legitimacy of, 102; club solutions, 226–227; history of, 35–36; intent and omissions, 59–60; neutralizing potential Arctic conflict, 144; polar perceivers, 87(table); polar peripherals, 88(table); polar powers and polar players, 86(table); polar typology, 79–80, 83; potential for polar conflict, 135; Putin's claims on the Arctic Shelf, 37–38; Russia's Arctic military policy, 93; treaty-oriented stability model, 126–128; US Arctic policy, 112

Arctic Crescent, 208–209

Arctic Ocean, 5–7

Arctic region: Alaska's WWII strategic importance, 24–25; China's Arctic policy, 98–103; competition-to-conflict trajectory, 69–70; defining the polar regions, 4–7; four Cs framework, 45–46; great power competition over resources, 14; ice pack, 22(n33); NATO concerns, 34–35; Russian control of navigation, 71(n8); Russian expansion under Putin, 36–41; Russia's renewed militarization, 15; telecommunications, 65–66; territorial claims, 51–54, 71(n25); transactional balancing, 191–193; US military strategies, 124–126; US POLCOM-North, 213; warming temperatures, 17

Arctic rim powers, 78

Arctic Shelf, Russian claims on, 37–38

Argentina: Falklands War, 205–206; military operation in Antarctica, 33–34, 62; polar perceivers, 84; territorial claims in Antarctica, 31–32, 55

Armed Forces Network (AFN), 67

Army, US: Arctic operations and strategy, 125

Ascension Island, 207

Australia: Antarctic claims, 55; China's expanding relationships, 106–107; concerns over China's Antarctic expansion, 204; Five Eyes Alliance, 158–159; polar perceivers, 84; resource extraction, 223–224; US partnership, 223; US polar military units, 214–215

authoritarian regimes: great power competition, 10–11

Barents Sea: US freedom of navigation exercises, 39

battlespace compression, 150

BeiDou global satellite system (China), 68, 104, 196

Belgium: polar peripherals, 84

Belt and Road Initiative (China), 97–98, 107, 152, 156–157, 168(n71), 194, 229

Bering Sea, 5, 7, 21(n6)

Biden administration: great power competition, 10–13; potential for polar conflict, 133–134; transactional balancing model, 183–184, 229

biological resources, 7, 9, 33

bipolar world order: as alternative to US hegemony, 173–175; China's ambitions, 171; transactional balancing, 178–179, 189; US lag in polar policy, 141. *See also* China; Russia

"Blue Arctic" strategy, 124–125

border states: Russian claims to the Arctic shelf, 54

borders and boundaries: Arctic shelf claims, 51–56; Peace of Westphalia creating, 49–50; sovereign claims in the Arctic Circle, 7; US coastal states, 71(n20)

Brady, Anne-Marie, 63–64, 67–68, 77–78, 103–107, 151, 196

Brown, C.Q, 105, 138(n44), 151–152
Buchanan, Elizabeth, 78, 98
Bush administration (George W.), 115–116, 184
Byrd, Richard, 26–28, 43(n11)

Canada: indigenous sovereignty in the Arctic, 135; Northwest Passage crossings, 191–193; US Polar Command, 212; US support of military expansion, 217–218
Canadian Forces Station Alert, 217–218
Canadian Rangers, 69
capability, state: polar typology, 80–83, 85
Chile: Antarctic claims, 55; military operation in Antarctica, 62; polar perceivers, 84
China: Antarctic policies, 103–108; Arctic policies, 98–103; balancing Arctic and South China Sea access, 227; claims on the Antarctic, 59; delegitimizing international institutions, 127–128; expanding the Polar Silk Road, 222–223; fishery exploitation, 217; great power competition, 12–13, 15–16; hegemonic ambitions, 153–154, 158–159; militarization of Svalbard, 60–62; military presence in Antarctica, 62, 67–68, 151–152, 219–220; nuclear weapons states, 1; polar conflict, 133; polar interest and orientation, 4; polar powers, 76–77, 85, 96–103; polar typology, 83; potential for future polar confrontation and conflict, 63–64, 225–226; research stations in Antarctica, 73(n55), 104, 106, 158–159; Sino-Russian polar alliance, 41–42; South China Sea expansion, 71(n8); threatening US hegemony, 177–178; the Thucydides Trap, 155–156; transactional balancing in the polar regions, 130–132, 189–191, 196–197; undermining US strength in the Arctic, 145–146; US defense of the commons, 48–49; US military Arctic strategies, 124–125; US policy under Trump, 119–121; US view as strategic competitor, 203–204; wedge-driving in small and weak states, 194
Chosin Reservoir, the Battle of, 43(n27)
claims. *See* territorial claims
climate: Antarctica, 8–9; Russian Arctic tundra, 54
climate change, 17, 203, 228–229
climate refugees, 228–229
Clinton administration, 114–115, 184
Coast Guard, US, 123, 192
Code for Unplanned Encounters at Sea (2014), 59–60
Cohen, Eliot, 48, 177, 203
Cold War: Arctic Council, 35–36; Arctic security concerns, 34–35; great power competition, 11; US interest in Greenland, 29–30; US polar policy, 113–115
commons, 18, 46–49; control of the space domain, 65–68; history of control in the polar regions, 153–154; potential for polar conflict, 63, 134; transactional balancing model, 129–132, 179–181; treaty-oriented stability model, 126–128; US polar policy, 112–113, 116–117
competition. *See* great power competition
conflict, great power, 2
conflict and confrontation: Antarctic Treaty, 57; apathy over, 69–70; Arctic advance towards, 66; avoiding confrontation, 143–145; great power competition in the Arctic, 54; inevitability of, 171, 176, 229–230; over Antarctic claims, 55; over sovereignty, 49–50; potential for future conflict in Antarctica, 62–65, 72(n32); potential for future polar conflict, 132–137; reduction through transactional balancing, 187; the rise of strategic competition, 153–154; Russian Arctic aggression, 162–163; Svalbard Treaty, 61; the threat of rising powers, 173–175; the Thucydides Trap, 154–155; transactional balancing, 180–181, 193–197; US-China competition spurring, 225–226
conflict avoidance and prevention, 171–172, 219–222

confrontation. *See* conflict and confrontation
conspiracy theories: Hitler's expedition to Antarctica, 26–27
continental shelf, Russian claims on, 52–54
cooperation: Arctic Council, 36, 59; avoiding the polar trap, 174; China's polar policies, 98, 100–102; the global commons, 49; global democracy promotion, 175–176; history of US policy, 114–115, 117; move to a competitive dynamic, 63–64; polar covenants, 56; Russia's Arctic policies, 89–94, 94(table); Sino-American relations, 196; transactional balancing and, 228–230; US military policy, 124, 147, 153; US-Canada cooperation on the Northwest Passage, 192
cosmos, 18, 65–68
counterinsurgency, 3
covenants, 18; Antarctic Treaty, 56–59; Arctic Council, 59–60; enforceability, 56; future crumbling, 62–65; Svalbard Treaty, 60–62; transactional balancing model for conflict prevention, 129–132
Covid-19 pandemic: cancellation of the Antarctic Treaty consultative meeting, 134; economic effect in Australia, 107
Crimean Peninsula, Russian annexation of, 15, 50, 59–60, 128, 146–147
Cruzen, Richard, 26–28

Dangerous Military Activities Agreement (1989), 59–60
Daru Island, 159
deepwater ports, 159; Canadian Forces Station Alert, 217; polar perceivers, 87(table); polar powers and polar players, 86(table); polar typology, 83
Defense, US Department of (DoD), 67; apologist position on Arctic confrontation, 145; great power competition and polar policy, 120–121; US military Arctic strategies, 125
defense and security: alarmist position on Arctic importance, 145–148; Antarctic Operation High Jump, 26–28; Antarctica's role in, 10; Arctic Council failing to address, 59–60; border security and sovereignty, 50; Bush administration polar policy, 115–116; China's polar concerns and policies, 99–100, 103–104; Chinese and Russian hegemonic ambitions, 156–157; four Cs framework, 45–46; globalization as threat to, 70; great power competition, 12; historical context of the polar regions, 23–24; history of US polar policy, 113–114, 153–154; idealist and realist models of global interaction, 228–230; literature on, 33–34; polar actor typology, 78–80; polar balancing, 185–188; polar typology, 83; realpolitik and polar security, 225–227; Russia's Antarctic policy, 95–96; Russia's Arctic policy, 38, 89–95; the South Pole blind spot, 150–152; state capability and polar presence, 80–81; Svalbard Treaty, 60–62; the Thucydides Trap, 154–155; transactional balancing approach, 179–183; US Arctic concerns during the Cold War, 34–35; US lag in engagement, 141–142; US polar defense policies, 117–119; US prioritizing polar policy, 202–203; US 2020 presidential polar memo, 122–124. *See also* militarization
Defense Early Warning Line (Arctic), 35
Defense of Greenland Agreement (1941), 30
defensive armament, 123–124
democracy promotion, liberal hegemony and, 175–176
Denmark: Arctic shelf claims, 52; China's Arctic partnerships, 101; China's transactional balancing, 130; polar perceivers, 84; strategic value of Greenland, 216–217; US interest in Greenland, 28–30
deterrence strategy, 1, 3, 31–32, 194–195, 203–204
development, economic: Russia's Antarctic policies, 95
disruptors, 125–126

economic downturn: Australia, 107
economic expansion: China, 97, 104; Russia, 88–95
economic model: Russia's great power status, 75–76
economic opportunities: Arctic Ocean opening, 7; Russian Arctic claims, 54; Russia's dependence on Arctic resources, 38, 51, 54, 91, 161–162
economic strength: Sino-Russian transactional balancing, 187–188
economic zones: Arctic shelf boundaries and claims, 52–56
ecosystem preservation: China's Arctic policies, 101
Eielson Air Force Base, Alaska, 39–40, 164, 212–213
Eldorado complex in Antarctica, 57
Enhanced Polar System satellites, 66
environmental protection: China's Antarctic policies, 105; China's Arctic policies, 101
Esperanza Base, Antarctica, 16, 22(n14), 31
exceptionalism, Arctic, 143–144, 174
Exercise Northern Edge (Alaska), 39
external balancing, 176, 181, 187

Falkland Islands: EUCOM boundary and, 210; Falklands War, 205–206; US POLCOM-South, 213
Fang Li, 103
Finland: polar perceivers, 84; US Polar Command, 212–213
fishing: China's Antarctic policies, 104
Five Eyes Alliance, 158–159, 219–220
foreign direct investment: China's investment in Arctic states, 122
France: Antarctic claims, 55; nuclear weapons states, 1
frigid zones, 4

geography: China's foreign policy, 98, 101; effects of changing Arctic geography on the US, 195–196; opening in the Arctic Ocean, 7; polar perceivers, 87(table); polar peripherals, 88(table); polar powers and polar players, 86(table); US Unified Command Plan, 209–212
geopolitics. *See* defense and security

geostrategy: alarmist and apologist positions, 142–148; China's designs on Antarctica, 103–104
Germany: Hitler's expedition to Antarctica, 26–27
global commons. *See* commons
global positioning system (GPS), 68, 104
Gorbachev, Mikhail, 35, 114
governance: China's great power ambitions, 106; the global commons, 46–47; sovereign claims in the Arctic Circle, 7; transactional balancing model, 129–132; treaty-oriented stability model, 126–128
grand strategy. *See* transactional balancing
great power: China's Antarctic presence, 105; defining, 75
great power competition, 1(fn), 2; Antarctic Treaty, 33–34, 58; apologist and alarmist positions on polar confrontation, 143–148; Arctic competition-to-conflict trajectory, 69–70; bipolar balance replacing US hegemony, 173–175; Chinese and Russian hegemonic ambitions, 153–154; defining, 10–11; gaps in US polar policy, 111–112; the goals of, 13–14; historical path of, 10–13; impact of the war on terror, 11–12; increasing polar access, 10; increasing strategic interest in the polar regions, 141–142; polar regions, 16–18; potential for polar confrontation and conflict, 62–65, 69–70, 132–137, 138(n44); Russian military expansion in the Arctic, 36–41, 160–163; Sino-Russian relations, 15–16, 41–42, 75; the Thucydides Trap, 154–156; US polar policies, 119–122; US polar trap, 163–165; US posturing in the polar regions, 17–18; US shift from counterterrorism, 11–12; US use of productive competition in the polar regions, 202–203. *See also* defense and security; strategic competition
Greenland: China's Arctic partnerships, 101; defining the Arctic, 5; Nanook expedition, 27; strategic importance to the US, 216–217; US attempt to

252　Index

purchase, 28–30, 113; US Polar Command, 212–213; US Unified Command Plan, 210
Greenland-Iceland-United Kingdom Gap, 35, 60–62
gross domestic product: China as polar peer power, 96–97; China's meteoric rise, 159–160; polar perceivers, 84, 87(table); polar peripherals, 88(table); polar powers and polar players, 86(table); polar typology, 83

hegemonic power status: China's ambitions, 158–160; Chinese and Russian ambitions, 153–154; the goals of great power competition, 13–14; Russia and China threatening US unipolarity, 177–178; the Thucydides Trap, 154–155, 163–165; transactional balancing as alternative to, 173–176; US "exit" from, 113, 184, 221–222. *See also* great power competition; polar powers
History of the Peloponnesian War (Thucydides), 155
Hitler, Adolf, 26–27
Hope Bay base (United Kingdom), 16, 31–32
hypersonic missiles, Russian, 148–149, 162

Ice Curtain (Russian expansion posture), 38–39, 91–92, 162, 208
ice shelf, 17
icebreakers, 145–146; China's Antarctic policies, 104–105; China's Antarctic presence, 106; dubious nature of Chinese activities in the Antarctic, 151–152; icebreaker gap, 147–148, 207–208; indications of polar military power, 81; polar typology, 83; Russian posture in the Arctic, 162; US 2020 presidential polar memo, 123–124
Iceland: Keflavik Air Station, 208–209; polar peripherals, 84; US polar military units, 215
Incidents at Sea Agreement (1972), 59–60
India: nuclear weapons states, 1

indigenous peoples: polar typology, 79; potential for polar conflict, 135
infrastructure projects: China in the Antarctic, 104; China's Arctic partnerships, 101–103; Russia and China, 15–16; Russian Arctic military, 91
intent: China's Antarctic policies, 105–106; China's Arctic policies, 101; polar actor typology, 79, 81–82; polar perceivers, 84; polar powers, 85
Interim National Security Strategic Guidance, 10–11
internal balancing, 176, 181, 187, 196
International Geophysical Year, 32
International Maritime Organization, 60
international relations: China's Arctic policies, 98
international security. *See* defense and security
interventionism: liberal hegemony's policy prescriptions, 176–177
Iraq, US war in, 11–12, 38
isotherm: Bering Sea, 21(n6); defining the Arctic, 5
Israel: nuclear weapons states, 1

Jan Mayen Island, Norway, 60–62, 72(n44), 77, 218
Japan: polar perceivers, 84
Joint Base Elmendor-Richardson, 212–213
Joint Base Pearl Harbor, 215
Joint Task Force-Support Forces Antarctica, 215

Keflavik, Iceland, 208–209
Kinzhal ballistic missiles, 149
Kissinger, Henry, 113–114
Korean War, 30, 43(n27)

Lee Kuan Yew, 158
liberalism, global stability and, 172, 174–176
Little America bases (Antarctica), 27–28, 43(n11)
Lomonosov Ridge, 52, 130

MacDonald, David, 57
Madrid Protocol (Antarctic Treaty), 103, 151, 167–168(n52), 227

Mahan, Alfred, 97
mapping: Operation High Jump, 26–27
Marie Byrd land, 55
Marine Corps, US, 34–35, 39–40, 214–215
maritime commons: China's hegemonic ambitions in Antarctica, 159; potential for polar conflict, 134. *See also* commons; shipping, trade, and navigation
maritime law, international, 15, 51, 91; China's Arctic policies, 99–100
Matisek, Jahara, 138(n44)
Mattis, James, 119
McMurdo Station, Antarctica, 67, 104
Mearshiemer, John, 179
Mendeleev Ridge, 52, 130
milieu goals, 48
militarization of the polar regions, 2–3; Antarctic Treaty prohibition, 32–34; apologist position on geostrategy, 143–145; Arctic Council failing to address, 59–60; conflict prevention in the Antarctic, 219–221; great power competition in the polar regions, 16–18; history and context, 153–154; human settlement in Antarctica, 22(n14); increasing potential for polar conflict, 62–65; polar powers and polar players, 86(table); polar typology, 83; of the space domain, 65–68; Svalbard Treaty prohibiting, 61; transactional balancing outcomes, 131
militarization of the polar regions (China): Antarctic policies, 104; Arctic policies, 98–99; China's global ambitions, 151–152; Russia and China, 15–16; Sino-Russian polar alliance, 41–42
militarization of the polar regions (Russia): Arctic policy, 91–92; challenging US hegemony in the Arctic, 160–163; China and, 15–16; expansion, 15, 39–41; great power aspirations, 76; maritime reconnaissance aircraft in Alaska, 136; Russia as polar peer power, 88–89; Sino-Russian polar alliance, 41–42
militarization of the polar regions (US): Alaska's WWII strategic importance, 24–25; Arctic strategies, 124–126; focus on Asia and Eastern Europe, 203; interest in Greenland, 28–30; Operation Deep Freeze, 32; projecting military power into the polar regions, 205–206; response to Russian buildup in the Arctic, 121; undermanning polar regions, 168(n80); WWII Antarctic strategy, 26–28, 31–32
military power: Arctic alarmists advocating military strength, 145–148; Canadian Forces Station Alert, 217–218; defining polar presence, 80–81; preserving order, 220–221
military power, US: defensive armament in Antarctica, 123–124; icebreaker deployment, 207–208; limitations on US power in the Arctic, 148–150; Polar Command, 212–213; polar defense policies, 112–113, 117–119; polar units, 214–216; POLCOM-North, 213; POLCOM-South, 213–214; security interests in the Arctic, 115–117; Unified Command Plan, 209–212, 232(n40)
mineral resources: Antarctic Treaty governing extraction, 57–58; Arctic Ocean, 7; Russia's claims on, 38. *See also* natural resources
Mitchell, Billy, 165
Mulroney, Brian, 192
multipolar order: China and Russian ambitions, 128; effect on the Arctic Council, 135; effect on the global commons, 49; reality of, 13; revisionist powers, 119; transactional balancing approach, 189. *See also* China; Russia; transactional balancing
Murmansk Initiative, 35, 114

Nanook expedition, 27
Napoleonic Wars: security aspects of the polar regions, 24
National Defense Authorization Act (NDAA), 118, 120–122, 208
National Defense Strategy (NDS), 3–4, 12, 19, 119, 150, 203
National Geographic magazine, 69
National Military Strategy (US), 120

National Science Foundation (NSF), 67, 158
National Security Decision Memorandum (US), 113–114
National Security Strategy (NSS), 3, 19, 94, 116–117, 150, 203
nationalism: great power competition, 11
natural gas: Arctic Ocean, 7
natural resources, 9; China's Antarctic policies, 103–104; China's Arctic policies, 99–102; China's grant hegemonic strategy, 97; great power competition over, 14; polar balancing model, 185–188; Russia's Antarctic policies, 95–96; Russia's dependence on the Arctic, 38, 51, 54, 91, 161–162; Russia's great power status, 76; Russia's territorial claims, 90. *See also* mineral resources; oil
navigation. *See* shipping, trade, and navigation
Navy, US: Arctic operations and strategy, 39–40, 124–125; Operation High Jump, 26–27; polar military units, 215; SOUTHCOM purview, 232(n40)
neorealist approach to strategy, 172, 175–176, 179
New Zealand: Antarctic claims, 55; China's expanding relationships, 106, 222–223; communications systems with Antarctica, 67; Five Eyes Alliance, 158–159; polar perceivers, 84; POLCOM-South, 213; US alliance, 219–220
Nixon, Richard, 34, 112–113
nonaggressor state, 1
North American Aerospace Defense Command (NORAD), 135–136, 209
North Atlantic Treaty Organization (NATO): China's global partnerships, 156–157; concerns over Arctic areas, 34–35; concerns over Russia's anti-access areas, 204; Denmark's addition, 29–30; internal and external balancing behaviors, 187; military expansion in the Arctic, 39; Northwest Passage claims, 135–136; Norway's polar power status, 78; Russia's Arctic policy, 92; Russia's gains through military conflict, 144; Svalbard Treaty, 61–62; transactional balancing outcomes, 130–131, 181–182; US "exit" from hegemony, 184
North Korea: nuclear weapons states, 1
North Pole: defining the polar regions, 4; Russia's territorial claims, 90. *See also* Arctic region
North Warning System, 35, 40, 49, 148–150
Northern Fleet Joint Strategic Command (Russia), 39, 120–121, 162, 212–213
Northern Sea Route: China's use of, 100; Russian Arctic policies, 94(table); Russian-Canadian relations, 193; Russia's aggressive posture, 15, 71(n8), 91, 94, 147, 161, 217–218; strategic value of, 116; Suez Canal and, 99(fig.), 110(n58)
Northwest Passage, 116, 135–136, 191–193, 217
Norway: Antarctic claims, 55; China's Arctic partnerships, 101; China's transactional balancing, 130; cold weather military exercises, 39–40; Jan Mayen, 72(n44); as polar state, 77–78; Russia's anti-access areas, 204; Russia's Arctic policy, 92; Svalbard Treaty, 60–62; transactional relationships, 182–183; US bilateral basing program, 34–35; US Polar Command, 212–213; US polar military units, 214–215
nuclear weapons states, 1–2; deterrence threat for great power competition, 155–156, 173; polar perceivers, 87(table); polar peripherals, 88(table); polar powers and polar players, 86(table); polar typology, 83; Russian Arctic deployment, 15
Nye, Joseph, 178–179

Obama administration: global inaction, 17; polar policy, 115–117; US polar defense policies, 117–118
oil: Antarctic Treaty governing extraction, 57–58; Arctic Ocean, 7; great power competition in the polar regions, 17. *See also* natural resources
Operation Deep Freeze, 32, 67

Operation Frostbite (US), 28–29
Operation High Jump, 26–28, 113
Operation Ninety, 33–34
order, preserving, 220–221
O'Shaughnessy, Terrance, 66, 136, 147, 149–150
Ottawa Declaration (1996), 36

Pacific Air Forces (PACAF), 215–216
Pakistan: nuclear weapons states, 1
partnerships: China's Antarctic policies and ambitions, 106–107; China's Arctic policies, 101–102; China's Belt and Road Initiative, 41, 97–98, 107, 152, 168(n71), 194, 229; China's global military ambitions, 151–152; effect on US strategy, 222–223; Five Eyes Alliance, 158–159, 219–220; polar conflict and, 133; potential Sino-Russian alliance, 147; preserving order, 220–221; transactional balancing outcomes, 129–132, 181
Patterson, Robert, 29
Peace of Westphalia (1648), 49–50
peaceful intent: Russian Arctic policy, 90–93
peer powers: Russia, 88–89
Peloponnesian War, 155
planes, polar: China's Antarctic policies, 104; polar perceivers, 87(table); polar peripherals, 88(table); polar players, 86(table); polar powers, 86(table); Russia in the Arctic, 40; Russian reconnaissance in Alaska, 136; as threat to the US, 28; US power projection in Antarctica, 206
polar balancing, 20–21, 185, 194–195. *See also* strategy; transactional balancing
Polar Bear Expedition, 24
Polar Code (2017), 60
polar Cs: claims, 49–56; commons, 46–49; cosmos, 18, 65–68; covenants, 56–65; elements of, 45–46. *See also* commons; covenants; territorial claims
polar great powers: China, Russia and the US, 75–77
polar perceivers, 84; polar typology, 78–80

polar peripherals, 83–84, 88(table); China, 102; polar typology, 78–80
polar pivot: defining, 20–21. *See also* strategy; transactional balancing
polar players, 84–85; polar typology, 78–80
polar powers: China as polar peer power, 96–103; China's ambitions to, 174–175; polar typology, 78–80, 85–88; Russia, China, and the US, 75–77; Russia as polar peer power, 88–89. *See also* China; Russia; United States
polar regions, defining and characterizing, 4–10
Polar Silk Road policy (China), 41, 98–100, 103, 120, 158
polar states: polar powers and, 77–78
polar trap, 20; avoiding a US polar trap, 163–165, 173–175; bipolar balance replacing US hegemony, 173–175; Chinese and Russian hegemonic ambitions, 156–160; conditions for, 155–156; Russia's polar pivot, 160–163. *See also* conflict; hegemonic power status
polar typology, 78–80; capability and presence, 80–81; core dimensions and variables, 82–83; polar perceivers, 84, 87(table); polar peripherals, 83–84, 88(table); polar players, 84–85; polar powers, 85–88; polar powers and polar players, 86(table)
policy, polar, 33; China's Arctic policies, 98–103; gaps in US polar policy, 111–112; great power competition, 119–122; the importance of the US in balancing power, 202; military Arctic strategies, 124–126; polar actor typology, 81–82; polar perceivers, 87(table); polar peripherals, 88(table); polar powers, 76–77, 85; polar typology, 79(fig.); Russian Arctic policies, 89–95; stagnation of US policy, 112–113, 164–165; US apologist position on geostrategy, 143–145; US polar defense, 114–115, 117–119, 202–203; US presidential polar policies, 114–115, 122–124

political policies, China, 98
polycentric world order, 128
Pompeo, Mike, 99, 192
posture: great power competition, 13; polar perceivers, 84; polar posture indicators, 82; polar typology, 79(fig.); Russia's Arctic military policy, 92–93; US inaction in the polar regions, 17–18. *See also* policy, polar
power: Arctic alarmists advocating military strength, 145–148; indications of polar military power, 81; instruments of transactional balancing, 180; transactional balancing model, 129–132; US projecting military power into the polar regions, 205–206. *See also* great power competition
primacy, global, 111–112, 156, 173–174, 178–179
Putin, Vladimir, 14–15, 36–41, 76, 90–92, 95, 161, 194

Reagan administration, 114, 192
realpolitik, 157, 180, 225–229
reconnaissance sorties, 30, 136
Red Arctic propaganda, 34
regional power status: Russia's, 76; transactional balancing approach, 179, 189; US focus on Russia and China, 177–178, 203–204
resource exploitation: Antarctica, 57, 223–224; Arctic conflict, 146; China's polar policy, 100, 102–103, 106–107, 120, 151–152, 222; UNCLOS criteria, 52. *See also* natural resources
retrenchment, US, 171–172
revisionism, 12–13, 19, 47–48, 119, 126, 153–155, 163–165, 171, 202–203, 226
rising powers: China's Belt and Road Initiative, 97; indigenous sovereignty, 135; potential conflict with ruling powers, 154–155, 157–158, 173; regional hegemonic ambition, 153–154; Sino-Russian partnership, 164–165. *See also* China; Russia
rotational force concepts, US, 39, 164, 214–215

Russia: Antarctic policies, 95–96; Arctic apologist position on policy, 143–144; Arctic claims, 51; Arctic competition-to-conflict trajectory, 69–70; Arctic expansion under Putin, 36–41; Arctic policies, 89–95; Arctic shelf claims, 52–54; China's alliance, 98–99; claims on the Antarctic, 55–56, 58–59; control of Antarctic space, 68; control of Arctic navigation, 71(n8); counteracting military prohibitions in Antarctica, 151–152; defining the Arctic, 5; delegitimizing international institutions, 127–128; formidable military posture, 174–175; great power competition, 12–13, 15–16; hegemonic ambitions, 153–154; intent of expansionist agenda, 146–147; maritime reconnaissance aircraft in Alaska, 136; militarization of Svalbard, 60–62; military operation in Antarctica, 62; military superiority in the Arctic, 148–150; nuclear weapons states, 1; polar conflict, 133; polar interest and orientation, 4; polar powers, 75–77, 85; potential for future Antarctic confrontation and conflict, 63–64; Sino-Russian polar alliance, 41–42; threatening US hegemony, 177–178; the Thucydides Trap, 155–156; transactional balancing, 130–132, 189–191, 194; undermining US strength in the Arctic, 145–146; US defense of the commons, 48–49; US military Arctic strategies, 124–125; US policy under Trump, 119–121; US view as strategic competitor, 203–204; US-Russian security alliance, 187–189. *See also* Soviet Union
Russian Arctic tundra, 54

satellite communications, 65–69
Scandinavia: defining the Arctic, 5. *See also specific countries*
scientific research: Antarctic Treaty, 33–34; China in Antarctica, 73(n55), 104, 106, 158–159; China's Arctic partnerships, 103; the Chinese in

Svalbard, 60–62, 98; concerns over China's Antarctic expansion, 204; defining great polar powers, 77, 86(table); defining polar presence, 80–81; Operation Deep Freeze, 32; polar perceivers, 87(table); polar peripherals, 88(table); polar powers and polar players, 86(table); polar typology, 83; Russia's territorial claims in Antarctica, 161; satellite communications in the Antarctic, 67–68
sea ice: Arctic Ocean, 4, 6–7, 17, 47, 54, 203, 221
seabed resources, Russian claims to, 52–53
security. *See* defense and security
self-governing international organizations, 51, 183
Sfraga, Mike, 45–46
Shea, Neil, 69
shipping, trade, and navigation: Northern Sea Route and the Suez Canal, 99(fig.), 110(n58); Northwest Passage crossings, 191–193; preserving order in the polar regions, 220–221; Russia's Arctic militarization, 91; US Arctic status, 195–196; US control of Arctic interests, 217–218; US policy on "command of the commons," 115; US-Canada transactional arrangements, 217
Sino-Russian polar alliance, 41–42
source documents, 33–34
South Africa: polar peripherals, 84
South China Sea, China's claims to, 15; as analog for Arctic intent, 146–147; China balancing Arctic access, 227; China wedge-driving in small and weak states, 194; China's disregard to international law, 128; island building, 16–17, 71(n8), 204; Polar Silk Road policy, 99–100
South Pole: defining the polar regions, 4, 8–10. *See also* Antarctica
sovereignty: Argentina's military operation in Antarctica, 33–34; China's security concerns in the Antarctic, 103–104; Falklands War, 205–206; the global and polar commons, 46–47; Norway's polar power status, 77–78; potential for future Antarctic confrontation and conflict, 63–64; territoriality and, 49–51; transactional balancing model, 179; US base in Antarctica, 27–28; US presidential polar policy, 116–117
Soviet Union: great power competition, 11; Murmansk Initiative, 35; Red Arctic propaganda, 34; US interest in Greenland, 29–30; US polar policy, 114
space domain, military control of, 65–68, 127
special managed area (Antarctic): China's, 105
Spitsbergen, Norway, 60–62
Strategic Command (STRATCOM), 67
strategic competition, 1(fn), 3–4; US interest in Greenland, 28–30; US polar policy under Trump, 119–120. *See also* great power competition
Strategic Homeland Integrated Ecosystem Layered Defense (SHIELD), 149
strategic value of the polar regions, 14, 25, 68, 141–142, 194–195, 202–203
strategy: alternatives to US hegemony and retrenchment, 171–172; apathy over the polar regions, 141–142; the Arctic as a strategic resource, 93–94; conflict prevention, 219–220; expanding polar military presence, 207–208; Iceland's Keflavik Air Station, 208–209; the importance of Greenland, 216–217; the need for a pragmatic polar strategy, 197–198; preserving order, 220–221; protecting national interests, 216–219; realpolitik and polar security, 225–227; strategic framework, 205; thinking outside safe confines, 201–202; transactional balancing, 129–132; treaty-oriented stability model, 126–128; Unified Command Plan, 209–216; US need for military buildup and support, 204–205; US options, 171–172; US polar policy under Trump and Biden, 120–122; US projecting military power into

the polar regions, 205–206. *See also* transactional balancing
Suez Canal, 91, 99(fig.), 100, 110(n58)
Svalbard Island, 72(n44), 77, 101, 158, 218–219
Svalbard Treaty, 60–62, 92, 98, 218
Sweden: polar perceivers, 84; US partnership, 219

temperatures: Antarctica, 9, 16–17; during the Korean War, 43(n27)
territorial claims, 18, 49–56; alarmists' view of Russia's Arctic expansion, 147–148; Antarctic claims, 31–32, 54–56; Antarctic Treaty articles, 58; Arctic claims, 51–54, 71(n25); Canada, 135–136; China's special managed area in the Antarctic, 105; Falklands War, 205–206; the global and polar commons, 46–47; polar perceivers, 87(table); polar peripherals, 88(table); polar powers and polar players, 86(table); polar typology, 83; potential for polar conflict, 134–135; Russia's Arctic and Antarctic claims, 160–161; sovereignty and, 49–51; transactional balancing model, 130–131, 179–180
Thirty Years' War, 49–50
Thucydides Trap, 154–155, 163
Thule Air Base, Greenland, 29–30, 66, 209, 213
trade. *See* shipping, trade, and navigation
transactional balancing, 129–132; in Antarctica, 189–191; in the Arctic, 191–193; avoiding conflict, 193–197; China's transactional relationships, 224–225; climate change issues, 228–229; described and explained, 178–185; importance in avoiding the polar trap, 202; multipolar balance of power, 175–177; polar balancing, 185–188; polar region conflict as outcome, 132–134; polar security and the emergence of realpolitik, 225–227; predicted behavior, 185–188; as a probable outcome, 188–189; Trump administration approach, 183–185; US polar military units, 216; US support of Canadian Forces Station Alert, 217. *See also* strategy

treaty-oriented stability model, 126–128, 225
Truman, Harry, 26, 113, 216
Trump administration: attempt to purchase Greenland, 216; great power competition, 10–12; international relations approach, 183; Northwest Passage disagreements, 193; potential for polar conflict, 133–134; transactional balancing approach, 183–185, 188–189, 229; US polar policies, 119–120
tundra aeration programs, 90

Ukraine, Russian invasion of, 15. *See also* Crimean Peninsula, Russian annexation of
UN Commission on the Limits of the Continental Shelf (CLCS), 51
undersea surveillance capabilities, 150
undetermined sovereignty, 63–64
Unified Command Plan (US), 209–212
unipolarity: Arctic Council founding, 135; China and Russia challenging, 13, 36–41, 49, 128; China's ambitions, 160, 171; establishment of the current international order, 157; hegemonic stability theory, 153; neorealist perspective, 176; US military primacy, 177–178. *See also* hegemonic power status
United Kingdom: Antarctic claims, 55; Falklands War, 205–206; nuclear weapons states, 1; territorial claims in Antarctica, 31–32; US POLCOM-South, 214
United Nations: Russia's Arctic policies, 90; transactional balancing model for conflict prevention, 129–130
United Nations Convention on the Law of the Sea (UNCLOS), 51–54, 99–100, 129–130
United Nations Security Council (UNSC): polar perceivers, 87(table); polar peripherals, 88(table); polar powers and polar players, 86(table); polar typology, 83
United States: Alaska's strategic importance, 24–25; alternatives to global hegemony, 173–175; Antarctic research, 104–105; Antarctic Treaty,

32–33; Arctic territorial claims, 51; avoiding a polar trap, 163–165; building transactional relationships with access states, 224–225; China's Antarctic ambitions, 107–108; China's Arctic policies, 99–101; China's hegemonic ambitions, 158–160; China's militarization in the Arctic, 16; claims on the Antarctic, 55, 58; competition-to-conflict trajectory, 69–70; control of the space domain, 65–68; foreign policy and the command of the commons, 47–49; great power competition, 10–14, 17; human settlement in Antarctica, 22(n14); Keflavik Air Station, 208–209; lag in polar strategy, 164–165; limitations on military power in the Arctic, 148–150; loss of hegemony, 221–222; maintaining global power status, 188–189; military Arctic strategies, 124–126, 207–208; military operation in Antarctica, 62; military training in the Arctic, 39; Northwest Passage crossings, 191–193; nuclear weapons states, 1; omitting Antarctica from strategic competition, 152; Polar Bear Expedition, 24; polar policies and great power competition, 114–115, 117–124; polar powers, 76–77, 85; policy and strategy recommendations, 21; prioritizing polar policy for defense and security, 202–203; Russian and Chinese hegemonic ambitions, 154–156; Russian maritime reconnaissance aircraft in Alaska, 136; Russia's Arctic expansion under Putin, 36–41; stagnation of polar policy, 112–113, 141–142; strategic focus on Asia and Eastern Europe, 203–204; the Thucydides Trap, 155–156; transactional balancing assumptions and objectives, 180; transactional balancing in Antarctica, 189–191; transactional balancing in the Arctic, 194–197; treaty-oriented stability model, 126–128; Unified Command Plan, 209–212; US Polar Command, 212–214; WWII-era security interests, 28–32. *See also* strategy; transactional balancing

US Africa Command (AFRICOM), 209, 212
US Central Command (CENTCOM), 209
US European Command (EUCOM), 118, 209–210, 215
US Indo-Pacific Command (INDO-PACOM), 209, 211–212, 215
US Northern Command (NORTHCOM), 66, 147, 209–210, 215; US polar defense policies, 117–118
US Polar Command (POLCOM), 212–213, 215
US Southern Command (SOUTHCOM), 211, 232(n40)
US Space Force (USSF), 65–66

Van Atta, Lee, 28

Wang Yi, 41
war on terror, 3; great power competition, 10; onset and duration of, 11–12; Putin's Arctic expansion during, 37
wedge-driving behaviors, 157, 159, 178, 193–194, 214, 223
wildlife: Antarctica, 9
Wolfers, Arnold, 48
World War I, 24–25, 156, 163
World War II: Alaska's strategic importance, 24–25; great power competition, 155–156; security interests in the high north, 28–30; strategic indicators in the polar regions, 24–36; US Antarctic strategy, 26–28, 31–32
Wrangel Island, 149

Xi Jinping, 15, 77, 97, 100, 158

Yellow River research station, Svalbard, 98, 158

About the Book

ONCE IMPASSABLE AND INHOSPITABLE, BOTH THE ARCTIC region and Antarctica are rapidly emerging as geopolitically strategic hot spots. As Ryan Burke writes in *The Polar Pivot*, the ice is melting and the tensions rising.

In this new environment, what are the stakes? Why are Russia and China racing to increase their military capabilities and infrastructures in the polar regions? What is the United States doing to safeguard its interests and influence in response? Arguing that both poles are becoming contested military domains in an arena of great power competition, Burke tackles these questions and outlines the shift necessary in US defense policy to face a potentially looming crisis.

RYAN PATRICK BURKE is a professor in the Department of Military and Strategic Studies at the US Air Force Academy.